SERMONS ON THE
OLD TESTAMENT LESSONS
FROM THE NEW
LECTIONARY AND CALENDAR

AUGSBURG SERMONS

OLD TESTAMENT LESSONS
SERIES C

AUGSBURG PUBLISHING HOUSE
MINNEAPOLIS, MINNESOTA

AUGSBURG SERMONS — OLD TESTAMENT LESSONS —
SERIES C

Copyright © 1979 Augsburg Publishing House

Library of Congress Catalog Card No. 79-50092

International Standard Book No. 0-8066-1703-9

All rights reserved. No part of this book may be used or reproduced in any manner whatsoever without written permission except in the case of brief quotations embodied in critical articles and reviews. For information address Augsburg Publishing House, 426 South Fifth Street, Minneapolis, Minnesota 55415.

Scripture quotations unless otherwise noted are from the Revised Standard Version of the Bible, copyright 1946, 1952, and 1971 by the Division of Christian Education of the National Council of Churches.

Quotation from "The Sound of Silence" © 1964, 1965 Paul Simon, is used by permission.

Manufactured in the United States of America

Contents

Introduction   11

FIRST SUNDAY IN ADVENT
Jeremiah 33:14-16
The Lord Is Our Righteousness   Ronald M. Hals   17

SECOND SUNDAY IN ADVENT
Malachi 3:1-4
The Unexpected Visitor   Arndt Halvorson   21

THIRD SUNDAY IN ADVENT
Zephaniah 3:14-18a
Waiting for the Presence   Larry A. Hoffsis   26

FOURTH SUNDAY IN ADVENT
Micah 5:2-4
The Little Town of Big Beginnings   Walter Wegner   31

THE NATIVITY OF OUR LORD — Christmas Day
Isaiah 62:10-12
The Astounding Gift   Leopold W. Bernhard   36

FIRST SUNDAY AFTER CHRISTMAS
Jeremiah 31:10-13
A Song and a Dance   Walter C. Huffman   41

THE EPIPHANY OF OUR LORD
Isaiah 60:1-6
God's Light, Glory, Presence   Gerald C. White   45

THE BAPTISM OF OUR LORD
First Sunday after the Epiphany
Isaiah 42:1-7
We Are the Servant   August Wenzel   49

SECOND SUNDAY AFTER THE EPIPHANY
Isaiah 62:1-5
Finding Hope Amid Ashes and Ruins   A. Joseph Everson   53

THIRD SUNDAY AFTER THE EPIPHANY
Isaiah 61:1-6
Celebrate!   Alton F. Wedel   57

FOURTH SUNDAY AFTER THE EPIPHANY
Jeremiah 1:4-10
Help for the Hesitant   Thomas R. Lee   61

FIFTH SUNDAY AFTER THE EPIPHANY
Isaiah 6:1-8 (9-13)
Steps in the Calling of a Prophet   Daniel J. Simundson   65

THE TRANSFIGURATION OF OUR LORD
Last Sunday after the Epiphany
Deuteronomy 34:1-12
Seeing From Afar   Morris J. Niedenthal   70

FIRST SUNDAY IN LENT
Deuteronomy 26:5-10
A Creed of Word and Deed   Hagen Staack   74

SECOND SUNDAY IN LENT
Jeremiah 26:8-15
Sentence of Death; Summons to Life   Delmar L. Jacobson   76

THIRD SUNDAY IN LENT
Exodus 3:1-8b, 10-15
Surprise, Surprise!   Lester Meyer   81

FOURTH SUNDAY IN LENT
Isaiah 12:1-6
Joy During Lent   Robert H. Boyd   86

FIFTH SUNDAY IN LENT
Isaiah 43:16-21
God's New Thing   Mark E. Hillmer   91

SUNDAY OF THE PASSION — Palm Sunday
Deuteronomy 32:36-39
God's Power for His People   Frank L. Benz   94

MAUNDY THURSDAY
Jeremiah 31:31-34
New Lives for Old   Frank H. Seilhamer   99

GOOD FRIDAY
Isaiah 52:13—53:12
Rate It R   Paul W. F. Harms   104

THE RESURRECTION OF OUR LORD
Easter Day
Exodus 15:1-11
The Lord Is My Strength and My Song   Frederick J. Gaiser   109

SECOND SUNDAY OF EASTER
Psalm 149
Let the Faithful Rejoice in Triumph   Stanley D. Schneider   113

THIRD SUNDAY OF EASTER
Psalm 30
An Easter Recital   Frederick E. Hasecke   117

FOURTH SUNDAY OF EASTER
Psalm 23
Banquets in the Shadows   O. B. Fjelstad   121

FIFTH SUNDAY OF EASTER
Psalm 145:1-13
So—Sing!   Harold P. Krull   126

SIXTH SUNDAY OF EASTER
Psalm 67
The Priest's Easter Song   Ronald E. C. Grissom   131

THE ASCENSION OF OUR LORD
Psalm 110
The Coronation of God's King   Ralph W. Doermann   135

SEVENTH SUNDAY OF EASTER
Psalm 47
An Absent Presence   Diedrik A. Nelson   139

THE DAY OF PENTECOST
Genesis 11:1-9
Is Fame the Spur?   Walter R. Wietzke   142

THE HOLY TRINITY
First Sunday after Pentecost
Proverbs 8:22-31
Where Shall We Find Wisdom?   Carl Graesser Jr.   148

SECOND SUNDAY AFTER PENTECOST
1 Kings 8:22-23, 27-30, 41-43
God Is the Greatest   Richard D. Nelson   152

THIRD SUNDAY AFTER PENTECOST
1 Kings 17:17-24
Death Defeated   Mark A. Jerstad   157

FOURTH SUNDAY AFTER PENTECOST
2 Samuel 11:26—12:10, 13-15
You Would Be a Nathan   Terence E. Fretheim   161

FIFTH SUNDAY AFTER PENTECOST
Zechariah 12:7-10
In the Path of the Suffering Messiah   Paul D. Hanson   165

SIXTH SUNDAY AFTER PENTECOST
1 Kings 19:14-21
When God Breaks Silence   Foster R. McCurley   170

SEVENTH SUNDAY AFTER PENTECOST
Isaiah 66:10-14
Begin Again   Joyce D. Sandberg 174

EIGHTH SUNDAY AFTER PENTECOST
Deuteronomy 30:9-14
God's Gift—A New Heart   Wendell W. Frerichs 178

NINTH SUNDAY AFTER PENTECOST
Genesis 18:1-10a (10b-14)
An Old Promise Made Good   Herbert C. Spomer 183

TENTH SUNDAY AFTER PENTECOST
Genesis 18:20-32
Hidden in a Prayer   Ronald M. Hals 188

ELEVENTH SUNDAY AFTER PENTECOST
Ecclesiastes 1:2; 2:18-26
The Graceful Point of View   Wesley J. Fuerst 192

TWELFTH SUNDAY AFTER PENTECOST
Genesis 15:1-6
Is Anyone Else Up There?   Rolf Nestingen 196

THIRTEENTH SUNDAY AFTER PENTECOST
Jeremiah 23:23-29
The Word to Shatter Dreams   David B. Kaplan 202

FOURTEENTH SUNDAY AFTER PENTECOST
Isaiah 66:18-23
A Vision of God's Universal Glory   Ralph W. Doermann 207

FIFTEENTH SUNDAY AFTER PENTECOST
Proverbs 25:6-7
An Old Sickness: "Get-Ahead-itis"   Walter L. Michel 211

SIXTEENTH SUNDAY AFTER PENTECOST
Proverbs 9:8-12
Wisdom and Life   Thomas E. Ridenhour 216

SEVENTEENTH SUNDAY AFTER PENTECOST
Exodus 32:7-14
How Many Golden Calves Have You Made this Week?
James S. Aull 219

EIGHTEENTH SUNDAY AFTER PENTECOST
Amos 8:4-7
Quick Profit at a High Cost Richard D. Vangerud 223

NINETEENTH SUNDAY AFTER PENTECOST
Amos 6:1-7
Rich Man, Poor Man James Limburg 227

TWENTIETH SUNDAY AFTER PENTECOST
Habakkuk 1:1-3; 2:1-4
How to Live in the Midst of Trouble Allan H. Sager 232

TWENTY-FIRST SUNDAY AFTER PENTECOST
Ruth 1:1-19a
The Lesson of History Barbara Jurgensen 238

TWENTY-SECOND SUNDAY AFTER PENTECOST
Genesis 32:22-30
The Blessing of Struggle Jack C. Leininger 242

TWENTY-THIRD SUNDAY AFTER PENTECOST
Deuteronomy 10:12-22
The Chosen Sheldon Tostengard 246

TWENTY-FOURTH SUNDAY AFTER PENTECOST
Exodus 34:5-9
Stories of God Walter R. Bouman 250

TWENTY-FIFTH SUNDAY AFTER PENTECOST
1 Chronicles 29:10-13
A Doxology Richard Simon Hanson 255

CHRIST THE KING
Last Sunday after Pentecost
Jeremiah 23:2-6
What Kind of a King? John Victor Halvorson 260

PREFACE

"Do I dare to preach a whole year's sermons on the Old Testament lessons?" That might seem an appropriate first question for a pastor making plans for an approaching church year. But there is another question which deserves priority, "Do I dare not to?" Theoretically, we confess that the Old Testament is authoritative for Christian faith and life; when it comes to choosing the text for Sunday's sermon, however, it becomes a decidedly second-class citizen all too often. Only you know how it is with your people and with your own heart, but it has often been observed that each generation must do battle against the temptation to demote the Old Testament from any functional place in the canon.

Since 1958 the current generation of Lutherans has made tremendous strides overcoming the dubious heritage of its immediate predecessors which had denied the Old Testament its appropriate place. It was in 1958 that the *Service Book and Hymnal* made the reading of an Old Testament lesson common practice for Lutheranism in America. With the coming of the new three-year lectionary in 1973 an even wider range of Old Testament material became standard diet for our congregations. And now that large numbers of pastors have rejoiced in and profited from working their way through the Gospel and Epistle pericopes, the time is ripe to commit ourselves to preaching on the Old Testament lessons of Series C. (In order that Old Testament texts might be provided for the entire year, the Psalms for the Sundays of Easter have been used as sermon texts to replace the lessons from the book of Acts prescribed for that season.)

There will be the same joy and profit to be found here. Actually, both joy and profit will likely be greater! The fact that by and large both pastor and people are less familiar with most Old Testament texts is a powerful advantage. We are all curious about the unfamiliar—and curiosity means enjoyable learning and attentive listening! And, as each of us knows well, when we ourselves genuinely rejoice at new insights which have broadened our faith, that joy as well as the insight has a stimulating effect on what we say—and even the way we say it! To make the hearts of hearers burn within them as the Scriptures are opened is surely a pattern that stands in the very best tradition.

But if I do dare to preach the Old Testament lessons, how do I go about it? Are there special methods? No, there are only the same methods that apply to the study of any biblical text. Every text should be interpreted in the light of its historical and literary context. Every text should be examined to determine the type of literature it represents (e.g., a parable), the outline it has and the setting in life it may have had. Naturally the extent to which such questions may provide the preacher with information useful for sermonizing will vary from case to case, just as it does with New Testament texts.[1]

Nevertheless, although there are no special methods for studying Old Testament texts, there certainly are special considerations that apply to their proclamation. Because we are Christians, we hear these Old Testament texts speak in the light of God's further revelation in Jesus Christ. He is the one in whom God's purposes for his people found and continue to find their true shape and their ultimate realization. And this fulfillment occurs not just where the New Testament happens to point it out. The New Testament does not provide us with an exhaustive list of what fulfillment involves. When Psalm 2:7 says, "You are my son, today I have begotten you," this finds significant fulfillment in Jesus' baptism as the New Testament affirms, and also in every Christian baptism, even though the New Testament never happens to apply the passage in that way. This is only a sample of how God's former words help us understand his latter acts. In fact, many times the Old Testament passages guide us to discover aspects of New Testament truth which would otherwise remain obscure. Again by way of brief example, the one who sees in the old exodus the twin stresses on grace and faith in "The Lord will fight for you, and you have only to be still" (Exodus 14:14), will have new insight into why the same twin stresses on grace and faith are so automatic in Paul's presentation of the new exodus.

As indicated above, the linking up of old and new does not by any means imply that the old is only secondary and abrogated. Sometimes, though, it has been superseded and a Christian preacher must be bold enough to point it out, even if it might offend cherished notions. Sunday, for example, is *not* the Christian sabbath, and to apply sabbath laws to Sunday can only lead to grief. Luther's model of transforming and expanding the meaning of the Ten Commandments so that all of them express a positive word as well as a negative is a good one. But it should be noted that only in part did he do this on the basis of New Testament authority. The emphasis on the study of God's word as the way of fulfilling the Third Commandment is not rooted in either Old or New Testament directives, but stems from the extra-biblical Jewish tradition reflected in Luke 4:16.

In many cases the Old Testament is simply *assumed* by the New Testament writers. In fact, sometimes—as is especially evident in the prophetic preaching about social justice—the Old Testament message is far more directly suited to our situation than is the New Testament treatment of the same area. Today's cultural situation of affluent independence is far closer to that of eighth-century Israel than it is to that of the powerless minority who made up the early church.

But all of this is simply to say that the preacher is called to *listen* both to the intention of the text and to the crying needs of our own day. The text records what happened once, but because already its first listeners stood within the stream of generations of the people of God, even that ancient text was constantly reinterpreting the very message it preserved. Abraham is portrayed as the called of God, and his experience under God is in many ways paradigmatic for all whom God calls, since his God is our God, and since the purpose in history of this one and only God is still blessing for the world.

A special part of the context out of which an Old Testament lesson is to be understood is its contemporary liturgical context. Our lessons have been picked normally to relate to the Gospel for the day. The Gospel is the reading from the New Covenant in the light of which the word of the Old Covenant now speaks anew. The two illuminate each other. Rather than something new which rejects and supersedes the old, the New Testament lessons far more often show us a new thing which is in fact the old word spoken in a new time and place. In some cases already within the Old Testament itself we find both the old and the new in this same sort of relationship. The return from Babylon is already a new exodus. The prophets already brought words of judgment and deliverance, death and life-out-of-death (e.g., the dry bones in Ezekiel 37:1-14).

In Jesus all this happens one more time, but with a finality heretofore unknown. As the name Yahweh (Septuagint *kyrios*) revealed to Moses was put back into the patriarchal narratives dealing with a time long before that name was revealed in order to affirm who the God of Abraham really was, so the New Testament's labeling of Jesus as *kyrios* has a similar intent. The God who "spoke of old to our fathers . . . has spoken to us by a Son," (Hebrews 1:1) and has "bestowed on him the name which is above every name . . . that every tongue confess that Jesus Christ is Lord" (Isaiah 45:23 and Philippians 2:9-11). When we preach the Old Testament we proclaim an old word, and we do it in the light of the ultimate Word, but we know from experience that this light of fulfillment often shines both ways. The old is not only illuminated by the new, but itself sheds a light that makes the new shine forth more clearly. To let the light shine is and always was the calling of God's people (Isaiah 60:1-3 and Matthew 5:14) and *the* characteristic of God's word (Psalm 119:105 and 2 Corinthians 4:6).[2]

RONALD M. HALS
TERENCE E. FRETHEIM

---

1. Foster R. McCurley Jr., *Proclaiming the Promise* (Philadelphia: Fortress, 1974) is an extremely useful work on the Christian use of the Old Testament in preaching, treating both methods and specific texts.

2. For further exploration of the theological relation of Old and New Testaments along the lines suggested here, see Gerhard von Rad, *Old Testament Theology* (New York: Harper and Row, 1965), II, 319-409.

THE LORD IS OUR RIGHTEOUSNESS

First Sunday in Advent
Jeremiah 33:14-16

A young man in California wanted to be a highway patrolman. He almost made it, but near the end of his training he was, as they say, washed out. But this young man bought his own uniform, his own motorcycle, and had copies made of the official patrolman's citation form on which tickets are written. They eventually caught this phony patrolman, because all the tickets he gave out bore the same number. Amazingly, though, no complaints were received from the people who came in to pay their fines. That meant, the other patrolmen concluded, that these were "righteous" citations. The people must really have committed the violations for which they were cited. That's one of the meanings of "righteous." It can mean "genuine" or "true," and that's part of what it does mean in this passage where a true king is promised, one who will be called "the Lord is our righteousness."

When in Advent we celebrate the coming of Jesus and his kingdom, it is this kind of king that we welcome.

Jesus Is Our True King Who Brings True Obedience

That's the way the Gospel reading in Luke 19 describes him. Jesus came to be the true king, the one promised. Our text talks about God's fulfilling the promise he made. On Palm Sunday it's plain that Jesus made a definite effort to show he was fulfilling that promise, that he came as the true king, the Lord our righteousness. In the Gospel for today we hear people saying, "Blessed is the king." In Mark's version of the same story he mentions "the kingdom of our father David," and in his account Matthew speaks of the "son of David."

But what really happened on Palm Sunday was the start of a long argument that is still going on. The leaders of the people who saw Jesus march into Jerusalem that day said, "No, he is not the true king, the Messiah." And to this day most Jews continue to say that. How do we account for this? Didn't Jesus live up to the promises? Let's look at those promises. They start with a promise to David about his descendants sitting on his throne. The label "branch" comes into use as a way of talking about that descendant of David. Our text talks about "a righteous branch to spring forth for David." It's a lot like the way we talk about a branch on a family tree. The king in Jeremiah's day claimed to be the "rightful king." In fact his name, Zedekiah, means "the lord is my righteousness." But just having the name doesn't necessarily make it so. After all, there are a lot of used car dealers named Honest John.

What did happen in Jeremiah's day was that God took a hand in the argument. Through his prophet he said "No" to the king in Jeremiah's day and for a long time after that! He had Jeremiah announce about the last king of Judah, "Write this man down as childless; none of his offspring shall succeed in sitting on the throne of David" (22:30).

Because there wasn't a righteous king, God said to his people, "Now you're going to have no king." But not having a king just meant that there would be some pinch-hitters who would try to carry on God's promise of justice, for God had promised more than a king, he had promised justice and righteousness. In our text the focus has shifted from the king to his city; Jerusalem is given the label "the Lord is our righteousness." "And this is the name by which *it* will be called: 'the Lord is our righteousness.' " In the days of the prophet Zechariah the branch idea was handed over to the priest, and finally in the Christmas carol, "Lo, how a rose e'er blooming" we see how that song talks about Mary as the stock from whom Jesus comes as a branch. But even though there were all kinds of pinch-hitters, God didn't say "Yes" again to his promise until Christmas.

But at Christmas all this happened, the promise was fulfilled. That must mean that our Advent task then is just to remember. No, that's not true, not yet! Even though we recognize in the Palm Sunday Gospel how "peace in heaven" and "glory in the highest" really happened at Christmas, and even though Mary was told before her son's birth how he would sit on the throne of his father David, just saying so doesn't mean everybody would believe it. The argument goes on. We don't see the genuine fullness of this true king until he comes again. That's why there is an alternate Gospel for this day, Luke 21, where we read about Jesus' second coming. Until that time there will always be room for argument. After all, in spite of Palm Sunday, Jesus' glory was hidden, and only revealed in part. He never did receive the genuine response of true obedience that the true king should get. He himself spoke about how "the very stones would cry out," but that didn't happen. No, true obedience will come to this true king only on that day when every knee shall bow, and every tongue shall confess that Jesus is Lord. Then we shall see the true king, but then we'll see him as even more than a king. Then we'll see clearly how the Lord is our righteousness.

Jesus Is Our True Savior Who Brings True Security

"In his days . . . [his people] will be saved and . . . will dwell securely." Now, of course, Jesus already is true king and Savior, but it is only in hope that this is completely fulfilled. That's why there is to be a second Advent.

His first coming was real and true. He did save us, even if we weren't there. That salvation is real, even if our lives don't always show it. He was and is the true king, even if the sign on the cross, "the king of the Jews," was meant as a cruel joke. The reason the argument still goes on, is that Jesus was different from what had been expected. In him, God gave more than he had promised. It wasn't just to *show* us righteousness, but to *be* our righteousness that he came. He *gave* us his righteousness, so that we can sing: "Christ's crimson blood and righteousness my glory are, my spotless dress. In this before my God I'll stand and enter heaven, my fatherland." And also the security which Jesus offers is a better one than had been promised. He has changed the place where his followers live from being a city to being a church. He comes as king and Savior and not just of a land, but of a spiritual kingdom, one without any boundaries. And he comes so that we should find our security not just in our feelings about him, but in his gift to us of himself. He is our true Savior who brings true security.

But the second Advent remains our hope. Luke 21 talks about Jesus "coming in a cloud with power and great glory." Advent means coming, and Jesus will come again. But that is not something to be feared. It seems as though we have the idea that we ought to be afraid of the return of our Lord. I think we get that idea because we talk about his coming in judgment. But "judgment" is not a bad word. That passage in Luke 21 says, "when you see these things taking place, look up and raise your heads, because your redemption is drawing near." How can judgment and redemption be the same thing? Redemption means salvation. That's what we mean by Jesus' kingdom. Well, the second Advent brings the promise of full salvation. It brings the promise of a hope that becomes reality. Judgment means setting things right, and that is good news for God's poor and oppressed people. Justice and righteousness are not here now in their fullest sense, but then, at Jesus' return, everything will become "right." Then it will be true that the Lord is our righteousness, fully true in a way it never has been before.

Then there will be no more argument about what is true or who is true, for Jesus will be clear as our true Savior who brings true security. We are sure about that now, but then there will be no doubts anywhere. And that changed scene will last forever. At Jesus' second Advent there will be no more traveling music, but his people will begin to sing the songs of home. Then we will have true security in a greater way than ever before. It will be true security, because there will be no more opposition outside. The people in Jerusalem always hoped for true security, and so they built big walls. And they dreamed of a greater wall. In Zechariah's day they looked for a wall of fire. (Try to prop a ladder up against that!) In one of our hymns the writer speaks of God's people like a city "with salvation's walls surrounded." Luther wrote about the church as "a mighty fortress." All that security meant protection against enemies outside. But when Jesus comes again there will be no opposition outside. The New Jerusalem will never need to close its gates.

But the greatest part of the true security that comes from our true Savior rests in his promise that at his return there will be no more opposition within either. Let's face it, we are God's real problem. He has no other opposition that causes him trouble. Our stubborn hearts are the only places where God's will runs into trouble. But Jeremiah promises that God will make a new covenant with his people, and then he will put his word in his people's hearts. He will write it on our hearts, so that there will never again be any clash between his will and our will. Instead our will will always be his will. When that final opposition is overcome, then God and his people can rest and rejoice forever.

In the Eucharist today we get a pledge, a down payment, a foretaste that our Lord's promise is true about his kingdom. We need that kind of assurance, because this is a strange kind of kingdom. Our Lord has come, but he will come again. We really ought to be getting used to that strangeness, for it has been a long time that we have been praying in the Lord's Prayer, "The kingdom, the power, and the glory are yours," while we have still been praying in that same prayer, "Your kingdom come." This is what Advent is about: We celebrate our true king and Savior, who has come and who will come again. Amen.

RONALD M. HALS
Trinity Lutheran Seminary
Columbus, Ohio

THE UNEXPECTED VISITOR

Second Sunday in Advent
Malachi 3:1-4

The issue this text addresses is:
"Is this a moral universe?"
The question it raises is:
"If so, what is the nature of judgment by a Holy God?"
The purpose of the sermon is:
"To let God's searching love have its way with us in our innermost selves."

Do we live in a moral universe?
 Most of us would answer "yes."
 We might say, "The non-responsible life is not worth living."
 We might say, "If there is no judgment, how can you believe in God?" We say this in proverbial ways:
 "He had it coming."
 "He made his bed, now let him lie in it."
We say this in psychological terms:
 "Repressed guilt will express itself some way, even in the form of physical disorder."
 "This illness is psychosomatically induced."
We say this sociologically:
 "Crime does not pay."
 After Watergate, the nation was bathed in self-righteousness. We said, "It served the rascals right."
 Everybody seems to agree. This is a moral universe.
 This includes the people to whom Malachi was preaching. It was a commonly held belief that evil will be punished in this lifetime and good will be rewarded. If this did not happen, they believed, it would happen after death.
 Yet, these same people were now challenging this assumption.
 They said, "Morality doesn't pay." They saw evil people prospering and good people suffering. So they asserted their "freedom." They ignored the rules about marriage and divorce. They neglected the poor and the lonely. They were careless about Sabbath worship and tithing. Even the priests became careless.
 They said, "It doesn't work." They had expected to return from their Babylonian exile to a land of plenteous rainfall, bountiful crops and an expanding population. The land they came to was tiny, rocky, arid, unfruitful.
 We 20th century folk say also, "It doesn't pay, it doesn't work."

But we have a new way of saying this. We say, "Times have changed."

We assume we are thus acknowledging that history is a moving river, not a stagnant pool. Actually the reverse is true. This commonly used phrase has become a beaver's dam on history's river.

We use the phrase as if it were a new, fixed dogma. We seem to be saying history has now reached us, and the changing times have now revealed their true intention.

And we are now harvesting our weed crop.

"Commitment" is a bad word. Expedience sounds better.

To "give your word" seems to be more a mode of seduction than a binding force.

Don't tell the truth if a lie will help.

Fornication and adultery are old language. "Make love."

Love is permissiveness—a way of indulging our feelings without guilt.

Happiness is becoming Number One. Happiness is self-indulgence.

Worship and prayer are options.

God is a debatable concept.

Forgiveness is thus a cheap word—a way of getting approval for what we have done and want to do.

Do we live in a moral universe? No—all is relative.

How strange! How did this happen?

It did not happen by an overt act of rebellion. It did not happen because we decided to scrap morality.

No. It happened, as it always will, because we lost our relationship with a holy God.

For to say "life is moral" is not to say that morality pays or works.

Morality is not the gear case which makes our human machine work.

To say "life is moral" is not to say that moral people find success. Morality is not the magic key to happiness.

Jesus was killed for it.

The prophets were stoned, derided, imprisoned for it.

No—righteousness is right, morality is right, simply because it is *right*. It is right only because our loving God is holy. He supplies our needs only out of his holy love.

How did we forget this?

As we said, we broke our contact with him.

At Christmastime all of us go through that difficult moment of deciding whether to send John or Mary a Christmas card this year.

We pause in our work to reminisce, to remember the friendship we once enjoyed. The memory is pleasant. We smile. Then we frown.

The friendship is only a memory. We have lost contact. Regretfully we decide not to send a card. There is no relationship.

This is how we lose contact with our holy, loving, Father-God. We simply drift apart. Anxieties and pressures move in. Fatigue and boredom take over. When there are times of success and pleasure, we might say, "I've deserved it, after all I've been through."

Self-centeredness displaces worship. Practical concerns displace prayer.

"Is there a judgment?" Is this a moral universe?" someone asks. We frown. We're not sure. All is relative.

How did this happen?

We simply forgot our baptismal covenant. In baptism we were united with God in a *mutual bond of friendship.* Friendship.

He promised never to leave us.

We promised never to leave him. We promised to keep our contact alive by prayer and obedience.

He promised to keep the contact by never withholding his love. He would always be in our corner. He would always be available. He would always give us a second chance, and the power to take it. But we forgot.

God became a memory.

What is the result?

Our lives get out of focus. We don't know what is wrong.

We are like runaways whose freedom is spoiled by always having to look over their shoulder.

We read the news with foreboding. We turn on a TV comedy or a football game.

We excuse ourselves, rationalize our actions.

We act like people who have lost something. Frantically we look among old papers for whatever it is we have lost.

We even look in the garbage bin. For without the friendship of God our lives feel like rubbish bins. Once in a while we dig in deep, but we quit the search. The rubbish bin is so dirty.

We are rotten before we are ripe.

What is God doing all this time?

He is keeping his promise. He is looking for us. He keeps coming back, through memories, incidents, people.

This makes us very nervous, apprehensive. We feel spied upon. We say, "Why are you judging me?" Notice: it is we—we the hunted and lost—who use the word "judgment."

God says "visit."

He is coming simply to love, help, redeem us.

This sounds fine until he gets close to us. Then we are like the unfortunate spouse who was interrupted in an illicit love affair by the return of her husband. He had only come to make sure she was all right, to say he loved her. But she screamed:

"Don't you trust me? Why do you check on me?"

So it should be no surprise that there is a judgment. Yet, when he does come, it always takes us by surprise.

Why:

1. It is a surprise in its timing.

He comes when we most need him, which is, ironically, the time we think we are getting along quite well alone. He does not wait for us to be aware of our need of him. He comes to awaken in us the long dead awareness that we do need him. He does not always wait for us to ask. He comes to create the desire. He does not place himself at our mercy: He accommodates his mercy to our need.

So he comes to us every day.

Judgment does not refer to one great mass future court trial.

It refers to his daily visit.

Look for him today.

2. It is a surprise in its form.

Love is seldom aesthetically appealing. There was no "beauty in him that we should desire him" when he hung on the cross or groaned in the Garden.

They called him insane, demon-possessed, immoral, radical.

That is because he was bearing our sins. He was saying, "God loves you."

Love always takes on itself the pain and the ugliness of the sinner being loved. It may make you prematurely old, broken, undesirable.

Malachi says that to be loved like this is to be washed in fuller's soap. The fuller had to remove all the oily substance from the new wool. The cleaning substance was rancid, strong, and made a terrible stench. Therefore, the poor fuller always carried that stench in his skin and clothes. Jesus, God seeking for us, is the fuller.

3. It is a surprise in its goal.

He comes to heal, not expose, to restore, not cast out.

Yet, this is not always pleasant for us. It means a return to the rubbish bin, among other things. We are quite self-satisfied.

Must fellowship with God come through such pain?

Yes, says Jesus, not because pain is necessary but because fellowship is so important.

For he wants to give us something far greater than a new form of behavior. He wants to give us himself.

We can trample on him if we wish—but once we have understood his mission, it hurts too much.

We can ignore him if we wish, but then life is so empty.

4. It is a surprise in its method.

He does not talk to us of our sins, but of his suffering. His cross, his death, his resurrection, are shown us. We are a bit annoyed, with this talk of his suffering, until we hear that the real emphasis is upon his resurrection.

He seems to want to give us something we can't get any other way.

He is tender, caring, understanding—yet it only annoys us.

What is going on?

"Leave me alone," we cry out.

But we can't. The purging fire has been burning too long. We are being cleansed, something is happening in us that must be completed.

We are in the fire, the purging fire of judgment.

We look to him, but we cannot find him.

He is not sitting dispassionately on the sidelines giving advice and watching our spiritual progress.

He is in the fire with us!

He is sharing our griefs, bearing our sins.

As we become more and more naked, he says, "You **don't need** the mask any longer."

Closer and closer we come, until the broken cord is healed.

We are in fellowship with him.

But he is looking at us ever so intently.

"What are you looking for?" we ask, still **afraid.**

"My image," he replies.

Sometimes goldsmiths would test the purity of the refined metal by seeing when it gave them back a clear image.

"I'm not good enough," we sob.

"Yes you are!" he says. "I see myself in you. Now always look for yourself in me."

The wall is broken down.

We are one with God.

We are well again.

We feel like singing and weeping and dancing. So he takes our hand and leads us in the celebration.

Indeed. "Who can abide the day of his coming?"

ARNDT L. HALVORSON
Luther-Northwestern Seminaries
St. Paul, Minnesota

WAITING FOR THE PRESENCE

Third Sunday in Advent
Zephaniah 3:14-18a

The key in today's Old Testament reading is "On that day it shall be said . . . 'The Lord, your God, is in your midst.' " With these words, we are invited to join with all the people of God in an age-old Advent activity—"waiting for the presence."

I wonder what you children heard when I said, "waiting for the presence?" Did you think I meant p-r-e-s-e-n-t-s? Caught up in the spirit of these weeks before Christmas, it would be understandable if you did. I know you can hardly wait for those presents!

You parents and grandparents might have heard it the same way. These are the weeks of your preoccupation with choosing, buying, wrapping, and, in some cases, sending the right presents. Perhaps you can hardly wait for the presents to be over and done with!

Your thoughts are absorbed with such things and so I understand if that's what you thought I meant.

Presence, Not Presents

But I meant p-r-e-s-e-n-c-e! Our language has many words that sound alike but have different meanings. "Presence" and "presents" are two such homonyms. They sound alike but there is a vast difference in their meaning. Keeping this distinction clear is the essence of Zephaniah's counsel for God's people. It's striking how true they ring for our times.

The secular calendar may have captivated us once again this December in the waiting for things, but the Advent calendar lifts us from our captivity to things and would have us wait for a person. Thus a prophetic, counter-cultural claim is made that such a "presence" is more to be desired than all the "presents" in the world.

It goes without saying that the words of our text were first addressed to people of God in a captivity more visible than ours. They had been physically transported to Babylon from their homeland in Israel. In many cases they were separated from their families. In most cases they realized that they had become separated from God. Reflection on their situation was a reminder that they had ignored the warnings of many prophets before Zephaniah—not to confuse their priorities. Indeed, they had, in their shortsighted way, opted for the acquiring of temporal "presents" as being more important than acknowledging the divine "presence." How easily they had turned from God. In their desire for things, any gods would be tried, even the Eastern astral deities currently in vogue.

Now, in exile, the vision of God's people could clear. They had not been created primarily for a relationship to things, but for relationships with persons—a relationship with God himself, the highest priority. It did not take long before they began to realize that they had been in a spiritual exile even before they were forcibly separated from their homeland. As a matter of fact, anyone away from God is in exile—separated from one's true homeland.

So it is not at all far-fetched to suggest that in some ways we are in exile just as surely as were the people to whom the prophet Zephaniah first addressed his words. If this December finds us separated from God, exile may best describe our condition. And, if exile is the case, we certainly do not need more presents. They may simply widen our separation.

The Presence of God

The needs of the people of God in Zephaniah's day could not be satisfied by giving them things, no matter how impressive. We can list their needs. They are the same as our needs now. They wanted protection from their present enemies. (We call it security.) They wanted peace. (We know that people are not meant to live in constant conflict, even when winning.) They wanted a pleasant life, life filled with praise and good times. They wanted prospects for a meaningful future.

In our better moments we know that these needs cannot be met by coveting and acquiring more things. But, oh how Israel had tried—seeking the favor and presents of the powerful of this world. (For them, it was the Assyrians and their gods.)

What the people sought could not be bought from any world power. How disillusioned Israel must have been when Assyrian protection, peace, pleasures, praise and prospects for a bright future were short-lived.

The lessons of history come hard, even to the people of God who know that history well. This year we will once again send our array of "presents" to do what only a "presence" can accomplish. Someone will be given a specially-coded electronic garage door opener to insure protection from enemies. Someone will receive an expensive present with the accompanying hope that the thing may make for peace between the two parties. Someone will get a household gadget or some other a golf club, a tennis racket, and it will be obvious that the giver desires the thing to make life pleasant and pleasurable. Other presents will be given with the hidden agenda of evoking the acclamations of praise we so desperately seek. Some son or daughter will open that red bank envelope with the oval framing the portrait of Hamilton, Jackson, Franklin or Grant. The giver will be pleased if the thing is placed away in the college fund with the ultimate aim of making bright the prospects for a future.

Although we can testify that a great deal of time and money is expended in choosing just the right presents, we know that none of these things can substitute for the "presence" for fulfilling our basic needs. It is a sign of our continuing exile as God's people when we send presents to do what only a "presence" can do.

Well do I remember how it was during the Decembers when my youngest brother and his wife served as Peace Corps volunteers in Fiji. Not being together as a family to celebrate the festival gave us a feeling of kinship with all exiles. True, we did eagerly await the packages from Fiji which we knew contained our presents—exotic items from the South Pacific. And, it was hard to wait for the time to pass until they could be opened. Upon opening our treasures, we were for a while enthralled with those unusual things. But my father was wiser, "This is fine, but it's not like having Jim and Diane with us." His point was similar to the point of the prophet. No presents could take the place of their presence. The pleasure we derived from their gifts, as with all things, would prove each year to be transitory.

More vividly than opening presents from them do I remember their coming home from Fiji to be with us. We ran from the car through the airport parking lot. Each minute of waiting seemed like an hour. Then we saw them coming down the walkway and everyone ran to meet them, engulfing them with hugs and kisses. They had no presents for us—their luggage limitations not allowing for any such extras—but they needed none. For all that we desired was fulfilled by their presence.

Recently, in going through her things, one of the elderly members of our parish discovered letters that her father, a German immigrant, had received from his parents still in the homeland. The letters were in a German script too difficult for me. A seminarian of our parish was able to decipher them. After translating the letters he checked with me before sharing their contents, so poignant were they. They described the pain of separation, of exile, one might say. Beyond that, some mistrust had ensued, possibly over the circumstances which prompted the son's leaving for America, and possibly intensified by the fact that he had not written. It was clear that life had been hard since he went away, and not knowing for sure how each felt about the other, the family was not at peace. The parents felt less than confident about their security and their prospects for the future, now that their son was gone. They were not waiting for the son to send back presents from America; they wanted the reassurance that could be theirs only by his presence.

Such was the desire of the ancient people of God in exile. They knew that they didn't need things, they needed God. Now they waited not for presents but for God's presence. But was this waiting being done in vain? Having abandoned God, had he also abandoned them?

The prophet's words came as great comfort to them. "It shall be said . . . 'Do not fear. . . . The Lord, your God, is in your midst." All that they needed was supplied in the assurance of God's presence. Protection? Oh, yes! Real security is in God. He is a "warrior who gives you victory." "He has cast out your enemies," Zephaniah wrote. Peace? Oh, yes! "He has taken away the judgments against you." Prospects for the future? Oh yes! "You shall fear evil no more." Pleasure and praise—so seldom heard amidst the laments of the exiles? Oh, yes! It comes out loud and clear, in the imperative, "Sing aloud . . . shout . . . rejoice and exult with all your heart." And what makes it even better, Zephaniah states, is that their pleasure shall pale next to God's. Mark well—when God's children are reunited with him, no one celebrates more than he! So the prophet noted that God would "rejoice over you with gladness, he will renew you in his love, he will exult over you with loud singing." It will be like a festival. When the prodigal and his father are together, the father's celebration is something to behold!

The Presence of God in Christ

The prophet's verbs are interesting in that they employ all three tenses. Sometimes he uses the past . . . "has taken away the judgments." Sometimes he uses the present . . . "The Lord is in your midst." But many of his verbs are cast in the future tense "you will" or "he will." All of which is a reminder that though God's presence was a reality for Israel at the time, nonetheless, they were seeing through a "glass darkly" for the prophet was pointing to an even clearer manifestation of God's real presence.

That clearer manifestation we are privileged to know in Jesus Christ. In Christ, God has graced us with his presence. Our time of exile, no matter how wide our separation from God may have become, is brought to an end in Christ. Believing in Jesus as Christ and Lord we can never be without God's presence.

If the exiles of the Old Testament, living before Christ, could greet Zephaniah's words as welcome news, what must they be for us who live in the New Testament era? They are pure Gospel! Good news! Nothing less. We can see all that they saw in these words . . . and more! Much more!

They could hear "The King of Israel, the Lord, is in your midst"; we too can know this Lord in our flesh, Jesus, the King of all kings. Gathered in his name and around his table, we know that he is in our midst.

They could hear peace in the words "The Lord has taken away the judgments against you," and we can see peace with God, offered by the Lord with nail-printed hands outstretched.

They could assume divine protection with these words, "He has cast out your enemies." We can see it in the empty tomb, knowing that the last enemy, death, has been destroyed.

They could hear prospects of a future in these words; we can see it as we watch him ascend into heaven, his earthly exile over, assured that where he is, there we shall be also.

They could hear, "let not your hands grow weak"; we can see down through the centuries, hearts strengthened and made courageous by his abiding presence.

They could hear the invitation to sing, and we are caught up in the very song, sung not just by us, but by the "angels, archangels and all the company of heaven."

The prophet's words are fulfilled in Christ. Even so, there remains for us, too, the element of the future about them. Certainly all is not past in Christ. He points us to his coming again. He is in our midst now, of that we can be assured. But there is a nearer presence still to come, when we shall have our final homecoming with God. That will be a greater celebration than when my brother came home; a higher festival than when the prodigal returned.

Advent remains for us, as exile for God's people before us, a time of waiting for the presence. Knowing Christ we can be sure of the fulfillment of God's promises. And so may this Advent be a time of festival, the festival during which people sing, exult and rejoice as they wait, not for the presents of a glittering Christmas, but the presence of God in Christ.

LARRY A. HOFFSIS
Trinity Lutheran Church
Columbus, Ohio

A LITTLE TOWN OF BIG BEGINNINGS

Fourth Sunday in Advent
Micah 5:2-4

Today's Old Testament Lesson invites us to think about the "little town of Bethlehem." It invites us to reflect on the significance of Bethlehem for God's people in times past as well as the significance of Bethlehem for you and me today.

A Big Beginning in David's Day

"Bethlehem Ephrathah, you are *little*," says the prophet. "Insignificant" would, in fact, be a good word with which to translate the adjective Micah uses to describe this little town. That's what Bethlehem actually was—"little, insignificant"—until the days of great King David when the great King of heaven and earth made a divine decision which singled out this little town of small significance and made it the locale of a big new beginning in David's day.

What was that big new beginning? It was the beginning of a new kingly family which started with David whose family home was located at Bethlehem. It was the beginning of a new royal house, a new dynasty to rule over God's people through which God would share great blessings with his chosen nation.

It all began when God moved the prophet Nathan to bring a message to David shortly after David had been established as king in Jerusalem. David had decided that he would build a "house" for the Lord. But Nathan was directed to inform David that his plan would not materialize. It would, in fact, be the other way around: God would build a house for David. Nathan's prophetic message to David is recorded in 2 Samuel 7, beginning with these words:

> Thus says the Lord of hosts, I took you from the pasture, from following the sheep, that you should be prince over my people Israel.

Notice, by the way, how Nathan's words refer to the little town where David grew up. Nathan doesn't even mention Bethlehem by name. It's only a "pasture town."

> Nathan's message from God to David continues: "Moreover the Lord declares to you that the Lord will make *you* a house. When your days are fulfilled and you lie down with your fathers, I will raise up your offspring after you, who shall come forth from your body, and I will establish his kingdom. *He* shall build a house for my name, and I will establish the throne of his kingdom for ever. I will be his father and he will be my son. . . . I will not take my steadfast love from him, as I took it from Saul, whom I put away from before you. And your house and your kingdom shall be made sure for ever before me; your throne shall be established for ever" (2 Sam. 7:5-16).

And that's how insignificant little Bethlehem became the place of one of God's big new beginnings. Bethlehem, the birthplace of David, became the beginning-place of "the house of David," the place of origin of the Davidic dynasty, which reigned on the Jerusalem throne as long as that throne existed. Each king who ruled there traced his ancestry back to David's hometown, the little town of Bethlehem in the district of Ephrathah. That insignificant little pasture town surrounded by its shepherds' fields achieved new significance because its royal sons, descended from David, became the "shepherds" through whom God himself provided royal direction and kingly protection for his ancient people.

In all of that, God was acting in a very characteristic way. It has always been characteristic of God to use that which is small, plain or ordinary to accomplish his will. It's typical of him to take that which is insignificant in people's eyes, even that which is ridiculed or despised, and to use it to accomplish his beneficial purposes for his people. Do you recall how the Apostle Paul expressed it? In his First Letter to the Corinthians Paul stated that "God chose what is foolish in the world" to carry out his plan of salvation! Yes, Paul says, to carry out his saving purpose for the world "God chose what is weak in the world"; he "chose what is low and despised in the world, even things that are not."

The outstanding example of all that was God's use of the "stumbling block" of the cross—of all things, the *cross*, an instrument of death—as the means of effecting forgiveness, life and salvation for all! And through the powerful, life-changing message of the cross of his Son, he is able to take people like you and me—regardless of how insignificant we may be—and through us accomplish great new beginnings in his church and in his world. Remember, he once took an insignificant lump of clay, molded it into a human being, and used that little lump of clay as the big beginning of humanity. And he's still doing that today. He still takes lumps of clay—like you and me—breathes new life into us, and makes us into a new creation in Jesus Christ. Yes, our great God who initiated a big new beginning in insignificant Bethlehem back there in David's day is still the God of big new beginnings even today.

Another Big Beginning in Micah's Day

Let's look again at today's Old Testament Lesson, this time to see how it looks to Bethlehem as the place of another big beginning that was foreseen in Micah's day. But first we will do well to face up to a problem that confronts us as we try to determine precisely when this particular paragraph of Micah's book was written.

Micah lived during the turbulent last half of the 8th century before Christ. That was the time when Micah's people were politically dominated by mighty Assyria who threatened to ride roughshod over Jerusalem and to obliterate the kingly rule of the house of David. It is possible that it was in response to that threat from Assyria that Micah spoke these prophetic words about the coming of a new king who would deliver his threatened people: a king who would shepherd his people "in the strength of the Lord," a king who would be "great to the ends of the earth" and under whose kingly rule his people "shall dwell secure" (Micah 5:4).

But it's equally possible that these words became part of Micah's book at a much later time, as much as two centuries later than Micah's own days. These words of prophetic hope and promise that constitute today's Old Testament Lesson may very well have been composed and added to Micah's book during the time when the people of Jerusalem and Judah were in exile in Babylonia. That certainly was a time when God's people were in travail (to use the terminology of verse 3 of the text) waiting eagerly, like a woman in childbirth, for her delivery and the joy that would follow. If the words of this text come from that period of the Babylonian Exile, then the "return" and the "restoration" referred to in verse 3 would be the return of God's people from their exile in Babylonia and the restoration of Jerusalem and Judah which followed.

In either case, what we have here is a prophetic oracle that looks at the bleak situation of God's people in a time of crisis and insists that the situation is *not* hopeless! God is in control, and under his guidance there *will* be a new beginning. And that new beginning will be brought about by the coming of a new king of the house and lineage of David, one who traces his ancestry and origin back to little Bethlehem Ephrathah. And so the prophetic oracle addresses the little town of Bethlehem and says:

> But you, O Bethlehem Ephrathah, who are little to be among the clans of Judah, from you shall come forth for me one who is to be ruler in Israel, whose origin is from of old, from ancient days.

You see, back of this prophetic statement is the underlying conviction that God will be true to his promise. God had made a promise long ago to David whose origins in ancient days had been in Bethlehem Ephrathah. Down through the centuries there were those faithful folks who held on to that promise in firm trust, confident that God's promise would be fulfilled. Not even long decades of despair could undercut their faith in God. Even when they as a nation had to walk through the valley of the shadow of death they held on to that promise in faith. They feared no evil; they were convinced that God was with them as a faithful Shepherd; they were confident that they would be comforted and guided by his rod and staff.

The confident, trusting faith in God's word of promise which this prophetic oracle reflects serves as an inspiring example for you and me today. It's the kind of example we need to look to when we find ourselves going through long nights of despair, when we are in the midst of periods of dire crisis or seemingly hopeless situations. When this text refers to "the strength of the Lord" it refers to a present reality in our lives today. His strength, which was able to create big new beginnings for his people in days of old is still the strength with which he directs our lives today. It is still the strength whereby he is able to create big new beginnings for his people today and beyond. "The steadfast love of the Lord never ceases," says the book of Lamentations; "his mercies never come to an end; they are new every morning!" How's that for a big new beginning with which to start each day of your life?

The Biggest Beginning of All in Jesus' Day

Now let's take still another look at this text from Micah, this time to see it as a reference to Bethlehem as the place of the biggest beginning of all in Jesus' day.

Through the centuries of the Old Testament era, the promise of God spoken by Nathan to David lived on. God's people lived in the expectation that the house of David would provide the kind of kingly leadership envisioned in words like those of this text. Theirs was an expectation which looked to each new king on the Jerusalem throne as one "who shall stand and feed his flock in the strength of the Lord, in the majesty of the name of the Lord his God." But the history of Judah's kings, portrayed so frankly in the Old Testament, makes it clear that one king after another disappointed the people's expectations as king after king failed to live up to the great ideals of kingship envisioned in Nathan's words to David.

Nevertheless, those expectations, based on God's promise, continued to live. They lived on, even after the monarchy itself had come to an end. They lived on because God's people had faith in what God had promised. They lived on in and through the intertestamental period, but now with a new shade of meaning. The new king who was expected became more and more a figure of a future age. The expectation was that he would in "the coming days" restore the kingship of the house of David and that in his royal reign all the ideals of Davidic kingship and all the promises made to the house of David would at last be fulfilled.

The question is, did it happen? Were those promises at last fulfilled? They were indeed! But they were fulfilled in ways that went far beyond the expectations that looked merely for a new king who would reestablish the house of David. According to Matthew's Gospel those promises were fulfilled when Jesus Christ, whom Matthew expressly calls "the Son of David" was born "in Bethlehem of Judea." The expectations expressed in Micah's prophetic words found their crowning fulfillment in the birth of him whom we worship as King of kings and Lord of lords and who was and is and ever shall be "great to the ends of the earth" (Micah 5:4). The promises of God on which today's Old Testament Lesson are based are promises which for us find their fulfillment in the birth at Bethlehem of the greatest Shepherd-King of all: in the birth of Jesus the Good Shepherd who continues to this day to "stand and feed his flock in the strength of the Lord, in the majesty of the name of the Lord his God" (Micah 5:4).

Our gracious God has always been, and continues to be, a God of big new beginnings, beginnings that are often made in events that are inconspicuous or unimpressive—like the birth of a little Baby in an out-of-the-way stable. Beginnings that are often made with people who are quite ordinary—like you or me. Beginnings that often occur in places which to human eyes are quite insignificant—like the little town of Bethlehem.

But remember what great things can happen when God makes his new beginnings with people like you and me! Remember what a great salvation can come with the birth of a little Baby like the one whose birth we will again celebrate in the coming days! Remember what great blessings—blessings of forgiveness, life and salvation—can come into God's world when God chooses to make a place like Bethlehem the starting point of his great new beginnings for you and me!

The little town of God's big beginnings certainly deserves a spiritual pilgrimage visit from you in the coming Christmas Season. The God of big beginnings deserves your undying gratitude and praise. The Baby of Bethlehem deserves your worship and adoration.

> To Bethlehem hasten with joyful accord:
> Oh, come, let us adore him, Christ the Lord!
> Amen.

WALTER WEGNER
Grace Lutheran Church
Pagedale, Missouri

THE ASTOUNDING GIFT

The Nativity of Our Lord—Christmas Day
Isaiah 62:10-12

What Did You Get for Christmas?

One question we are likely to ask our friends and to hear from them today is: What did you get for Christmas, or, did you get for Christmas what you had hoped for? It's a good question really, when you think about it, especially for Christian believers; for God has promised us salvation. The birth of the Savior is the fulfillment of that divine promise. That is the Christmas message.

So we look at the baby in the manger. Is he really the gift we had hoped for? Do we recognize in him the fulfillment of God's promises for which we hope and pray every day of our lives? Or do we find it difficult, perhaps even impossible to receive this child as God's gracious gift to us?

It would by no means be the first time that God's people were startled, yes appalled by God's response to their needs and prayers. In fact, when God freed his people Israel from captivity in Babylon more than 2500 years ago, they were terrified by the fulfillment of God's promise. So fearful was their experience when they returned home and were free to rebuild their lives and God's Temple that they nearly forgot how they had longed and prayed for their return home.

Our text from the Book of Isaiah urged God's people to discern in their liberation God's powerful faithfulness to his promise and the effectual gift of his love. That's what makes this text a real Christmas text although it comes to us from a time more than half a millennium earlier than the birth of Christ. For at Christmas it is our chief concern that we recognize in the child born of Mary God's mighty faithfulness to his promise and the all conquering effectiveness of his love.

Out of the Depth We Cry

So let's look at our text. The prophet who wrote under the name of Isaiah lived at the time when some of the first groups of Israelites returned to their homeland from their captivity in Babylon where after their defeat by Nebuchadnezzar God's people Israel had lived as slaves for about 60 years. Upon his victory the Babylonian king had destroyed Jerusalem including God's Temple where alone his chosen people were permitted to offer their sacrifices as prescribed by God's Law. To make sure that the Hebrews would never again plot and fight against him, Nebuchadnezzar had carried off into servitude in his capital city the leaders of Israel and their families. The old, the sick, and the feeble had been left behind. Most of them had perished within a few weeks or months.

In the course of the years much of the land of Israel had again become barren wilderness. The tumbledown ruins of its cities had been overgrown with nearly impenetrable thickets. Bent to slavery, uprooted from their homeland, unable to perform their acts of worship the exiled people had lived in misery and shame without comfort or hope. What kept them going was the fact that God had given them a new prophet known to us as Isaiah like the earlier prophet whose words are recorded in the first 39 chapters of the biblical book of Isaiah. The Second' Isaiah had implored the unhappy beaten-down people not to despair, for he had promised that God, the God of their fathers, would not forsake them, not even in this strange land in which they were unable to sing their Lord's song. God, the Second Isaiah had said, would send his Anointed One, his Messiah to set them free, that they might return home and rebuild the Temple for lawful and proper worship. How they had longed and prayed for the fulfillment of this promise.

God's Response

Finally a new figure appeared on the world scene, Cyrus, the King of Persia. He had defeated Nebuchadnezzar. Without knowing that he was doing God's will, Cyrus served as Israel's liberator and sent home the captives he had found in Babylon, and encouraged them to worship their own gods. The children of Israel felt as if they were dreaming when Cyrus set them free. Quite literally, their salvation had come. They would return home. How unspeakably beautiful and wonderful it would be! God had come through for them according to his Word!

Yet the practical task was exceedingly complex. Fortunately Cyrus had been astute enough to release the Israelites over a period of several years one tribe after the other. The advance groups had tried to prepare for the arrival of the others. The first tribe to arrive in the Holy Land had found nothing but wasteland. The returnees had to conquer the wilderness all over again. They found that life was so hard that they could barely endure it. Progress was so slow that when the next group of returnees arrived, they simply did not know what to do. The more groups of returnees reached the homeland the more desperate the situation grew for all. Starvation and epidemics ran wild. Was this the freedom they had hoped and prayed for? Was this the fulfillment of God's promise for which they had yearned with such fervor? And what about the Temple? Not only the Temple buildings were razed to the ground, even the broad access roads to the Temple had been swallowed up by the wilderness. That meant that none of the prescribed processions could march. Lawful worship would not be possible until those roads had been rebuilt. Even the new prophet, called the Third Isaiah who is the author of our text, had a different message for God's people. No longer did he call for the people to prepare the way for the Lord and his Anointed One who would set them free from their captivity in Babylon as the old prophet, the Second Isaiah, had done.

God's Gift as Harsh Reality

The Third Isaiah urged to prepare the way for the people, not just in some symbolic way, but quite literally to prepare those access roads to the Temple, that God's people might process in accord with the Holy Law to worship God in his Temple. And when the people protested that they had not bargained for this, the prophet bade them to remember and to look ahead in faith.

As they would recall their misery in Babylon, the divine promise to set them free, and the unspeakable joy of their return home, they would realize, the prophet said, that God is the God who keeps his word in his way. And as the returnees would lift up their eyes from the heavy, often seemingly futile labor to force the barren land to yield food for their ever-increasing numbers, they would by God's grace catch a glimpse of what was to come. Their return from Babylon would be an indication of the salvation God had prepared for them when he had chosen them as his own by giving them a new name which would ever remind them and tell the world who they were destined to be, namely the holy people, the redeemed of the Lord, sought out, a city not forsaken. Their memory of Babylon, of their sufferings, and of their wondrous liberation would affirm the validity of their vision and give them defiant hope now. In the power of that hope, which would be fed until the end of time by God's Word and by their worship, God's people will live and labor as those who have experienced God's mighty help and trustworthiness; and their commitment to God's praise and to justice and love of their neighbors will endure through all hardships and in spite of the murderous hatred of the world and the apparent futility of their dedication and their faith.

The Strange Christmas Gift

At Christmas that is also our story. We who today celebrate the birth of Jesus our Savior and the Redeemer of the world, we too wonder what kind of fulfillment Christ's coming really is. For if Christ is the Savior, then salvation is different from what we had expected. At least, that appears to be the case, since peace on earth clearly eludes us, and good will does not determine the relationships among us humans. Nor do the prospects look good for either of them. In fact, serious-minded, well-informed, and morally decent persons keep telling us today, as they have done for at least 200 years, that so long as human nature is what it is, there can be no peace on earth and no effective good will among men. We have learned that these people are telling the truth, which is thoroughly frightening in these days of nuclear bombs. No wonder God's promises at Christmas puzzle and distress us.

Remember and Look Ahead in Faith

The prophet's admonition to the people of Israel who were puzzled and distressed by the fulfillment of God's promise to set them free, applies to our bewilderment at the fulfillment of God's promise of salvation in the Christ child. To heed the prophet's words to ancient Israel today, we remember and look ahead in faith at Christmas time. We celebrate Christmas in order to remember that the God who gave us in Mary's firstborn son our Savior and the Redeemer of the world, is the God who keeps his word in his own way. We recall that God's way of fulfilling his promises more often than not is quite different from our expectations and dreams. Yet God's way of keeping his word, no matter how strange it may look to us, accomplishes his loving purpose and always preserves our humanity. Our total dependence on God does not reduce us to puppets on a string. God gives us his blessed gift in such a way that we may respond to him as responsible human beings; much like the exiles who returned from Babylon were able to respond to the gift of their liberation by walking through the gate of his grace and by spending themselves in building the access roads to the Temple on which other returnees could process to worship God with them. The God who gave us Jesus of Nazareth is the God who keeps his word. Christ guarantees to us as it were the effectiveness of the promises of God no matter how illusionary they sound and how fragile he looks.

In accord with the prophet's instruction to ancient Israel we also look ahead in faith at Christmastime. He who came as Mary's son is the one who will come again as Lord and King of all. Only as we live with that certainty today are we able to commit ourselves now to the doing of the will of him who through Christ has made us his own. All appearances to the contrary notwithstanding, that's what our life and the life of the world are all about, that we move in spite of resistance, pain, and futility into the future of his design under the banner of the cross.

Living with God's Christmas Gift

At Christmas too God deals with us in such a way that he gives us the opportunity to respond to his gift and to prove by our mode of living what he has made of us in his power and love. We are God's own, his beloved; we are his people, holy, made righteous by his mercy; we are his royal priesthood who praises his name forever. We are all of it and more by God's will and grace. As such we live among other humans who like us need God's grace and salvation. God's grace opens the mercy-gate for us by giving his Son to us and for us. We who by faith have passed through that gate are now called to give ourselves to clearing the road for others that they too may approach the gate, and together we may enter God's presence with thanksgiving.

Christmas Hope

God's Christmas gift, the newborn infant in the manger, looks fragile and strangely inadequate as God's response to the human condition. On Christmas we confess that in this child God has fulfilled his ancient promises. At Christmas God calls us once again to build the road on which with our fellowmen we shall move into the future which God's grace has designed. Our Christmas celebrations praise and thank God; but above all they enable and inspire us to live every day as the Redeemed of the Lord who patiently bring Christ's light of healing and hope to the world until he returns, and God is all in all.

LEOPOLD W. BERNHARD
Lutheran Church of the Reformation
Washington, D.C.

A SONG AND A DANCE

First Sunday after Christmas
Jeremiah 31:10-13

"I am sometimes asked to explain the success of *Roots*," said Alex Haley, "to pinpoint what it is that this book has touched, and the answer is really very simple. In all of us there is a hunger, marrow-deep, to know our heritage—to know who we are and where we have come from. Without this enriching knowledge, there is a hollow yearning . . . a vacuum, an emptiness, and the most disquieting loneliness" (from *Reader's Digest,* May 1977, p. 73). Attempting to understand something of the unprecedented reaction to his book and the award-winning television series, Haley points to the great need of all people to have a sense of lineage and ancestral foundation. This knowledge of roots not only enables one to live confidently in the present but it is the raw material for dreams of the future. Such are the genetics of life: the past is the key to the future.

In one of those inevitable book-signing appearances, Haley tells of a pregnant black woman who handed him two copies to sign. "One," she said, "is for me; the other is for him"—and with that she patted her stomach. For countless thousands, the book became "my history" affecting "my present" and "my future."

Every biblical text has an important past, present, and future. One can hardly appreciate a passage spoken to us as an isolated word. Nor is it sufficient to merely describe the historic situation of the prophet or the nation of Israel at that time. Texts contain great themes in Scripture that encourage powerful memories as well as dreams for the future. We will, therefore, listen to the lyrical words of Jeremiah with an ear to the past and an eye to the future.

The Prophet Sings

It is a little strange to hear words of good news—of singing and dancing—from Jeremiah. He was a prophet who continually predicted Israel's doom. Because of the nation's faithlessness, he believed God had raised up foreign powers to punish and shame them into submission. Jerusalem is described as a desperate harlot relying on her power to seduce in order to stay alive. Israel's leaders are like vines without grapes, barren cupboards, wells that run dry. Like a potter dissatisfied with his work, God will take his clay, his people, to unmake and remake them. Violence, lament, judgment, punishment—Jeremiah's themes were very unpopular in his day and hardly qualify him as a joyful minstrel man of Scripture.

"Love and joy come to you" sings the old Christmas carol. It is inevitable for those who read Scripture and know the God of Scripture that "love and joy" eventually counterbalance and reverse the weeping and gloom so prevalent in the sermons and oracles of Jeremiah. And so, even this prophet, carrying one of the heaviest rebukes for Israel, leads us into a moment of ecstatic "love and joy." His secretary and prophetic friends preserved a "book of comfort" as a collection of cheerful words of hope and consolation. They knew that the ultimate purpose of Jeremiah's ministry of doom was to lead a faithful people into the promised joy of their Lord.

In the Beginning a Song

The song of Jeremiah has many ancestors. One could look to the account of creation in the first chapters of Genesis. Claus Westermann writes:

> The first chapter of the Bible strikes one who reads it for the first time like a mysterious song, like a festal celebration—one could almost say, like a heavenly liturgy.
> (*The Genesis Accounts of Creation,* Fortress, p. 6.)

In the beginning a song!

In another "creation passage" God answers the questioning of Job by calling him to consider the wonder of creation, to praise his maker rather than trying to reason with him. The beginning of life is described as a time ". . . when the morning stars sang together, and all the sons of God shouted for joy" (Job 38:7).

According to biblical scholars, the real beginning of Israel's history is not found in Genesis but in the exodus from Egypt. There, on the other side of the sea, after plague and Passover, with the people now safe from the pursuing hoard of Pharaoh's army, they sang and danced. A prophetess named Miriam took a timbrel in her hand and sang:

> Sing to the Lord, for he has triumphed gloriously;
> The horse and his rider he has thrown into the sea.

And, reports Exodus, women joined Aaron's sister in a dance for joy. In the beginning, a song and dance to celebrate the saving acts of Yahweh, the Lord.

The Old Testament is punctuated with such singing and dancing as Israel encountered the steadfast love of their creator and redeemer. David, "the sweet psalmist," was a prototype of every ideal man in his ability to praise God. So prevalent is this theme that one is tempted to say of Scripture that it is more singable than readable—a Song of Songs rather than a Book of Books!

The Glad Refrain

Nowhere does the Old Testament's promise of joyful song find more obvious fulfillment than in the opening chapters of St. Luke. Jeremiah's hopes are realized

Young women will dance for joy,
and men young and old will make merry.

(*LBW* Canticle 14)

Young Mary, old Zechariah break into eloquent singing—in canticles that formed part of the earliest Christian hymnal. In Luke the birth narrative is a veritable concert of praise.

Today's Gospel is a perfect complement to the Jeremiah text. Old Simeon "looking for the consolation of Israel" was the kind of man that Jeremiah longed for in his own day. A faithful Israelite who was righteous and devout, whose hope and confidence was in God alone.

As if by coincidence their paths cross, the old man and the little family with the infant Jesus. In the great spaces of the Temple that meeting would go unnoticed. Later ages, however, would see it as a momentous intersection of Israel's hope and the answer of God in the gift of his Son. The brief encounter precipitated a song which, in our communion liturgy, is called the Nunc Dimittis. For thousands of years the church has treasured Simeon's song as a sign of the great-promise-come-true in the incarnation of Jesus Christ. Each time we commune we taste something of the joy and peace that Simeon experienced.

The Final Chorus

Of all the specters in Charles Dickens' *A Christmas Carol,* none scared Ebenezer Scrooge as much as the last, the "Ghost of Christmas Yet to Come." That phantom showed Scrooge the inevitable outcome of his malignant personality.

> The Ghost of Christmas Yet to Come conveyed him . . . into . . . a churchyard. Here, then, the wretched man, whose name he had now to learn, lay underneath the ground. Walled in by houses; overrun by grass and weeds; choked up with too much burying. A worthy place!
>
> The Spirit stood among the graves, and pointed down to one.
>
> Scrooge crept towards it, trembling as he went; and, following the finger, read upon the stone of the neglected grave his own name, EBENEZER SCROOGE.

Scrooge was scared into goodness. It was a fortunate if elaborate bit of dreaming that changed that man's life and led him into acts of charity and goodwill, but such tactics do not always assure us of a happy ending.

Jeremiah's prophecies of destruction could not frighten Israel into righteousness. Foreign armies overran the land as the leaders were carried off into exile. During the prophet's lifetime, the story ended in death and destruction. But that was not the last word.

The prophet, knowing God's loving purpose could sing:

> He who scattered Israel will gather him,
> and will keep him as a shepherd keeps his flock.
> I will turn their mourning into joy,
> I will comfort them, and give
> them gladness for sorrow.

As we celebrate the glad tidings of Christmas, we join a great song that began at creation and will continue into eternity. The melody is pure joy; the words tell of one who died and rose again for us. God's love song. Our love song. So dance, sing: Alleluia, Alleluia.

WALTER C. HUFFMAN
Trinity Lutheran Seminary
Columbus, Ohio

GOD'S LIGHT, GLORY, PRESENCE

The Epiphany of Our Lord
Isaiah 60:1-6

Let's talk about light. We all know something about it. Scripture also speaks about light. It uses the concept to help us understand something about God and about what God has done for us.

Lights Can Attract Us

One night we found it rather hard to concentrate on our driving. The road, the car, and the weather were all very good. The problem was a magnificent display of the northern lights. Their beauty attracted our attention and distracted us from the business of driving. We solved the problem by taking turns at the wheel. That way, at least one of us could give undivided attention to the scene.

The shopkeeper, too, knows how lights can attract. The elaborate displays of lights outside the business places and/or shining through the windows are evidences that merchant knows the importance of attracting attention to his place of business.

Lights Can Guide Us

The shopkeeper's lights and others, like the old-fashioned Coast Guard light stations, can serve to guide the traveler to his destination. Lights can identify the place for which we seek and can reveal danger spots we need to avoid.

Lights Dispel the Darkness

We have all experienced this fact when we light a match or turn on a light switch. It is more dramatic and inspiring to experience this reality in the beautiful candlelight service on Christmas Eve. All the lights of the sanctuary are extinguished. Then a lighted candle appears near the altar. It is only a single light and very small but it cannot be overwhelmed by the darkness. Then ushers light additional candles and distribute them to all the worshipers. A warm and gentle glow pervades the entire place which once was dark.

God's work, God's truth, God's self-disclosure is something like that. Listen to the prophet of old:

> Arise, shine; for your light has come, and the glory of the LORD has risen upon you. For behold, darkness shall cover the earth, and thick darkness the peoples; but the LORD will arise upon you, and his glory will be seen upon you. And nations shall come to your light, and kings to the brightness of your rising (Isa. 60:1-3).

The Old Testament Witnesses

The prophet spoke of God coming to his people as a light and as a glory. We need to explore that concept of God's glory. The term is used to describe some visible evidence of the presence of God. During the days of the exodus, as Israel wandered in the wilderness, they sensed the glory of God in the fire and the cloud atop Mount Sinai; they sensed his glory and used the term in reference to the pillar of cloud by day and the pillar of fire by night. It was by this light that they were led and when that glory settled on the tabernacle Israel could worship in the way and at the place that God had chosen. It was a "tabernacling presence" among them. Centuries after the wilderness wanderings, when Solomon built the Temple, the glory made its home there.

Several centuries after the erection of the Temple, a prophet called Ezekiel, by birth and training a priest, found himself in exile far from his home in Jerusalem. As he pondered his plight and that of the other exiles, he saw a vision of that glory near the river Kebar in Babylon. As the visions continued he came to realize that God cannot be caged in a box. He came to realize that God had reacted to the rampant iniquity in Jerusalem by forsaking both the Temple and the city to dwell among the needy exiles far from home. He grew in faith in a God who cares and who would eventually lead his people in a new exodus from Babylon and dwell among his people in a new and better Temple.

The passage from Isaiah needs to fit in the plan of God at this point. He envisioned, as did Ezekiel, that the effect of Israel's restoration and the presence of God among his people would be that the nations would be drawn to worship the God of Israel and gifts of gold and frankincense would be brought.

Isaiah

The message of Isaiah for his own time was that God is faithful. God keeps his promises to judge and redeem his people and to dwell among them. Such a message is relevant for any age. But there was more!

God is faithful and therefore the future is hopeful. There was hope of restoration to the land. There was hope of prosperity and recognition by the Gentiles. But there was more! Ultimately, the prophet insisted, the nations would be drawn to Israel and to her God who now dwelt among his people.

Later Witnesses

The obvious meaning for the prophet's time does not exhaust the divine intention which would be interpreted by other inspired writers. Hundreds of years after the prophets spoke, a light appeared in the heavens. Wise Men from the east beheld it and inspired by it came to visit the infant Jesus with his parents now in Bethlehem. They brought with them gifts of gold, frankincense and myrrh.

We do not know for certain who these men were. Some have suggested Zoroastrians from Persia, others have suggested that the visitors were Jews living far from home and yet others have proposed that they were kings. Their identity matters little.

The Gospel writers saw in the visit of the Wise Men from the east a fulfillment of the divine promise and in so doing made a most astounding claim—that in Jesus, the infant of Bethlehem, God's glory had come to Israel in a unique way, and because this was true the men came and brought the appropriate gifts (Matt. 2:1-12).

John is even more specific. He wrote of Jesus saying, "the Word became flesh and dwelt among us, full of grace and truth; we beheld his glory, glory as of the only Son from the Father" (1:14). He spoke of Jesus as the true light, the light from heaven, the light that enlightens every man, the light that shines in the darkness and is not overwhelmed by it (1:1-9).

We could continue to heap up phrases from the Gospels too to show how profoundly the New Testament writers were influenced by the Old Testament imagery and vocabulary and how convinced they were that Jesus was the ultimate fulfillment of the prophetic hope.

Arise, Shine, Your Light Has Come

These words of Isaiah take on a new significance in the light of the incarnation. We have received a message from him of whom it is written, "He reflects the glory of God and bears the very stamp of his nature" (Heb. 1:3).

What is the significance of this for us? Jesus said, "You are the light of the world. A city set on a hill cannot be hid. Nor do men light a lamp and put it under a bushel, but on a stand, and it gives light to all in the house. Let your light so shine before men that they may see your good works and glorify your Father who is in heaven" (Matt. 5:14-16).

How shall we shine, we who have no light in ourselves? We are like the moon which has no light in itself but reflects the light from the sun. We have such a light source in Jesus Christ. It is our privilege, our duty, and our delight to reflect his light to all around us.

Jesus has shown most dramatically that God does keep his promises, that God is concerned about his creation, that God is, indeed, with us. We are never alone, even though we may be lonely. God is concerned about his people. He meets us in our need and redeems us and draws us to himself.

That marvelous light of God's revelation not only draws us to him, but also guides us. His word is a "lamp unto our feet and a light unto our path." That's why we are so interested in studying the Scriptures and in trying to teach them. All the schools of the church exist for this reason. The mission work of the church attempts to teach all to observe all that our Lord has commanded (Matt. 28:20).

Finally, that revelation of God is taught in order to dispel the ignorance that prevails where this truth is not presented. That truth which is in Christ gives to each of us a sense of self-worth and a deep appreciation of the freedom that our God bestows on us. The events of the exodus show us that God is concerned about all facets of freedom, even the political and economic. We also know that he is concerned about our freedom from the bondage to sin, guilt, and death. God's Son has set us free and we are free indeed.

In our freedom we seek not only to teach the Word of God as it has been revealed to us but we also seek to order our lives as the Spirit reveals, inspires, motivates, and empowers. In this way God is glorified in the lives of his saints, not only by word, but also by deed.

So rise and shine! We have cause to rejoice—we are remembered by God. We have cause to rejoice because God is faithful to his promises and has sent his light into the world. Our God has come to us in Jesus Christ our Lord. That's the word of fulfillment for all nations and for all time.

GERALD C. WHITE
McIntosh, Minnesota

WE ARE THE SERVANT

The Baptism of Our Lord—First Sunday after the Epiphany
Isaiah 42:1-7

Have you ever thought of the possibility that each of us may be the servant of the Lord described in the text?

That possibility may seem presumptuous, but as we are identified as a child of God in our Baptism, we are also called in righteousness as his servant. We are chosen and upheld by him in that act and God's promises concerning it. As we are called in righteousness and his spirit is placed upon us, we are commissioned into his service, like the servant of the text. As we are taken by the hand and kept by him, the mission to which we are sent is made plain.

On this day, the day of the Baptism of our Lord, let's reflect on the proposition that we are the servant of the text to the extent that we are both identified as a servant, and commissioned into his service in our baptism.

We Are the Servant—Identified in Our Baptism

Feel for a moment some of the emotions and attitudes surrounding this text. There must be a feeling of loneliness for a word from the Lord, an experience of its absence. One can sense the longing of the prophet in this text as he reflects on those who have gone before him with courage and conviction. They proclaimed the word and way of the Lord with power. Now he waits for another to come and fill that role.

There is about this text a sense of yearning for somebody, definitely expected, but not yet present. One can almost see the prophet peering into the hazy horizon of time. One can imagine his standing on tiptoes, so to speak, to get a better view of that which lies in the distance. He is yearning, longing for one who would come, and in coming fill those expectations by being such a servant. One in whom the Lord would find great delight and would come as a gift, a sign of God's faithfulness to the people.

It is possible that the writer has experienced the word and ministry of several great prophets, or one great prophet. It is possible that he is referring to the prophet Isaiah. There may be a shortage of such people at this time in the nation's experience and they need somebody—somebody of flesh and blood, somebody to be that servant again. Whatever may be the case, there is a desire for a real person, somebody who would come and serve.

From our vantage point in history, we can see more clearly that he came. In this latter part of the twentieth century we can say with certainty that he came in human form, walked this earth, and fulfilled completely the yearnings expressed so eloquently in this text.

Today, as we celebrate the Baptism of our Lord, one of the most thoroughly documented events of his life and ministry, we have the opportunity to reflect on that event and on our baptism as well. We can see a connection between the servant of the text and Jesus of Nazareth.

We can see also that you and I have a place in that continuing drama. We can see that we, too, are chosen, named, and identified in our baptism in a similar manner. We are one of his. By virtue of that act of baptism we stand in the tradition of the servant awaited by the prophet in the text and the servant of the Lord, Jesus Christ our Savior.

In our Gospel for today, we see the transition beginning in the ministry of a most unusual character, John the Baptist. He is bearing witness in his own body and life to the continuity from the old covenant to the new.

There is John the Baptist, standing with one foot in the history of the Old Testament and stepping with the other into the New. He and Jesus came forth from the waters of the ancient

Jordan into a new era. A new period of the history of God's people was being initiated. Jesus went forth from that day performing his ministry as that chosen servant anticipated from the days of antiquity.

The writer of the Gospel for today noted the transition in this manner: "This is my own dear Son, with whom I am well pleased." The dream of the prophet has been realized, the prophecy fulfilled. The servant of the Lord had come and he is well pleased.

Our Baptism brings us into that history and makes that tradition ours as well. That wonderful story told around the camp fires at night and proclaimed to the people in their public places of worship, is our story. We stand in that tradition and their hope and its fulfillment in Jesus Christ becomes our hope and fulfillment as well.

There is a continuing stream of development in the plan of God, a historical succession, an unbreakable tradition that comes from the anticipated servant of the text, to the servant Jesus Christ at the river Jordan, to our identification in baptism.

We are the servant. We are taken by the hand, kept by God as his soul's delight, having his spirit placed upon us, and sent on our way with a definite ministry to perform.

We Are the Servant—Commissioned Into His Service

In the movement from the waters of the Jordan into the dawning of a new era, all of the preceding hopes and dreams, prophecies and aspirations were openly identified, claimed, and placed upon Jesus as the one anticipated by the text.

The spirit was put upon him and we can hear the echoes of the prophet coming down to us through the centuries.

> Behold, my servant, whom I uphold,
>   my chosen, in whom my soul delights;
> I have put my spirit upon him,
>   He will bring forth justice to the nations.

In the movement of the waters of our baptism and God's word concerning it, his spirit is placed upon us, and that which was anticipated from of old becomes our experience as well. We are sent forth in his name with a ministry to perform. The outline for that ministry is placed before us in language that is painfully precise and unmistakably clear. Our baptism marks the ending of our life and ushers us into the new as we are reborn in the water and his word. The implications are overwhelming.

In short, our lives are to be given as we are sent,

> ... as a covenant to the people,
> a light to the nations,
> to open the eyes that are blind,
> to bring out the prisoners from the dungeon,
> from the prison those who sit in darkness.

As servants, according to this commissioning, we are given by God to his people and that is an act of his keeping his word.

The results are demonstrable. The people of God should be better off because we have been sent to them. That puts it bluntly and to the point. The people of this world, of our nation, community, and family, should be better off because we are here. The affairs of his kingdom should be in better order because we are here. There is really no other way to put it.

- The Gospel of Jesus Christ and the continuing experience of human injustice are incompatible.
- The Gospel of Jesus Christ and the enslaving of people whether in mind or body are incompatible.
- The Gospel of Jesus Christ and the violation of human dignity, whether publicly or in private, are incompatible.

It has always been a mark of the servant's ministry that the people ministered unto should have some relief and justice. That the tyranny, hunger, suffering, and death so common in our human experience be confronted and overcome.

- If we are among those who are his servants, we are to be gentle and not break the bruised reed, nor quench the dimly burning wicks.
- If we are among those who are his servants, we will not fail or become discouraged until all has been done and justice has been accomplished upon the earth.
- If we are among those who are his servants, called in righteousness then we have little choice left in the matter. That is, unless, we choose unfaithfulness.
- If we are among those who are his servants, we may have courage and confidence because God's purposes and promises are dependable.

His promises are clear. His support is always present and his spirit will not be taken away. He has taken us by the hand and promises to keep us. And God keeps his promises. Ask the faithful saints in your midst.

We are the servant. In our reflection on our Baptism today, as we celebrate the Baptism of our Lord, remember he was identified as the one who would bring it all to pass. Remember also, that he in his good time and his way, finally, alone and in anguish on the cross paid the full price of being the servant. In his faithfulness he experienced and absorbed the ignorance, injustice and human hatred directed towards him, and they extracted their full price. Remember also his being raised from the dead, even though the hopes and dreams of the centuries were frustrated for a moment, to come forth again as that final and great sign of God's faithfulness to his people.

All of that comes to pass before us as we reflect on our Baptism today. In that act we became one with the servant in the text; one with this one who stood in the Jordan and hung on the cross; one with him as he came forth from the grave. Have no fear and be of good courage for he is the one who comes to us, calls, claims, identifies, and commissions us into his service as his servants sent forth into the world. He has taken us by the hand and he will keep us.

May God bless us in this ministry, both as clergy and lay, as we are supported by the promises made to that servant so many years ago, and as that same spirit is placed upon us. Let us pray that we may be upheld and that we may be his soul's delight as his servants.

AUGUST E. WENZEL, President
The Southern District—ALC
Austin, Texas

FINDING HOPE AMID ASHES AND RUINS

Second Sunday after the Epiphany
Isaiah 62:1-5

Think about people you have known who have come through great tragedies in life with the ability to maintain a spirit of hope. That ability or disposition is most certainly a gift from God. It is truly a gift when people are able to recover from grief and despair, when they are able to turn from the pain and suffering of a past event to discover healing in new community life and wellsprings of hope for the future.

The Aftermath of War

I remember an evening in West Germany in 1961. I was a student at the university at Heidelberg and had been invited to visit at the home of a German friend in Mannheim, an industrial city on the Rhine river some 15 miles away. The bomb damage that had been inflicted on Mannheim during World War II was almost unbelievable. From the streetcar stop, we walked through block after block of bombed-out apartment buildings. Brick skeletons of buildings loomed up around us with their open doorways. Hollow window openings were like eye sockets lined with the jagged remains of broken glass. Sixteen years after the end of the war, these bombed-out buildings remained. Through the open doorways, we could see huge piles of bricks, broken only by the shadows of occasional roof beams which cut off the light from the open sky above. We entered one such doorway and made our way through the rubble. We climbed on what had once been an enclosed stairway to a third floor level where by some strange chance, an entire apartment remained intact. There my friend's family had made their home. There they were seeking out new life. There they were seeking for new wellsprings of hope amid the ruins and remains of war.

Such a situation can help us understand with greater clarity the text from Isaiah before us. This beautiful poem of celebration and hope for Jerusalem comes from a similar situation long ago. Jerusalem had been leveled to the ground in 587 B.C. by the Babylonian armies. In slavelike caravans, most of the population (some think 100,000 people) had been marched northward around the so-called Fertile Crescent down into the Tigris and Euphrates river valley areas. There they lived in exile for the next fifty years. There many of them died. Not until the rise of Persia and the new emperor, Cyrus, did the situation change. In 539 B.C., Cyrus issued an edict allowing Hebrew people to return to their homelands. Some did. At first there were only a few, then others followed.

These events were obviously on the mind of the author of our text. We fool ourselves if we think that this was a romantic era. Far from it! The indications from this section of Isaiah, as well as from Ezra, Nehemiah and other contemporary writings, indicates that life was very bleak. Some obviously returned to their homeland with great optimism. But their optimism was quickly challenged by almost overwhelming economic difficulties. From all indications, the Persian authorities provided very little if any real help. With almost no resources, meager food supplies and amid the harsh realities of summer heat, drought, and winter winds, the people found the task of rebuilding their once-proud capital city almost impossible. Hidden amid the words of our text is the fear that the people are almost at the point of abandoning this task. Jerusalem simply looked like something forsaken, abandoned, the ruins of a bygone era. Just such realities provide the backdrop for us as we hear this text. And yet they are realities that are not unfamiliar for many people in our day as well.

Hope for Tired People

For Zion's sake I cannot keep silent,
For Jerusalem's sake I will not rest,
until her vindication goes forth as brightness,
and her salvation as a burning torch.

The prophet feels compelled to speak to his people. He knows very well the earlier traditions of the faith of Israel. His faith demands that he speak a word of comfort and encouragement to this weary and tired people. Focusing on the city of Jerusalem, the prophet plays on several Hebrew names to proclaim a new basis for hope. He declares that Jerusalem will be called by a new name. No longer shall this city be called Azubah "forsaken" (cf. 1 Kings 22:42) or her land Shememah "desolate." Rather, the city will henceforth be called Hephzibah "my delight is in her" (cf. 2 Kings 21:1) and the land Beulah "married to the Lord." By using the marriage imagery, the prophet is clearly reminding the people of their ancient covenant relationship with God. The time in exile may indeed have seemed like desolation. And without question, other peoples must certainly have laughed and mocked them, suggesting that their God had abandoned them. But the people of faith knew that this was not the case. It was the people who had abandoned their God, not the other way around. It was the people who had brought trouble on their own heads. But even so, the God of Israel, the Lord of all creation, had not abandoned them.

The Faithfulness of God

The prophet directs the people to their own heritage of faith. Precisely there in their own heritage, the people can find a wellspring for new hope in their own time. The Lord, your God, delights in you and you shall be married. You, holy city, are to be adorned as a bride for your husband. There has been no divorce. God has not forsaken you. In just this way, the prophet speaks to the people.

Jerusalem: People of God in Every Age

Now it is important to note that when the prophets speak of Jerusalem, they are almost always thinking about the welfare of people. A city exists to serve people. A city is intended to be a place of blessing . . . a place of order, harmony and service to people in their various needs. It is exactly the same with government—government in any form is intended to be of blessing to people. The Bible judges a city and political leaders again and again by the way in which they serve people. Because this is so, these marvelous poetic words are not just an interesting monument from a time and place long ago. Nor are they just words for people who happen to live in the city limits of Jerusalem today. Rather, these words belong to every community that seeks to live out of the heritage of biblical faith. They are words which are particularly at home with people who have known deep struggles, people who have been confronted with the temptation to give in to discouragement and fatigue. They are words for people who feel threatened by a loss of energy in the face of overwhelming odds. They may well be words for all of us as we think about the challenges of this Epiphany season and the year ahead.

In Christ Jesus, we are part of the people of faith who are the recipients of this tradition of faith. We are citizens of Jerusalem, the holy people of God. We are invited to draw our sustenance and new energy from the same source that nurtured people long ago. We are invited to live today with the confidence that the Lord of heaven and earth rejoices over us when we are about the business of building community. The promise of our God is certain even when we find our world in disarray. The promise is sure even when we find ourselves surrounded by ashes and ruins.

Not many of us have had to live amid the actual ashes and ruins of a city devastated by war. But many of us know all too well what those feelings are like. In whatever place we find ourselves, let us take comfort and find strength in knowing that our business is the business of building a city. Our business and our calling in life is to build our community and our congregation in ways that can bring blessings . . . blessings for those around us and blessings for ourselves. Our hope and our energy rest in secure trust that God is for us.

> As the bridegroom rejoices over a bride,
> so does our God rejoice over us.

A. JOSEPH EVERSON
Hope Lutheran Church
St. Paul, Minnesota

CELEBRATE!

Third Sunday after the Epiphany
Isaiah 61:1-6

What are we waiting for? Let's get the celebration started. We have been waiting long enough, it seems to me—like several thousand years on stand-by, but not much has happened. We had been told that God would come, but there is little to suggest he ever has or ever will. There are those who want to pawn off that poor baby in the manger and that central criminal at Calvary as God, but a likely God he is! That God has gone seems more of a reality than that he came or comes or ever will come.

Centuries ago the prophet Jeremiah, scratching at the bottom of despair, cried out to God, "Why are you a stranger in the land?" He had waited and God didn't show. And another prophet named Habakkuk screamed, "Lord, how long shall I cry, and you will not hear?" When the Jews returned from exile in the land of Babylon where they had spent those decades weeping at the memory of Zion (there were at least a few who did), they put their waiting into song, "My soul waits for the Lord more than they that watch for the morning," but when the morning came it didn't look much like the Lord. Things hadn't changed much when they landed in Jerusalem. And then one day there was that strange parade that came across the Mount of Olives and the people sang "Hosanna!" But less than one week later this poor spectacle who called himself the Son of David, great King David, wore a crown of thorns and was enthroned against the black skies of Judea on a cross.

If God Can't Deliver

True enough, there were a few who said that he had risen from the dead, and they staged a mission celebration, rushing out across the world to spread the story of the resurrection and to warn that he would come again in clouds of glory. But he never did and never has. Will he never learn? If God can't deliver what he promised—good news for the afflicted, liberty for captives, a garland instead of ashes, the oil of gladness instead of mourning, the mantle of praise instead of a faint spirit—he surely can't expect us to just sit here waiting patiently, hoping vaguely that there ought to be a silver lining somewhere, while our hopes are shredded and our expectations disappointed. We will have to go it on our own, and isn't that what we've been doing anyway? We will have to find another mission and another purpose in our lives, and isn't that what we've been doing anyway? We will have to find another content for the Christian faith, and isn't that what we've been doing anyway? Epiphany! That *God* has shown himself? It's another one of those exaggerated preacher claims!

What Is There to Celebrate?

But let me tell you that the Bible is an honest book that tells it like it is—the afflicted and the broken-hearted and the captives and the prison house, the mourners and the folks who sit in ashes of burned hopes. There is little cause for outward joy. There is nothing of that smiley froth and foam of simulated piety and joy that one is fed by hucksters of religion on the Sunday morning tube, "Smile! You're on camera now!" The Bible is an honest book, for it's about the human fears and doubts and sorrows and the peace of God that never quite comes off. It's about the Christmas blues and the mid-winter blahs and the Easter-time depression and the darkness that seems always to close in on us when everything should be the brightest. The Bible is about some folks called "us." So what is there to celebrate? The peace achievements of the world's big wheels, or perhaps the breakthrough that enables us to find our way around the darkness with a flashlight, or the January white sale and the new fur wrap to comfort those who are cold?

Good News in Judah

But now let's see if we can get located here and find a better way to celebrate! There was little cause for celebration when those weary exiles had come home from Babylon to see the ashes and the rubble of their holy city, to nurse their grieving hearts, to mourn the glory of the land that had been lost. But there appeared a prophet on the scene in Judah with good news from God. Certain that he had been sent from God with that good news, he put it this way as we read it in the lesson, "The Spirit of the Lord God is upon me, because he has anointed me to bring good tidings to the afflicted, to bind up the broken-hearted, to proclaim liberty to the captives, and the opening of the prison to those who are bound," to proclaim that God is faithful to his covenant and promise. He is coming with salvation, with relief, with comfort. He will restore your cities that still bear the marks of desolation. He will compensate the glory and the wealth that has been lost. He will plant you once again as oaks of righteousness. And to describe the difference that will make, the prophet reinforces the good news like this, a garland instead of ashes, the oil of gladness instead of mourning, the mantle of praise instead of a faint spirit. And by the preaching of that word, the celebration started. The salvation he proclaimed began to happen. The wounds were healed. The captives were freed. The bondage broken.

Good News in Nazareth

There had not been much to celebrate when down the centuries Jesus came to Nazareth. His people were in bondage yet again beneath the heel of Rome. Poverty abounded. Hopes were desolate. The God who had made a covenant with them seemed distant from the scene. The least likely place he might appear was Nazareth. Then in the synagogue one Sabbath day, when he was handed the Isaiah scroll to read, he read this lesson, and to everyone's astonishment, "Today this Scripture is fulfilled!" He had been anointed with the Spirit to proclaim good tidings, sent from God to free the captives and to bind the broken-hearted, to bring the day of our salvation. But they didn't celebrate when Jesus made that claim in Nazareth. The hometown boy made good was not to be received in his hometown. No prophet is acceptable in his own country. They provided usher service for his exit and tried to throw him from a cliff. But in that man of Nazareth, the Son of Joseph, still wearing on his hands the callouses of carpenters, the Son of God appeared, salvation's day had dawned, the promises of God had ripened to fulfillment, and the celebration of the new age started. It was Epiphany!

Good News for Us

That's the celebration, and it's our celebration now! In a world where there is little genuine to celebrate, we celebrate God breaking through, God coming to our level where the sorrows and the ashes are, the sin and guilt and death. This day this Scripture is fulfilled. Our Lord is here in Word and Sacrament. He comes to us in our despair of ever finding freedom from that sin and guilt and death with good news of forgiveness, chains of bondage broken, and eternal life. He comes to us when everything seems wrong and we despair of ever being right—he comes with righteousness, his gift for us. He comes to us when we are down, defeated, sick all over, and sick mostly of ourselves, and promises, "You are my child. I have my hand on you and I will never let you go. Fear not!" He comes to us with an entirely new life, a life no longer measured by our own performance, but by his, and only that can make a difference in our own. What was it Mary sang in her Magnificat? "My soul magnifies the Lord, and my spirit rejoices in God my Savior: for he who is mighty has done great things for me, and holy is his name."

What Are We Waiting For?

What, then, are we waiting for? Let's get the celebration started. God has come and God is here and God will come again. Christ has died, but Christ is risen. Christ will come again. That's solid joy, and in the noises of our celebration we can let the world know why we celebrate. Read on a little farther in this prophet's word and you will hear his reason, "I will greatly rejoice in the Lord, my soul shall exult in my God, for he has clothed me with the garments of salvation. He has covered me with robes of righteousness." And Habakkuk whom we mentioned also came to that, you may recall, for I don't care how bad things get, he said, "I will rejoice in the Lord, and I will joy in the God of my salvation."

Two little children who had suffered through the tragedy of separation by their parents, one of those disastrous things so many children suffer, were desperately ill and fevered, hovering close to death. They hadn't had a smile, hardly a sign of life for many days, when they were told one evening by their Daddy as he visited and sat with them, that as soon as they were well again they would discover that he had returned to them. And at that promise there were tiny smiles, and from that moment on the battle with their sickness had been won. The celebration had begun. We have an even better promise, haven't we? We have the promise that our God has never left us, that the God who came in Jesus Christ has come because we thought that he had left us, when in fact, we had left him. But now the celebration can begin, and let the priests of the Lord and the ministers of our God shout Hosanna! Alleluia! Amen!

ALTON F. WEDEL
Mount Olive Lutheran Church
Minneapolis, Minnesota

HELP FOR THE HESITANT

Fourth Sunday after the Epiphany
Jeremiah 1:4-10

It begins with a phone call. It's a phone call through which we learn that a close friend or neighbor or colleague has met with tragedy, lies seriously ill or is in grave emotional distress. It's one of those calls that leaves us sick inside and numb all over as we slowly hang up the receiver.

Our immediate reaction to the news such a call brings is, I suppose, the desire to reach out to that person, our friend. We want to be there with him or her. We want to say something, do something, anything, that will be of help. But then it hits us, and we say to ourselves: What can I do? I have no special skills, no special training for dealing with this kind of situation. As a friend, as a Christian, I want to do something. Yet when it comes to matters of how my faith might be able to speak to the grief and pain of a dear friend, I am at a loss for words. So while we truly want to do something of value, we feel incapable of it, and perhaps more often than not, we end up doing nothing at all.

Oh, it may be that we'll send a greeting card—one of those humorous ones with a get-well-quick message—or we'll pay a visit and talk about the weather, about the kids, about last night's ball game. But we're careful to avoid talking about what really matters: their burden, their pain, their grief. For though we might want to speak to these in some way, we're hesitant, afraid. And when the visit is over, when we leave the bedside, we feel that tinge of guilt down inside. We wanted so to touch the pain, the hurt, the grief—but we just couldn't bring ourselves to do that.

Such feelings, however, are not unique to us and our generation. For in past centuries there have been those who believed that they were called to respond to the needs of those around them, but like us, they felt themselves incapable of such a task. And it is in today's text, from the first chapter of Jeremiah, that we meet someone who felt then as we do today. In this narrative, wherein Jeremiah describes how he was called by God to be a prophet, we too find him hesitant to answer that call. Thus it may be that as the call of God addresses this reluctant Jeremiah, there will be a word from the Lord for us reluctant folk as well.

The Call

As we turn to the text, it seems to fall into three parts, three scenes or movements. In the first of these we hear those words with which Yahweh called Jeremiah to be his prophet: "Before I formed you in the womb I knew you, and before you were born I consecrated you; I appointed you a prophet to the nations" (Jer. 1:5). With these words, then, Jeremiah's identity is changed. Prior to this moment he was simply the young son of Hilkiah, one of the priests exiled in Anathoth just outside of Jerusalem. From now on, however, he's no longer to be known as Hilkiah's son. Rather people will know him as one whom God had called and to whom he had given a new identity as a prophet. Jeremiah would now be one with Isaiah, who had been called from his worship in the Temple (Isa. 6:1-13), he would be at one with Amos, called from cultivating his fig trees (Amos 7:14-15), at one with Gideon, called from the job of threshing wheat (Judg. 6:11-17), and he would be at one with him who was called from tending his father-in-law's flocks to be the first and greatest of the prophets —Moses himself (Exod. 3:1-12). And not only will Jeremiah share their identity, but also the responsibility that comes with it—a responsibility outlined in the words with which our text closes: "See, I have set you this day over nations and over kingdoms, to pluck up and to break down, to destroy and to overthrow, to build and to plant" (Jer. 1:10). In other words, Jeremiah—like Isaiah and Amos and the other great prophets who had gone before—would speak Yahweh's words of judgment and of grace. Or to put it a bit differently, Jeremiah was called to be a part of God's saving acts for his people.

Now I suggest that there is a moment in each of our lives that parallels the experience that Jeremiah, Isaiah and the others had at the moment they were called by God to be his prophets. The moment I have in mind is when we too were incorporated into his saving activity—the moment of our Baptism. St. Paul, for example, speaks of Baptism in these terms where in Romans he writes of our being baptized *into* Christ's death and resurrection (cf. Rom. 6:3-11). We, through our Baptism, have become a part of those events by which God chose to make his salvation known. And like Jeremiah, who was known no longer as Hilkiah's son, but as a prophet who shared the same lot as Isaiah and Amos and Moses, we, through Baptism, have a new identity. We are "neither Jew nor Greek, slave nor free, male nor female" (cf. Gal. 3:28), but rather, to use a phrase from the baptismal liturgy, we are "members of the priesthood we all share in Christ Jesus" *(LBW,* p. 124). And with this new identity, a new responsibility is ours. Like Jeremiah, who was to proclaim judgment and grace—"to pluck up and break down, . . . to build and to plant"—baptism calls us to "proclaim the praise of God and bear his creative and redeeming Word to all the world" (ibid.).

The Objection

So far this is all well and good. To talk about Jeremiah's call to a new identity and a new responsibility as having a parallel in the event of our baptism sounds great in theory. But when that phone rings, when we hear of the pain and grief and distress of someone whom we love, when we're faced with the question of whether or not we can bring a word of grace, of healing, of comfort to that person, we may very well protest that we're not up to that responsibility. For to conceive of ourselves as somehow a part of God's saving activity is overwhelming. Yet note what our text does at this point. For as we move from that first scene where Yahweh calls Jeremiah, to the second scene in which we hear Jeremiah's words of response, we discover that Jeremiah too feels incapable, incompetent: "Ah, Lord God! Behold I do not know how to speak, for I am only a youth" (Jer. 1:6). Moreover, Jeremiah's protest is not an isolated one in the prophets. Those prophets who preceded him likewise expressed their objection to God's call on the ground of their inadequacy. Isaiah, when called, protested that he was too much of a sinner to be a prophet: "Woe is me, ... for I am a man of unclean lips" (Isa. 6:5). And Gideon responded to the call to save his people from the Midianites with the plea, "Pray, Lord, how can I deliver Israel? Behold my clan is the weakest in Manasseh, and I am the least in my family" (Judg. 6:15). And of all people, even Moses objected to God's call by lamenting, "Who am I that I should go to Pharaoh, and bring the sons of Israel out of Egypt?" (Exod. 3:11).

There's a pattern, then, in how the Scriptures present the experiences of those who had been called to be prophets, to be a part of God's saving activity. And the pattern suggests that to be overwhelmed by the responsibility, to have those feelings of inadequacy is normal, understandable, even appropriate. For the feeling of hesitancy we share with Jeremiah, was known even by others long before Jeremiah's time. Yet—and this is important— as Jeremiah reflected on the experiences of those prophets who preceded him, he knew that Yahweh had not left Isaiah to lament about his sin, he had not left Gideon bemoaning the weakness of his tribe, nor had he left Moses in despair over the magnitude of the task before him. Rather, in each case Yahweh had dealt with those feelings; he had addressed the protests which had been raised. And knowing this, Jeremiah was ready for that which Yahweh was prepared to do in the third scene of our text.

The Reassurance

It is here that Yahweh chose to answer Jeremiah in the same way that he had answered the objections of those prophets in past ages—with a word of reassurance: "Do not say, 'I am only a youth'; for to all whom I send you you shall go, . . . Be not afraid of them, for I am with you to deliver you, says the Lord" (Jer. 1:7-8). Moreover, that spoken word of reassurance was backed by a sign, a symbolic gesture. Jeremiah had the sensation that Yahweh had touched his lips, placing in them the very words of judgment and of grace he would henceforth be called to speak. And of significance here is that as Yahweh did this, he accompanied his gesture with the phrase used in Deuteronomy about the coming prophet whom God would raise up to be like Moses. Of that prophet, that new Moses, the Lord said, "I will put my words in his mouth . . . " (Deut. 18:18), and to Jeremiah he says, "Behold, I have put my words in your mouth" (Jer. 1:9b). Our reluctant prophet, then, is assured that when he speaks, he will speak with the power and authority of Moses himself. Despite his own feelings of incompetence, he is told to not be afraid. For in making him a part of his saving actions on behalf of Judah, God would not leave Jeremiah up to his own feeble resources. Rather he promises that he will supply him with the grace to fulfill his calling.

And if God chose to do that for Jeremiah—and for Isaiah and Gideon and Moses—can he not do it for us as well? For called to be part of his saving activity through our Baptism into Christ's death and resurrection, he will not leave us without help in our moments of hesitancy. His word for us is likewise a word of "Be not afraid . . . , for I am with you." He is with us, each day, every day, in that daily forgiveness of sins promised in Baptism. And armed with that assurance, then, can we not risk taking that step in reaching out to that friend, that neighbor in pain? No longer need we feel paralyzed by our lack of competence, our not knowing just the right words. Rather we stand forgiven of those things we lack, and we're assured that his grace will be with us nonetheless, even if all we can do is to offer our friend a handclasp, an embrace, a halting prayer and a few simple words in the Lord's name.

So when the phone rings and we hear that news which none of us wants to hear—news of tragedy and pain, suffering and despair—and we wonder what we possibly can do . . . Remember Jeremiah! Remember the Jeremiah who, when called to be a prophet felt himself unequal to the task. Remember the Jeremiah who said, "Ah, Lord God! I do not know how to speak, for I am only a youth." But remember as well the one who answered him with the words, "Be not afraid of them, for I am with you to deliver you, . . ." For he who gave such a promise to a hesitant Jeremiah, will surely do the same for you and for me.

THOMAS R. LEE
University of Montana
Missoula

STEPS IN THE CALLING OF A PROPHET

Fifth Sunday after the Epiphany
Isaiah 6:1-8 (9-13)

How does one come to be a pastor? The church has always needed, and continues to need, dedicated leaders—persons of intelligence and compassion and deep spiritual insight. In every generation, the church has the important task of encouraging qualified young people to consider the possibility that they have a call from God to serve as a full-time leader in the church.

But how does one know whether or not one has the call? It is difficult enough these days to come to clear decisions about any vocation—and the prospect of serving the church seems to cause more hand-wringing and tortured self-analysis than for most other occupations. Rightly or wrongly, we look at the task of the pastor with a sense of awe. This is not just an ordinary job. Why would anyone take on this kind of work? How can you know that you have what it takes to succeed at such a demanding task?

The Old Testament Lesson today gives us an opportunity to reflect on the process of becoming a pastor. The autobiographical account of Isaiah's own call gives us some insights into the inner process, what goes on between the potential prophet and God, when the idea of being a special representative of God was first presented. Isaiah does not speak for everyone who has ever had the notion that he or she ought to be a pastor. But he does raise the significant questions. He highlights the important steps in the process that will be part of the experience of everyone who has at some time or other contemplated a call from God.

1. The Religious Experience

Isaiah tells us about his confrontation with God, probably in the Temple, accompanied by visions of God himself and strange creatures flying around, singing hymns, and touching him with a burning coal. With that kind of vivid encounter, Isaiah was reasonably assured that something had really happened.

Most of us do not have such extraordinary religious experiences. Few of us have actually seen God and, since seraphim are not something we are very familiar with, we probably would not know one if we saw one. We long for some sort of confirming, absolutely clear experience, like Isaiah had, so that we do not have to blunder along without ever really knowing what God is up to and what he wants us to do. We wish that he would simply tell us—as he told Isaiah. Then it would be so easy to respond. How can you respond if you are never sure that you have been asked?

We have been so conditioned by stories like this one from Isaiah that we expect that the call should always come in such spectacular ways. Many a promising young person has decided that the ministry was not the right calling because there had never been any glorious experience when the angels sang the Hallelujah Chorus and the feeling of euphoria was overwhelming and God spoke in plain English, "Go to the seminary; I need you."

The experience of the call comes in different ways. Isaiah's is not the only way. For most of us it is slower and less dramatic and the feelings of uncertainty continue. Nevertheless, even though it be more modest, the inclusion of this step in the process is absolutely necessary for one who would serve God and the church. That is, there must be a genuine experience that the calling is from God—that one is not simply doing a job for a group of people in a local place or even for a larger institution. There must be a spiritual dimension to the task, a certainty that one is ultimately responsible to God for what one is doing, the reality of an ongoing relationship with God that can sustain a person in the most difficult situations.

So, some kind of religious experience, a spiritual dimension, is a part of the process of becoming a prophet, even though an individual's experience may not be as colorful as Isaiah's. In our Second Lesson for today, Paul sheds some insight on his own spiritual experiences. It is significant for our first point that he declares that he would rather speak five intelligible words with his mind than ten thousand words in the language of tongues. The word that the prophet speaks on God's behalf is more important than the kind of experience which led to the assumption of the office.

2. The Reaction of Inadequacy and Fear

It is a serious business when God comes to you and lays a heavy task on you. When we are confronted by God, there is generally an overwhelming sense of inadequacy, even fear, that, as sinful human beings, we will be destroyed in the presence of God and his righteous demands. Isaiah says, "Woe is me. I am lost. For I am a man of unclean lips and I live in a society that had not lived up to God's demands. We are all lost." Similarly, Peter, in our Gospel, is terrified at the sudden realization that this man Jesus is not just another itinerant Galilean preacher, and he cries out, "Depart from me, for I am a sinful man."

How can I speak for God? I am only human. I am a sinner like everyone else. I have my hang-ups and my petty biases. I cannot possibly love people like a pastor should. And I am so stupid. I don't know anything, and God doesn't give me easy answers. If I take on the task of attempting to speak for God, will I not be in danger of even greater punishment because I have presumed to know something about holy things?

This is a common step for the person who is contemplating a call from God. Isaiah shared it with Moses, Jeremiah, Peter, and other great heroes of the faith. To go through this step in the process is not unusual at all. Rather, one would worry about a potential prophet who was so insensitive that he or she would not stand in fear and trembling before the awesome task of speaking God's word to the world that so desperately needs to hear it.

3. Cleansing and Providing a Word

God does not leave us in our state of inadequacy and fear. One of the seraphim touches Isaiah's lips with a coal and declares that his sins are forgiven.

Two important things are happening in this symbolic act. Isaiah is forgiven so that he can dare to stand before God and speak his word to his people. Further, his mouth has been touched —now he will have a word to speak, a word that is from God and not simply his own subjective, human word.

No one is good enough to serve as a pastor. No one is wise enough. Our own personalities get in the way so that, even when we say the right words, our actions and true feelings say more to our listeners than our words. We cannot love as we ought.

But we are forgiven—not just at the beginning, at the time of the call, but throughout our life. A person can dare to be a prophet because of the sure knowledge that sins will be forgiven. The wrong that one does, the hurts that are caused, the pain that is not eased, the words that are inappropriate—all that can be forgiven so that one dares to do anything at all.

The mouth is cleansed. That is significant. The word that is to be spoken should come from God. It is not enough simply to speak one's own mind if one is to be a spokesperson for God. It is not always easy to find that word, but God does not leave us without resources. The greatest resource, of course, is the Scripture and the promise that God will continue to speak through our prayerful study of the Bible. The modern day aspiring prophet will spend many years studying that Word in order to learn the word that God wants him or her to speak.

4. A Personal Decision to Accept the Responsibility

At some point a person must say yes or no. God will not make you do it. But, finally, the potential prophet must either fish or cut bait.

Some of the biblical characters find it easy to say yes. Perhaps it is because their experience is so clear-cut that there is really not much choice. Maybe they are more impetuous personalities, those who are willing to leap before they have explored all the alternatives and consequences. Isaiah and those disciples who dropped all and followed Jesus are good examples of this type.

Others, most notably Moses and Jeremiah, are more reluctant. They argue against the call. Their sense of inadequacy is more profound and it takes more assurance from God before they are prepared to say yes.

Sooner or later, the prophet must say yes or not be a prophet. There needs to be commitment to the necessary preparation, to the study of the word that is to be preached, to the idea of service.

5. Discouragement at the Response

If we ended our Old Testament Lesson at verse 8, we would not get to step 5. Nevertheless, it would be less than honest to stop too soon.

In verse 9 to 13 there are some strange and difficult words that describe the way in which Isaiah will be received. In short, his word will not be heeded until disaster strikes, until it is too late to avert some terrible consequences.

The prophet has to be prepared to face rejection. All the great prophets—Jeremiah, Ezekiel, Amos, for example—had a problem in understanding why God called them to preach a word that no one would hear. This was also a difficulty for the followers of Jesus. Why was Jesus not accepted by everyone? In an effort to understand this, Isaiah 6:9-10 is quoted in all four gospels and the book of Acts.

One ought not to take up the role of prophet or pastor without clearly looking at this step in the process. Isaiah and Jeremiah and Ezekiel were prepared for seeming failure in the words they heard at the time of their call. No wonder some of them were hesitant to take up the burden.

In our own day there is a disillusionment among many who have become pastors. They feel that no one pays attention to what they say, and they struggle to find some word that will get through to people and strike a responsive chord. There are widespread feelings of lack of fulfillment and identity problems among the clergy.

We see this same sort of struggle already in the call to Isaiah. The words of the preacher are not always met with instant approval and acclaim. Often people do not care, and sometimes they are even hostile. If one knows that at the beginning, there is less possibility of disillusionment later on. God's grace is sufficient for the task. But the task is not one of constant euphoria and success. There will be pains and self-doubts and failures. The need for God's word of forgiveness and support does not end with the ordination vows.

So, our text from Isaiah gives us five steps in the calling of a prophet. Isaiah's account of his call can be a helpful word to those of us who have assumed leadership roles in the church or who are thinking about it. It can help us to understand our own struggle with the call to be God's messenger. But it is not a text only for the clergy. Laypersons need to have some awareness of their pastor's struggle to be an obedient and effective servant of God. And they need to think about their own response when God speaks a word to them. This text invites us to think about these important matters in the life of the church.

DANIEL J. SIMUNDSON
Luther-Northwestern Seminaries
St. Paul, Minnesota

SEEING FROM AFAR

The Transfiguration of Our Lord—Last Sunday after the Epiphany
Deuteronomy 34:1-12

Imagine standing on a hill overlooking a calm and beautiful lake. Your heart is pounding inside as you anticipate getting to the shore, and then possibly diving into the water for a refreshing swim, or skipping pebbles across the water, or rowing a boat out on the lake and casting out a fishing line. But, for some reason, you can't get to the water. You can only see it from afar.

There's something disconcerting and frustrating about such an experience. Maybe that's why we try so desperately to deny that that is an accurate picture of our human life and experience. Note the penchant we have these days for instant success, instant gratification, instant sex, instant community—yes, even instant education. Who wants to see anything only from afar? We want vivid and lively experiences immediately. None of this seeing from afar for us, none of this petty pace of tomorrow and tomorrow and tomorrow. We want to experience it all *now*. I suspect that you know the craving and the feeling I'm talking about.

And, of course, it can affect our life with God, too. Most of us, I think, want to experience God's graciousness and goodness fully, here and now. We hanker after an awareness of God's Spirit alive and active in our lives, convincing us beyond a shadow of a doubt of his reality. "Quicken and warm our hearts. Make them tingle and delight in the assurance that You are with us." That might be the prayer that some of us pray. And some of you may even have had that prayer answered—at least on occasion in your life. But there are other people, including myself, who have seen only intimations of God's goodness, only hints of his presence—no tingling sensations, no mingling with that goodness. They've had to see it from afar.

The Inconsolable Secret

My impression is that all of us, at one time or another, have had to experience God's goodness from afar. This condition should not surprise us, for it points to what one writer has called the "inconsolable secret" in each one of us, namely, our "sense of exile on earth as it is." We cannot permanently enter in and mingle with the splendors and beauties we encounter. They come and go. We can neither possess them nor make them endure. Have you ever wondered why tears often come to our eyes during our moments of greatest happiness? Tears and happiness, what a strange combination. But it points to the "inconsolable secret," our sense of exile on earth as it is. We cannot make experiences last permanently, and we cannot be permanently at home here. We stand on a hill overlooking a lake, and we cannot get to the water.

People of faith in all generations have sensed this truth of life. Near the end of his career as Israel's greatest prophet, leader, lawgiver, and judge, Moses stood on Mount Nebo and the Lord showed him all the land which the Lord had promised to give to Moses' ancestors. It must have been a magnificent sight. At long last, the land which had been promised for centuries was lying stretched out before Moses' eyes. His whole life and career had been given to God in an effort to bring Israel, God's people, to this land. It was Moses who alone had seen God face to face. It was Moses who had delivered the law to the people after his encounter with God on another mountain, Mount Sinai. He kept leading, and judging, and interceding for this rebellious people, ever trying to reach the promised land. Finally, there it was stretched out before his very eyes. His life of leadership and devotion had not been spent in vain. His heart must have been pounding as he anticipated not only seeing the promised land but also moving into it, grabbing a handful of its soil and letting it sift through his fingers, settling down on the land and, at long last, feeling permanently at home.

But it was not to be so. Even the greatest of Israel's leaders and prophets, Moses, would finally see the promised land only from afar. For the Lord said to Moses, "I have let you see it with your eyes, but you shall not go over there." So Moses, the servant of the Lord, died there in the land of Moab, outside the promised land.

Traditions in the Bible give several interpretations as to why Moses was not allowed to enter the promised land. One says that he died outside the land because of his own sin and disobedience. Another claims that he died for the sake of the people's sins, so that the people might finally enter the promised land. And in and beneath both of these interpretations might be another: that all people of faith, even the greatest and most devout servant of God, can see the promised land only from afar. To be sure, some people entered the land which Moses saw, but they also had to learn that this was not their permanent homeland. All people of faith see the final promised land only from afar.

Lest you think that this is only an Old Testament perception of life and faith, one that has been superseded in the coming of Jesus Christ, consider then Luke's account of the Transfiguration. The setting is another mountain. Jesus and three of his disciples went up the mountain to pray. What began as an act of devotion and piety turned out to be an intense religious experience. In the vision, Jesus was seen talking to two Old Testament prophets, Elijah and Moses. The countenance and appearance of each was altered and changed so that the glory and splendor of the Lord became obvious. When Peter saw the glory of the Lord, he said, "Master, it is well that we are here; let us make three booths, one for you, one for Moses and one for Elijah." It's as though Peter were saying, "Master, let's make this moment of glory last; let's enshrine it in booths." But, of course, it wasn't to be. A cloud came and overshadowed them, and a voice from the cloud said, "This is my Son, my Chosen; listen to him." Then Jesus was found alone.

When Jesus and his disciples came down from the mountain, they met a father who pleaded with Jesus to heal his son who had epilepsy. The intense religious experience is over, and we are brought back down into the valley where we encounter the hard realities of life—sickness, suffering, rejection, and death. The disciples, once again, will have to see the glory of the Lord from afar.

Another New Testament writer underscores this same dimension of the life of faith for Christian men, women, and children. The author of Hebrews listed biblical characters who were examples of faith. Then he concluded, "These all died in faith, not having received what was promised, but having seen it and greeted it from afar, and having acknowledged that they were strangers and exiles on the earth."

Faith as a Not Having

All this testifies to the fact that our faith involves a certain not having, a certain not yet, a certain seeing from afar. And while this dimension of our faith might disturb and perplex us at times, it also points to the sustaining basis of our faith, namely, the faithfulness of God. That, I think, is what Moses recognized. He had known God's promise of land in days past. Now he was permitted to see the fulfillment of that promise from afar. It would not be fulfilled in Moses' time, but in God's time. The basis of faith is not Moses and his service to God. The basis of faith is the faithfulness of God to keep his promises.

And, you see, it is precisely God's faithfulness which delivers us from the compulsion to possess our own life, to secure it permanently in the here and now. No longer do we have to engage in frantic efforts to build little fortresses for ourselves and our lives, whether those fortresses be thought of in terms of financial security, or engratiating friends, or stellar reputations as civic minded persons, or simply keeping up with the latest fads and fashions. No, we don't have to spend our lives on these frantic activities because the faithfulness of God roots our lives elsewhere. One teacher put it this way, "Only as we come to know that this earth is not our true home can we ever find ourselves truly at home here."

The life and death of Martin Luther King Jr. bore witness to the truth of this contradiction. Martin Luther King had been to the mountain and had had a dream, a dream of a just and free society. To be sure, he saw it from afar because so little of American society confirmed his dream. Nevertheless, since his life was based on the faithfulness of God and was grounded in that dream which God himself had promised, King was free to be at home here and spend his life in the service of that dream. His dream, God's promise, was his final homeland.

And a pastor told me of a parishioner who came to know that this earth is not our true home and, therefore, came to be truly at home here. The parishioner had had polio as a child. One result of the polio was that one of her legs grew longer than the other, which finally caused spinal problems. A fusion was done but it brought only temporary relief before other problems developed. Her hopes for recovery were followed by repeated disappointments. Finally it became obvious that she would face a life of diminished activity. Nevertheless, she continued to trust in a faithful God, and she found that she had time to do things which she had always wanted to do. She learned the truth of Jesus' words that life is more than clothing, shelter, and health. She had life, and life, she said, is good. One day she confided to her pastor, "Pastor, I always thought of faith in God as meaning that everything would turn out all right as I conceived of all right. Now I know that God cares for me even when things don't turn out all right. He is my God." One woman who saw that her final home was not here and, therefore, could finally be at home here.

Each of us has a vivid reminder that our true home is elsewhere when we celebrate the Sacrament of Holy Communion. We sometimes call it the feast or the supper of our Lord. But what a strange feast! The courses are limited, the portions are small—a morsel of bread and a sip of wine, hardly enough to satisfy our appetites and fill us up. No, this certainly is not the heavenly banquet. No mistaking that. But what we are given at this feast is enough to sustain us on the way to the heavenly banquet, and enough to enable us to be truly at home in this puzzling, fascinating, and often tragic world.

We see the promised land and the heavenly banquet from afar when we participate in Holy Communion, but we also taste the goodness and faithfulness of God in Jesus Christ our Lord. And through both, the seeing from afar and the tasting, God forms his parish in the world. And you know what a parish is: it's a group of *aliens* who are at *home* in any community.

MORRIS J. NIEDENTHAL
Lutheran School of Theology at Chicago
Chicago, Illinois

A CREED OF WORD AND DEED

First Sunday in Lent
Deuteronomy 26:5-10

"Do we have to say the Creed, every Sunday?" So we ask. It seems so repetitive, so redundant, so superfluous. Don't we know what we hold as our faith?

First of all, we will have to learn that our creed does not originate with us. We formulate, we put the content God gives us into human words. But that content is from God. He is the original beginner of it all.

Even in a simple prayer, he gave first and we respond to that gift. He is God and we are his creatures. Under no circumstance are we creatures first.

And then we must never forget Jesus Christ was a Son of the Judaism of his time. He was in his upbringing nourished by the Torah, the five books we commonly call the Law.

When in the fourth century after our Lord's coming in the flesh, Jerome translated the Bible into the common Latin of that time he used the word "law" as also the translators had who used the Greek language in their rendering of the ancient biblical text centuries before Christ. Yet law is not Torah. We do not have a suitable word which combines instruction and tradition and also law.

Jesus our Lord grew up in the learning of those basic first five books of the Bible. He read many times the sentences of our lesson. They were for him a part of his creed as they must be a part of yours and mine.

What's confessed may seem strange to you. Jacob is the wandering Aramean. He is called father. He went to Egypt where there would be food for his growing family. And the groundwork is laid for the exodus.

Jacob as the father of the covenant people, the people of God, is certainly not an exemplary human being. He becomes great only in spite of himself and really only because of God's election.

We cannot argue with God's action of love, of mercy, of forgiveness. He is really "unfair" in our human sense. He gives as he wills. We pray so easily "thy will be done" in our Lord's Prayer and then resent the fact that he does what he wants to do.

Are we then simple fatalists who say we can do nothing on our own? No! But we say with Martin Luther "if you ever succeed spiritually it is God's gift, if you ever fail spiritually it is your own fault." Some like to call that a mystery, but it is more. We recognize in our confession of faith both the complete freedom of God and our own only relative freedom. We trust him. In this we have our certainty.

The "mighty acts of God" are told again and again. It does not matter that our lesson today is originally a part of the liturgy of the thanksgiving for the harvest in fall. We will always have to acknowledge the history by which God has brought us to the place and the conditions of where we are now.

"To forget" is the grave sin of any generation, not only as described in different form in the beginning of the Book of Judges. We are told those who forget their history are bound to repeat its mistakes, yet that is not the problem here.

The history of God's acts for us is human history because it happens in the human realm. But it is not our doing we talk about in the confession of the Creed. We confess the *Lord's* actions in our behalf.

God is the liberator. He made for himself a free people. And the Law is not a new enslavement. It is given as the instrument to become more and more his.

We Christians are in danger of concentrating only on the Second Article of our Creed. We tell of the basic steps in the life of Jesus Christ. He is our way of salvation.

We forget the foundation. Jesus Christ is an heir to the mighty acts of God. Only this way he can become the mightiest act of the Father.

And we forget the results. He wants to see the stewardship of our deeds. In our continuous recognition of God as the giver our life becomes a thanksgiving.

Without the foundations in the Old Testament and without the results in our own lives and the life of the church we only have words and never a true creed. Such a creed of word *and* deed is the confession of our faith.

HAGEN STAACK
Allentown, Pennsylvania

SENTENCE OF DEATH; SUMMONS TO LIFE

Second Sunday in Lent
Jeremiah 26:8-15

I

Martin Luther King Jr. came preaching, stirring up the people. Some said, "He is a Communist." Others said, "He is of God." Martin Luther came preaching, stirring up the people. Some said, "He is a heretic." Others said, "He is of God." Jesus of Nazareth came preaching, stirring up the people. Some said, "He is a blasphemer." Others said, "He is of God."

What about it? Were these men of God or not? How is one to know, especially in the day and age in which persons such as King or Luther or Jesus speak and act?

That was the situation in Jerusalem in 609 B.C. Jeremiah came preaching, stirring up the people. Some said, "He is a traitor." Others said, "He is of God." What, then, was he, true prophet or false?

One thing was sure: the temple priests, the official prophets, and the people as a whole didn't like what Jeremiah had to say. They brought him to trial before the princes of Judah. They accused him of speaking falsely in God's name; a crime, which according to Deuteronomy 18, was punishable by death. They said, "This man deserves the sentence of death, because he has prophesied against this city. . . ."

Jeremiah defended himself ably. His opening and closing words were the same, a double claim, a double challenge, "The LORD sent me to prophesy against this house (the temple) and this city (Jerusalem) all the words you have heard." In between this double claim and challenge he said, "Therefore, amend your ways and your doings. Obey the LORD. Then he will turn from 'the sentence of death' he has pronounced against you. As for me, do as you will; but know for certain that if you put me to death, you bring innocent blood on yourselves and this city" (a good defensive remark, for the shedding of innocent blood was also a crime according to Deuteronomy).

II

There are *three* things to notice in all this.

First, Jeremiah claimed to be delivering a message from God to the people of *his* day. He did not come with long-range oracles for the future. He did not come to make predictions for later generations. He came with a specific word from God for the people of *that* day, concerning the faith, life, and action of those people then and there.

It is important to understand this about Jeremiah, and about the prophets of Israel as a whole. They were not diviners, mediums, or mantics. They did not forecast the future with the aid of crystal balls, psychic wizardry, or ESP. Of course the prophets spoke of the future, particularly the near future. They could read the signs of the times. They had a sense of history. They understood the direction in which events were moving, and they spoke accordingly. They could even speak with hope of the far distant future, for they knew their God and his covenant purposes. But their responsibility was not to predict far distant events for future generations. It was much more difficult than that. It was to confront the people of their day—the king, the religious leaders, neighbors, everybody—with a pointed message from God.

This means that we cannot look into the biblical stories and writings of these prophets in order to discover predictions about specific events which are supposed to happen in the twentieth or twenty-first centuries. That is a misunderstanding of what the Bible is all about. Contrary to certain popular religious writers today, Ezekiel 38 does not predict the twentieth century actions of the Soviet Union; Revelation 16 does not predict the twentieth century actions of Red China; neither does Daniel 7 predict the present-day European Common Market. The prophets brought a message of God for the people of their own day.

Is there, then, no Word of God in the biblical prophets which speaks to our day? There is indeed! But quite frankly, it is only when we understand the historical situation in which a prophet first spoke that we can gain a proper appreciation of his message, and then apply that message to our own day.

This brings us directly to a *second* point that we should notice in this text: the meaning and purpose of this particular message which Jeremiah brought to his people.

Notice that Jeremiah stood in the temple courtyard when he delivered his message to the people (26:2). He did so for a specific reason: in order to attack the notion that the presence of the temple guaranteed the nation from being destroyed.

It was a cardinal teaching of the official state religion (the royal theology) that the LORD God had given two promises to David and his descendants that would never be broken: one, the kingdom of David and his descendants would continue forever; two, the LORD would dwell in the temple on Mount Zion forever. These promises are reproduced in a number of places in the Hebrew Bible, particularly in the Psalms. These twin doctrines were believed to be a guarantee (an eternal security) that no matter what, the nation would not be destroyed; threatened, perhaps; disciplined by God, certainly; but destroyed, never—not even if king and people failed to live up to their covenant with God.

Indeed, had not the LORD delivered Jerusalem from the Assyrians for this very reason? In that crisis one hundred years earlier, Isaiah had announced, "The LORD has founded Zion, and in her the afflicted of his people find refuge" (Isa. 14:32). In fact, Isaiah had urged the king and people of that earlier generation to refuse to submit to the Assyrians, for after all, the LORD fought for his people from Mount Zion (Isa. 29:5-8; 37:30-35). And so it had been. Was it any different now, one hundred years later? Could the armies of the Babylonians, or any army, be a match for the power of the LORD?

It is small wonder, then, that Jeremiah was hauled off to court as a false prophet. He had attacked a cherished, well-documented teaching of the royal theology. Listen to a summary of his courtyard sermon as recorded in Jeremiah 7:

> Hear the Word of the LORD, the God of Israel, "Change your way of living so that I may dwell with you in this place. Do not trust in that lie, 'This is the temple of the LORD, the temple of the LORD, the temple of the LORD.' Reform your ways. Treat each other fairly. Step oppressing foreigners, orphans, and widows who live among you. Stop following after other gods.
>
> "Look! You are counting on a worthless lie. What! Do you think you can steal, murder, commit adultery, perjure and deceive, burn sacrifices to Baal . . . and then come and stand in this house which bears my name, say 'We are safe,' and go on living in the same old way? No! Don't think you can make this place a hideout after you commit your crimes. This will not be a robbers' cave. Don't think I can't see.
>
> "Go to Shiloh, my first dwelling place in this land. That place is in ruins because of the sins of my people. And now, because you live as you do, because I have spoken and you have not listened, now this place in which you trust will become like Shiloh."

What a rabble-rousing sermon! I say, no wonder Jeremiah was hauled off to court. No wonder he was accused of speaking falsely in God's name.

This brings us to a *third* point raised by this text. How could the people know if Jeremiah's message was from God or not? How could they know if he was a true prophet or false? He was convinced that he spoke the truth, that was clear enough. But so were the official prophets who opposed him. Take note, then, that in the Hebrew Bible a false prophet is normally not one who intentionally lies or deceives, but one who, though sincere and dedicated, misrepresents God (Cf. Jer. 29:8-9; Lam. 2:14; Ezek. 13:6). Such a person may very well be false because he takes a Word once spoken by God and applies it to the wrong situation or the wrong persons or the wrong day and age.

So again we ask, how could the people know if Jeremiah was a true prophet or false? The answer is, only time would tell. As Jeremiah himself said, ". . . when the word of that prophet comes to pass, then it will be known that the LORD has truly sent the prophet" (28:9; cf. Deut. 18:22). Not one of God's prophets came with proof positive that his message was true. God's people are not coerced into accepting the truth. They are called to *believe* and obey, to walk by faith, not by sight.

Nevertheless the messages conveyed by God's prophets normally were reasonable, if not appealing. In the case of Jeremiah's message, it certainly contradicted the official theology regarding the temple and the kingdom of David. Yet his indictment of the people was as true as could be. The people *were* going through the motions of religious practice. Perhaps they were self-deceived. Perhaps they sincerely believed that saying prayers and offering sacrifices would make up for their sins and allow them to do the same old things in the coming week. In any case, they missed the message. They held on to the doctrine of eternal security represented by the temple, until the day the Babylonians leveled it to the ground. For time and events did prove Jeremiah was the true prophet of God.

III

Now, how does all this concern us, living as we do in the United States in the 1980s?

First of all, we can learn an important principle for interpreting the Bible. That is: The prophets were not soothsayers. They were messengers of God sent with a contemporary Word from God for the people of their day. And here is the principle: we can understand the prophet's message and apply it to ourselves only when we have studied that message in its historical context and have discovered the meaning and purpose of the message for that day.

Second of all, since we have now studied this particular message of Jeremiah in its historical context, and so have a basic understanding of its original intention, we can allow the central Word of this message to address us where we live.

We, too, are tempted to separate our church life from our everyday life. Prayers, liturgy, Word and Sacrament are intended to equip us for daily life, not to smooth over a failure to practice our faith in life. Of course, forgiveness is at the heart of our creed, but not so we can go on living in the same old way. A swindler is a swindler whether he is a deacon or not. A gossip is a gossip, choir member or not. Bitterness and resentment cannot be smoothed over by singing sweet hymns. They need to be dealt with straight on, face to face, with the people involved. That's the Christian way. Biblical faith is a relationship with the living God which involves the way we relate to the flesh and blood persons all around us, including the down-and-out, the unlovely, and those who just plain irritate us.

Let no one be deceived. God assures us of his love. He will never leave us nor forsake us. But we do not possess his love and forgiveness once and for all. The fundamentalist doctrine of once-saved-always-saved-no-matter-what is false. The popular understanding that once-you-are-baptized-and-confirmed-everything-is-fine simply does not hold water. Luther put it plainly, "Where there is no faith, baptism does no good" (*LW* 32:14). In other words, the new life created by God in Baptism must be nourished and renewed. This takes place as we exercise our faith in him—turning to him in prayer, responding to his presence through the Means of Grace, counting on him in daily life. By itself the sacrament of Baptism or a conversion experience is no more a guarantee of God's favor than Solomon's temple guaranteed God's protection of the ancient Judaeans. God's goodness calls for that ongoing response to him we know as faith. And surely, unless our faith in him influences the way we work, the way we treat people, the way we prepare our income tax, and everything else, that faith is questionable. Again, in Luther's words,

> Although he has justified us through the gift of faith and although he becomes favorable to us through his grace, yet he wants us to rely on Christ so that we will not waver in ourselves and in these his gifts . . . and so that no fool, having once accepted the gift, will think himself already con-

tented and secure. He does not want us to halt in what has been received, but rather to draw near from day to day so that we may be fully transformed into Christ (*LW* 32:235).

But perhaps there is a *third* word for us from Jeremiah's message, a word more basic and crucial than these others. It is this. God cares deeply for you and me and everything we are and do. That's the great truth which undergirds the message of Jeremiah, and of all the prophets and apostles. God wants us to be *his* people, yes, and his *kind* of people. That's why he calls us. That's why he startles us with this word of judgment and warning from his prophet Jeremiah. That's why he sends his Son to be one of us, to reveal his deep love and his judgment all wrapped up into one, on the cross.

When Catholic philosopher Baron Friedrich von Hügel was on his deathbed, he whispered a final word to his niece. He said, "Caring is everything. Nothing matters but caring."

That's the basic word which undergirds Jeremiah 26, God caring, and his call to us to care: for him, for one another, for his world.

DELMAR L. JACOBSON
St. John's Lutheran Church
Northfield, Minnesota

SURPRISE, SURPRISE!

Third Sunday in Lent
Exodus 3:1-8b, 10-15

The God of the Bible is full of surprises. He is always coming to those who do not expect him, at the least likely times and places. He is always saying and doing what no one could have predicted. He is not a God people can discover. He is a God who reveals himself.

Today's First Lesson is an example. Moses was a shepherd. He worked for his father-in-law, keeping the flock. Searching for pasture in a land where vegetation was sparse, he came to a mountain called Horeb. There he saw a bush, on fire but not consumed. When he went to investigate, God appeared to him in the flame of fire and called to him out of the bush. "Moses, Moses!" God called; urgency and authority are in that repetition. Moses could only answer, "Here I am." What began as an ordinary day became an extraordinary experience.

Who is this surprising God who came to Moses and spoke with him? What kind of God did he reveal himself to be?

The God Who Knows Our Suffering

He is a God who is alert to human suffering. Moses was, of course, a refugee from an oppressed people enslaved by the king of Egypt. The verses just before our lesson describe Israel as groaning under bondage and crying out for help, but it is strongly implied that they do not know where to turn. Now God speaks to Moses the refugee at Mount Horeb. The first thing he says to him, after warning him to show proper reverence, is this: "I have seen the affliction of my people who are in Egypt, and have heard their cry because of their taskmasters; I know their sufferings. . . ."

It is significant that God *first* sees the affliction of his people, and *then* hears their cry. God knows our need before we even express it. Quick as we are to complain about our troubles, God is even quicker. He knows our suffering from the moment we first experience it.

There is, I think, something even more significant hinted at here. God does not just *know* about the suffering of his people; it affects him. As he says to Moses, "I know their sufferings, and I have come down. . . ." Time and again, in the biblical story, God sees the affliction of his people and hears their cry—and comes down. The author of the Book of Judges says that God "became indignant over the misery of Israel" (10:16); or, as another translation has it, "he could bear Israel's suffering no longer" (Jerusalem Bible).

The culmination of God's involvement in our suffering is the cross. Jesus is one of us, our brother, and his crucifixion draws together and sums up all the misery and agony and sorrow of the human race. But he is also God's own Son, and when he suffers and dies, God suffers and dies with his people.

That is the Bible's profoundest answer to the "problem of suffering." The problem is never whitewashed. Through the pages of Holy Scripture walk men and women who experience floods and droughts and plagues and deformities and injuries and disappointments and death. Sometimes their afflictions, like ours, are the result of their sins. Sometimes they may be a test, and a prelude to great happiness. But in the great majority of cases, no such easy explanations are possible. Then it is simply affirmed that God sees our affliction, he hears our cry. "I know their sufferings, and I have come down. . . ."

The God of Our Heritage

The God of the Bible is full of surprises, but he is not capricious. His arrivals are unexpected and his words and deeds unpredictable, but they are not arbitrary. Those to whom he reveals himself recognize that he is consistent. When he first introduces himself to Moses, he says: "I am the God of your father, the God of Abraham, the God of Isaac, and the God of Jacob."

This mysterious God, who so astonished Moses out of the burning bush, is not an unknown God; he is the God of Moses' father. The God who has seen Israel's affliction and heard its cry is not a foreign God; he is the God of Israel's ancestors. He often shows himself in new ways. He repeatedly says and does novel and startling things. Nevertheless, he is the same God worshiped by generations past.

There is an old prayer which asks: "Deliver us both from stubborn rejection of new insights and from hasty assurance that we are wiser than our fathers." Today's lesson teaches us to avoid both of those extremes. Is there a God who is already completely known to us, who never leads us into fuller truth? That is not the God of the burning bush. Is there a God who is known to us only through our own personal experiences, about whom we have not learned from Scripture and from the confessions and liturgy of the church? That is not the God of the burning bush either. He is God of old and new. He is God of past and present.

The God of Moses is the God of Abraham and Isaac and Jacob. Similarly, the God who is the Father of Jesus Christ is the God of Moses. Christians have sometimes lost sight of that truth. There have been those, in ancient and in modern times, who would reject the Old Testament, as if the God of the Old Testament were someone other than the God of the New. Less radical souls have been guilty of neglecting the Old Testament or putting it in second place, as if it were not as much the Word of God as are the Epistles and Gospels. The authors of the New Testament present Jesus, his meaning and significance, in terms drawn from the heritage of Israel. Prophet, Priest, King; Son of man, Son of God, Messiah; the meaning of these titles can only be learned from the Old Testament Scriptures. Jesus is, to be sure, more than the sum of these; in him God has done a new thing. But Jesus' heavenly Father is not a new God. He is the God of Moses, the God of the patriarchs, the God of Israel.

The God of Our Future

Today's lesson points to the past; even more, it points to the future. After telling Moses that he knows his people's suffering, God continues: "I have come down to deliver them out of the hand of the Egyptians, and to bring them up out of that land to a good and broad land, a land flowing with milk and honey." He is a God with a purpose for the future, and his purpose is deliverance.

We should note that God's people are saved both *from* something and *to* something—and the emphasis is on the latter. Israel will be delivered from the hand of the Egyptians; Egypt is described only as "that land." Israel will be delivered to the land promised to their ancestors; it is described as "a good and broad land, a land flowing with milk and honey." Slavery will be left behind, that is true. Even more important, God will lead his people into abundance and security and peace. Our understanding of salvation should reflect this truth. It is not that we take lightly our deliverance from sin, aimlessness, and despair. But God's purpose is too generous, too gracious to be restricted to a negative. It is gathered up in a far more comprehensive goal: life in all its fullness.

God's purpose for the future is salvation. But he will save his people in his own way. That is the meaning of the most difficult part of this conversation between God and Moses. Moses says: "If I come to the people of Israel and say to them, 'The God of your fathers has sent me to you,' and they ask me, 'What is his name?' what shall I say to them?" That seems to be a perfectly innocent question. Consider, however, that in the biblical world to know the name of something was to possess it, to control it, to be able to call on it for one's own use. In the light of that fact, we may understand Moses to be asking for some sort of handle on this God, so that he and his deliverance will be at the disposal of Moses and the Israelites.

This makes sense out of God's answer to Moses. He does not refuse to give Moses his name. Indeed, he reveals for the first time his divine name, his personal name by which he is to be known from that time on. But he relates that name to an affirmation of his divine freedom. "I AM WHO I AM," he tells Moses. "Say this to the people of Israel, 'I AM has sent me to you.'" Old Testament scholars are not agreed about precisely how these words can best be translated. "I am who I am"; "I will be what I will be"; "I cause to be what is"—these are all possibilities. What is clear is that God's nature and eternal being remains a mystery, but his presence and action will be seen in historical events, in his own freely-chosen future acts.

When God confronted Moses on Horeb, he was setting in motion a story that includes exodus and wilderness and the land of Canaan; the dynasty of David and the Temple in Jerusalem and, we Christians believe, Jesus and his church as well. Nor has that story yet reached its end. Echoing Isaiah, St. Paul looked forward to "What no eye has seen, nor ear heard, nor the heart of man conceived, what God has prepared for those who love him" (1 Cor. 2:9).

God's people, then, cannot predict the course of future events. Still less can we compel God to do things our way. Our assurance is that the future is in God's hand, and his purpose for the future is salvation.

The God Who Seeks Our Response

So far, the emphasis has all been on God. He sees, he hears, he comes down, he speaks and promises to deliver. But it is not his intention simply to ease the burden of a group of slaves. He intends to create a community that will be his own people. He takes the initiative, but he calls for a response.

God begins with Moses. Speaking from the burning bush, he says to him: "Do not come near; put off your shoes from your feet, for the place on which you are standing is holy ground." This is a demand for reverence in a world where removing the sandals before entering a holy place was an ancient custom. Then God tells Moses: "Come, I will send you to Pharaoh that you may bring forth my people, the sons of Israel, out of Egypt." Moses is summoned to serve God's saving purpose.

Israel, too, is not to be just the passive recipient of God's deliverance. "When you have brought forth the people out of Egypt," Moses is told, "you shall serve God upon this mountain." *This mountain* is Horeb, or Sinai, where God will one day reveal his law to his people, that they might know his will and do it. When he reveals his name to Moses, he says: "This is my name forever, and thus I am to be remembered throughout all generations." Israel is called to serve God and remember him forever.

The point was made earlier that God does not just save us *from* something, but also *to* something. Now we can add that he saves us *for* something: that we may remember and serve him. To be the people of God means celebrating his gracious deliverance. It also means responding with obedience to his will. For God's people, freedom and service are the same. As St. Paul put it: "You were called to freedom, brethren; only do not use your freedom as an opportunity for the flesh, but through love be servants of one another. For the whole law is fulfilled in one word, 'You shall love your neighbor as yourself' " (Gal. 5:13-14).

God's Greatest Surprise

I said at the beginning that the God of the Bible is full of surprises. His greatest surprise of all is Jesus Christ: crucified for us; presented to us in Old Testament images; pointing us toward the future's final deliverance; calling us in the meantime to follow his example of service. Surprising as that is, however, we might have expected it of the God of the burning bush. For, in that surprising meeting with Moses, he already revealed himself as the God who knows our suffering, the God of our heritage and our future, the God who seeks our response.

LESTER MEYER
Concordia College
Moorhead, Minnesota

JOY DURING LENT

Fourth Sunday in Lent
Isaiah 12:1-6

Joy in the midst of Lent! Does this not seem rather incongruous? We are accustomed to thinking of Lent as a time of somberness and sober contemplation, yet today in the very depths of the Lenten season all the Scripture texts speak of rejoicing: the Old Testament Lesson that refers to drawing water with joy from the wells of salvation and concludes with an exultant cry: "Shout and sing for joy, O inhabitant of Jerusalem!"—The Psalm which begins: "Blessed (i.e. happy) is the one whose transgression is forgiven" and ends with "Be glad in the Lord and rejoice, O righteous, and shout for joy, all you upright in heart!"—the Gospel with its story of the prodigal son for whom his loving father prepares a feast on his return. It, too, terminates on a jubilant note with the father's joyous exclamation: "Let us eat and make merry!" Only the Epistle lacks a specific reference to joy, but it provides the basis for joy even in Lent—Lent with its reminder of the way of the cross. It says concerning the word of the cross that it is "folly to those who are perishing but to us who are being saved it is the power of God." Because of it salvation becomes available to us. Through the cross of Christ God's love becomes most clearly manifest. And that is what all the texts for today are about: forgiveness, salvation, the love of God. This is what ties them all together and provides the basis for the joy they radiate.

An Ode of Joy

It is the Old Testament Lesson which strikes the keynote of jubilation with its song of salvation, an ode of joy, written originally for the people of Israel. Although they had been languishing in captivity, they are here assured of a return again to their land. The verse immediately preceding the Old Testament Lesson clearly indicates this with its declaration: "There will be a highway from Assyria for the remnant which is left of his people, as there was for Israel when they came up from the land of Egypt." Against such a background the prophet declares: "You will say in that day: 'I will give thanks to thee, O Lord, for though thou wast angry with me, thy anger turned away, and thou didst comfort me.'"

God has directed his wrath against his people Israel because of their refusal to accept his loving guidance. He had sent many prophets to them, one of whom represents God as declaring: "From the day that your fathers came out of the land of Egypt to this day, I have persistently sent all my servants the prophets . . . yet they did not listen to me . . . but stiffened their neck" (Jer. 7:25f.). God in righteous anger had therefore permitted his judgment to fall. The land of Judah had been ravaged by the enemy. The city of Jerusalem had been destroyed, and many of the people carried into captivity.

God, however, never manifests anger simply to destroy. His ultimate purpose is always redemptive. He reveals therefore his love at the earliest opportunity. Like the loving father in the parable of the prodigal son, he is waiting to receive back with forgiveness any of his children who return to him in penitence. The cross of Christ is an absolute assurance of that fact. This is why joy is appropriate in the midst of Lent.

The fourth Sunday in Lent has had this accent of joy from ancient times. When Lent was first observed in church, the period of time was much shorter, confined to the three-week period following this Sunday. When Lent was later extended to forty days, the stern regulations of the church were relaxed for a day on this Sunday in mid-Lent. The ancient introit for this day, which was in the *Service Book and Hymnal*, sounded the keynote with its exhortation: "Rejoice and be glad with her, all that love her. Rejoice for joy all that mourn for her. I was glad, when they said unto me, Let us go into the house of the Lord."

In our Old Testament text for the day we also are being called to sing. Our song is the one Israel was urged to sing, when she returned from her captivity. But we have a more persuasive reason for singing it, because through Christ we have a far greater evidence of God's saving and redeeming power.

The hymn expresses in the exalted language of poetry the joy of salvation. The two stanzas in which it is written are held together by the promise: "With joy you will draw water from the wells of salvation." The first stanza describes *the joy of personal possession;* the second stanza *the joy of public proclamation.*

The Joy of Personal Possession

One of the vital features of a godly life is the joy it has, a happiness founded on salvation. Thanksgiving is its fundamental mode of expression. It demonstrates how the believer, comforted by the Lord, can manifest courage. All these features are evident in the first stanza of the hymn, whose primary theme is clearly salvation, as the repetitive statements in the first stanza clearly emphasize: "God is my salvation . . . God has become my salvation." These confident assertions stand out like two testimonial pillars, connected by a banner of joyous confidence.

"I give thanks to thee, O Lord!" is the opening statement of the hymn. "What better way to begin?" "It is a good thing to give thanks to the Lord . . . to declare his steadfast love in the morning and his faithfulness by night" (Ps. 92:1f.). We can never exhaust the possibility of expressing our thanks to God for the love he has manifested to us through his word: the written word and the Word that became flesh and dwelt among us. One hymnwriter in attempting to describe the love of God has pictured all men as scribes, trying to write on the heavens a full account of God's love by using pens dipped in an ocean filled with ink. In a burst of imaginative fervor, he concludes: "It would drain the ocean dry to write the love of God above, nor could the scroll contain the whole, though stretched from sky to sky." Hyperbole? Yes, but what language can we borrow to thank him for sending his only Son our Lord to die on a cross for our sins?

"Thou didst comfort me!" the hymn continues. Only the God we first meet in the Old Testament and come to know more intimately in Christ can provide such comfort. When we have sinned and done that which is wrong, we can come to his mercy seat and hear the consoling words: "Your sins are forgiven. Go in peace!" Our psalm for today reminds us of this with its statement: "I acknowledged my sin to thee, and I did not hide my iniquity; I said, 'I will confess my transgressions to the Lord'; then thou didst forgive the guilt of my sin." Herein lies comfort to know that God is "the Father of mercies and God of all comfort." He comforts not only in assuring us of pardon for our sins but in providing us with consolation in times of anxiety and sorrow. "For he gives us comfort in our trials so that we in turn may be able to give the same sort of strong sympathy to others in theirs" (2 Cor. 1:4, Phillips).

How shall one respond to God's saving love and gracious comfort? The hymn in our text provides the answer with its simple statement: "I will trust and will not be afraid; for the Lord God is my strength and my song, and he has become my salvation." The way to obtain God's salvation is to open our hearts to it through the power of his Spirit. By trusting in his mercy, it becomes ours. By trusting his saving power in Christ, we experience it and retain it as ours. He becomes our strength, so that like the Apostle Paul we can declare: "I can do all things in him who strengthens me" (Phil. 4:13).

He who puts his trust in God need not fear; for he who says: "I will trust" can also say with God's help: "I will not be afraid." Fear is something to which we are all heirs. We all have anxieties of every shape and form: fear of what is strange and new, fear of the future, fear of failure, fear of God, fear of death. God is aware of the many fears that haunt mankind. That is why there are so many words of assurance in the Bible, addressed to anxiety. Some of the finest verses in Scripture, worthy of being pondered again and again, are prefaced with the assurance: "Fear not!" The very first one was addressed to Abraham, the father of the faithful: "Fear not, I am your shield and your exceeding great reward" (Gen. 15:1). From then on this word of encouragement is repeated over and over again in both the Old and New Testaments. Check a concordance and see. They are still for us to claim in Christ.

We have a God in whom we can have confidence. If we put our trust in him and with conviction declare: "Behold, God is my salvation. I will trust." Then we will also be able to say with his help: "I will not be afraid; for the Lord God is my strength and my song." The strength for overcoming fear comes from God above.

The Joy of Public Proclamation

When one receives good news, one cannot keep it simply to oneself. The natural inclination is to want to share it. The second stanza of the hymn of our text demonstrates this by urging believers to share the joy they have experienced of God's saving grace, so others too may have the same kind of happiness. Indeed, the whole earth is invited to participate in the celebration of God's gracious goodness. "Give thanks to the Lord . . . make known his deeds among the nations . . . he has done gloriously; let this be known in all the earth."

The knowledge of God's saving action must never be selfishly kept to oneself. It should be joyously shared with everyone, as the hymn so effectively illustrates. The jubilant exhortations tumble over one another in rapid succession: "give thanks . . . call . . . make known . . . proclaim . . . sing praises . . . shout . . . sing for joy"—seven in all. What enthusiasm! Would that everyone who had experienced God's grace had such ardent zeal in sharing the good word of this wonderful Lord who meets us with his glorious saving power in his word and in our daily lives, whenever we let him.

If all believers really had been singing his praises and sharing what they had experienced of his goodness, then all the world long ago should have heard of his saving love. But too many of God's people are silent. Too few have been radiant proclaimers of what God has done. What about you? Do you love to tell the story of what a great God we have? Are you telling the story? Our text with its jubilant and contagious fervor brings us up with a start and forces us to take stock of our zeal.

The secret of how to become a more ardent witness for God is to take more time to think of his greatness: "Great in your midst is the Holy One of Israel!" is the concluding declaration of the hymn. We need to take more time to think of the greatness of our God rather than dwelling on the many little troubles and difficulties that so frequently beset us. What a great God he is, the Creator of the heavens and the earth, who has intimate concern for each one of us. He spared not his own Son but freely gave him up for us all, sending him to this world of sin to die upon the cross that we might live through him. Can you imagine what it would be like if you knew nothing of such greatness and love? Consider seriously the greatness of God. Ponder over the story of his love in Christ, as if it were something you were hearing for the first time. With joy draw water from those wells of salvation centered in his Word. As you reflect on the great and glorious acts of our Savior God, you will have the basis for a gratitude; for thinking is the prelude to thanking.

ROBERT H. BOYD
Luther-Northwestern Seminaries
St. Paul, Minnesota

GOD'S NEW THING

Fifth Sunday in Lent
Isaiah 43:16-21

It is not easy to be fully open to God. In fact, it is impossible. It is hard enough to receive in faith the message of how God has acted in the past. To keep up with what God is doing now and with what God will shortly bring about is to run a footrace with horses.

Yet if God would be God, if he would lead his people, he must do precisely that: he must lead. God must be ahead of his people, beckoning them on into the future he has prepared for them.

First Remember

Our text is the earliest biblical call for God's people to expect him to do a new thing, thereby setting a pattern which recurs in the biblical witness.

The 16 chapters of Isaiah 40–55 are admitted on all sides to be among the most profound words of Old Testament prophecy. The Babylonians had destroyed Jerusalem taking the best of Israel captive back with them to Babylon. That was 587 B.C. Shock and mourning turned to despair as the decades passed— 577, 567, 557, 547. The exiles could no longer sing, but they did ask, "Where is God?"

An answer came through a voice, the anonymous lyrics of one whom we call the Second Isaiah. Quite possibly he was one of the group of Isaiah disciples who were keeping alive the oracles once delivered by the 8th century Isaiah of Jerusalem.

Speaking with full authority ("Thus says the Lord") the prophetic voice makes bold to remind the despairing band of Israelites of their past saving history.

"Remember how the Lord once graciously set for us a way in the sea, how he cut a path for us right through the middle of the raging waters.

"Remember how Yahweh our God sovereignly summoned Pharaoh's army, as though it were his own, only to have horse and chariot sink helplessly in the foam.

"Remember, Israel, and take courage."

God's greater Exodus took place when Jesus passed on ahead of us, crossing the Red Sea of death. When we experience the loneliness of exile, the loneliness of having no roots, the loneliness of being misunderstood, the loneliness that sin brings, God calls us first to remembrance.

"Remember who I am, child. I am the one who brings out the stars at night, naming them as they appear.

"Remember that I have rescued my people for thousands of years—Abraham, Isaac and Jacob to name a few.

"Remember that for your tears I died, dear child. Remember that I experienced God-forsakenness as a remedy for your loneliness.

"Don't underestimate me my power, but remember and believe."

Then Forget

In a startling turnabout, the prophet then says, "Remember not the former things, nor consider the things of old." Don't remember. Forget. Forget what? Forget God's acts of creation? Forget God's saving acts like the Exodus? Forget the sins and rebellion which brought down Israel's house? The best interpretation is that the prophet is saying, "Forget all of what's past."

Forgetfulness is the first necessary step in being open to God's new thing. The Second Isaiah was sent to proclaim a new exodus. To do that he cleared the deck of remembrances of things past, both good things and bad things.

Paul caught the sense of this passage beautifully when he said, "One thing I do, forgetting what lies behind and straining forward to what lies ahead I press on toward the goal" (Phil. 3:13).

God is saying the same to you: "Forget *all* that lies behind. Do not let your sins haunt you. And forget your good deeds as well. Make a mental effort at not brooding over your past glories or your recent disasters. Do not be overcome by your past history. Cut it adrift. Be reborn to the fresh future I have in store for you, for I am about to act in your life, in your world."

God's greatest act was Jesus. Those who applauded that act and received Jesus were those who were not overly much in love with their own history. Those in Jesus' day who were in the business of remembering, the scribes and the chief priests, were not able to discern what God was doing in Christ before their very eyes.

We are not here being called to absent-mindedness. But on the strength of the prophetic injunction, we are being told, "Don't tie God down to the past. The Jesus who walked in history two thousand years ago has risen from the dead. The tomb is empty. He is risen. Look up and see what God is doing in Jesus right now, this very day."

Be Open to God's New Creative Act

Remember that God did act. Remember that God can act. Fix in your memory the pattern of his helping behavior. And then be ready for him to act again by forgetting the specific instances of his past help. Remember the pattern, forget the specifics.

"Behold, I am doing a new thing. I have done many good things which are now ancient history. It is the next new thing I want you to watch for. It is even now springing forth, like a crocus in the snow. Get to know it, become intimate with my next act, and take it up into your consciousness willingly."

At this point the Second Isaiah spells out the new act for his day, no longer merely alluding to it: "I am again going to make a way for you, not through a sea but through a desert. I am sending you back home to Jerusalem. You are worried about the journey, travelling through the dry and hostile desert? Don't be, I'll provide water for you, veritable rivers in the desert."

That's the spell-out of the new act the prophet sees Yahweh doing: providing a new exodus, another way out, a new salvation, a chance to go home, freedom from Babylonian bondage.

Each time has its own needs. The bondage in Egypt needed an escape from Pharaoh across the Red Sea. The exile in Babylon called for a release and a providential trip back home.

When the fulness of time came the whole world needed to be released from the power of sin, death, and hell. Jesus came at just the right time to set God's captives free. God has done his new thing in Jesus, and it never grows old, it always springs forth anew.

What is *your* need? To be set free from a past which nips at your heels with angry memories of failure? Remember that God has provided the way out in Jesus. Remember Calvary, but then let God be God so that he may, through the spirit of the risen Lord, release you today for energetic service.

What is *your* need? To be set free from the fear of death so that you may breathe quietly? Remember that Jesus died for you that you may live. Become more intimate with God's on-going action in Christ. Take up into yourself more willingly, more eagerly, that spirit which raised Christ Jesus from the dead. And live. Now and forever.

What is *your* need? To be set free from the specters of hell, those icy visions of total failure and rejection and the thought of an endless loneliness which ridicules with its steely laugh? Remember that God in Christ proved himself victor over the obscene laughter of darkness. Forget that it was done so long ago and remember only that he triumphed to give you the victory. You will not slip forever into darkness. He will draw you forth into light.

What is your need, church? To be set free from encrusted, outdated, unworkable tradition, to be renewed in faith, hope and love, so that you may do the works of him who sent you? Then remember your first love. Forget the coldness that has set in, forget the intervening centuries and remember that he sent you into the world to do greater things than he himself did. Let God do signs and wonders among you anew. He has not closed the book on the acts he intends to do through you, his church.

What is your need, world? To be set free from your bondage to decay? To experience the glorious liberty of the children of God? To find release from your self-destructing, from your wars, your greed, your pollution? Remember that God has created you. And learn that he can recreate you. O earth, be open to your maker.

What is the result of God's marvelous releases? All will declare his praise. Jackals and ostriches, magpies and poodles, men and women. All can now praise him. All will someday praise him, in one way or another, either with joy or with gnashing teeth. Every knee will bow and acknowledge his greatness and goodness. Someday all will recognize the new act that God has done in Christ.

But you needn't wait till then. You needn't wait another moment. You can praise him right now. Forget your past praises. Forget how often in the past you sang yourself hoarse with his praises. Forget too your many times of thanklessness.

Praise him anew, and keep praising him as you remain open to his ever new, ever thrilling new acts of freeing grace on behalf of you and his exiled world.

MARK E. HILLMER
Luther-Northwestern Seminaries
St. Paul, Minnesota

GOD'S POWER FOR HIS PEOPLE

Sunday of the Passion—Palm Sunday

Deuteronomy 32:36-39

"Rejoice, we conquer!" was the message of fleet-footed Pheidippides to the Athenians. He had run the 26 miles from the Plain of Marathon. He made that long run in order to announce that the outnumbered Athenian and Plataean forces had defeated the invading Persians. Athens therefore had no reason to surrender should the Persian fleet attack. Pheidippides' message of victory was good news to all the people of Athens.

The major part of our text is a messenger's report. It is cast as a prophetic announcement. It is the report of one who has stood in the council of God and now comes from there to announce a word of hope for God's people. That message of hope can be summed up in these words: God's power for his people!

He Delivers Us in Our Need

God's power for his people was the clear theme of the exodus. In their Egyptian bondage the Hebrews were oppressed slaves. They were forced to collect straw, mix clay, make bricks, build cities. Annihilation loomed ominously when the Egyptian authorities ordered the destruction of all Hebrew male children. Pleas for reasonable work brought only increased commands for higher production. The situation was desperate. It was a moment such as today's text reflects, ". . . their power is gone, and there is none remaining, bond or free."

Into that time of powerlessness and need came God's compassion for his people. He heard their cry for help and he sent Moses and Aaron through whom he worked the great deliverance. In the exodus experience, through awesome demonstrations of power, God wrenched the slaves from their taskmasters and flung them into freedom.

The Hebrews Remembered the Exodus

For centuries afterward the Hebrews remembered the exodus and they rejoiced over it. They sang of it and they celebrated it. For them it was an experience of God's power for his people.

"The Lord will vindicate his people and have compassion on his servants," our text announces. Do you notice that this good news is in the future tense? Of course, God's power for his people is a repeated experience. The exodus is not only a past event to be remembered. It is also a present reality and a future expectation.

In the days of David, when he finally put down Israel's surrounding enemies and brought rest to the land, the people had experienced God's power. Centuries later, through the Persian, Cyrus, God delivered his people from the Babylonian exile so that they could return to their homes in Judah. Their exilic tears turned to exultant songs as they felt the vindication of their compassionate God.

Jesus Demonstrates God's Power to Deliver People in Need

In New Testament times aged Simeon awaited it, and hymned it when he held the child, Jesus, in his arms and said, "... mine eyes have seen thy salvation which thou hast prepared in the presence of all peoples, ..." (Luke 2:30-31).

Jesus' own ministry of forgiving and healing was indeed a fulfillment of the promise that God has compassion on his servants. The Song of Zechariah exaults with the words,

> Blessed be the Lord God of Israel,
> for he has visited and redeemed his people,
> and has raised up a horn of salvation for us
> in the house of his servant David.
>
> (Luke 1:68-69)

When Jesus entered Jerusalem on Palm Sunday the hope in these words were like a descant to the song sung by the hope-filled crowd,

> Rejoice greatly, O daughter of Zion!
> Shout aloud, O daughter of Jerusalem!
> Lo, your king comes to you;
> triumphant and victorious is he,
> humble and riding on an ass,
> on a colt the foal of an ass.
>
> (Zech. 9:9)

That is the good news we still sing on this Sunday. For through the centuries of history the needy and oppressed have cried out to God. When their power was gone and hope was slipping they prayed. God heard. He responded. We know it too. We have experienced it. We claim it. We proclaim it. God's power is available in Jesus Christ. He is our king. He delivers us in our need.

He Asks for Our Trust

But what is a king whose people fail to give him loyalty and trust? What is God able to do for his people when they neglect to recognize his power to supply their needs? What can God do for us when we turn aside from him to seek help and protection elsewhere?

That is a critical issue in verses 37-38 of the text. God's messenger announces that God will put his people to the test when they ignore his ability and seek help from other gods. "Where are their gods, the rock in which they took refuge?" he asks.

"Let them rise up and help you, let them be your protection!" he challenges.

The point of the challenge is that God will let his people go to their other sources of security. But in their doing so they will learn that idols are powerless to assist. God hopes that they will turn again and trust him once more.

God's People Often Fail to Trust Him

Failure to trust God implicitly, falling into the temptation to go for help to other sources appears to be a common failing for God's people through the ages. The Book of Deuteronomy has Moses giving clear warning to Israel on the subject. Joshua is recorded to have said, "choose this day whom you will serve, whether the gods your fathers served in the region beyond the river, or the gods of the Amorites in whose land you dwell" (24:15). The prophets persistently were calling the people back to faithfulness and trust, to obedience and loyalty. Even the sensitive prophet of the Babylonian exile found it necessary to remind the exiles of God's ability to help them and of his willingness to do so. The collection of his proclamations of deliverance in Isaiah 40–55 is one of the Bible's most intense pleas to trust God and his willingness to help his needy people. They are filled with Gospel and direct our thoughts to Jesus.

In Jesus God Is Asking for Our Trust

Could we not say that God's most intense step to win our trust in his power and compassion is communicated in Jesus? What clearer message could he send than to give his Son in whom he has told and shown that he is able to help us? By Christ's demonstrative ministry of word and healing, of helping from hurts and pain, of freeing from rejection and guilt did he not say of God, the Father, "Trust me! I love you! Believe me! I love you! I want to help you. Turn back to me, for my power is for you. Give up your frantic searching for sources of help. Trust me for help! I love you! Trust me for help!

He Claims Total Superiority

"See now that I, even I, am he, and there is no god beside me"; our text goes on to say.

In these words God claims total authority, control and power in the world. There is no place for the question, "Does God exist?" There is no space for alternate claims to our allegiance and trust. God wants us to know that he alone is God.

At the same time God does not force us to believe. Nor does he compel us to trust. The last verse of the text we should notice is not a part of the messenger's speech as the first verses are. It is instead the first sentence of a divine argument which goes on through verse 42. The design of the entire passage is to persuade God's people to trust him and to have confidence in his power to deliver.

It is God's hope that all people will be open to him, but the choice of their allegiance is theirs. We too are free to reject or to accept. Therefore God's claim to total superiority waits for our response.

God Has Repeated His Claim to Superiority

As we read the Old Testament, particularly in the books of the Prophets, we find God again and again and again declaring his power and authority. By the prophets God set forth the folly of trust in other gods, in armies, in wisdom, in riches, in treaties between nations. In the history of Israel and of Judah a clear distinction is made between the welfare of each nation when they were ruled by a king faithful to the covenant with God and by kings who ignored or flaunted God's superiority. The Psalms have praises to God who in his superior power created all that exists and who looks with loving interest on the affairs of nations. The book of Proverbs which is a collection of ancient wisdom designed to help people make choices in life has a theme, "The fear of the Lord is the beginning of wisdom." That theme invites people to acknowledge God's superiority and it gives those who do a voice to show it, and shout it.

Turning to the New Testament we find that the triumphal entry of Christ into Jerusalem on Palm Sunday is a clear emphatic celebration of God's superiority. "Hosanna to the Son of David, Blessed is he who comes in the name of the Lord!" celebrates the power of God for his people. It is a moment in history when the people said, "Amen!" to God's authority. We can too, for God invites us to celebrate his power in Jesus the Christ.

God's Superiority Is Shown in Christ's Passion

On that high note we could stop, for Palm Sunday is the day on which we join the crowds in Jerusalem hailing Christ as the King. Palm Sunday is the moment in time when God's superiority seems clear and powerful.

But, Palm Sunday is also Passion Sunday. We need to see the reason. God's power and superiority spends itself in suffering and in death. We move down the slopes of the Mount of Olives with Jesus into the Via Dolorosa—the Way of Sorrows. There we truly see God's superiority. His loving concern for us, his compassion goes all the way to death. Therefore our song of celebration must contain the words,

> Ride on, ride on in majesty!
> In lowly pomp, ride on to die.
> O Christ, your triumphs now begin
> O'er captive death and conquered sin.
>
> *(LBW 121)*

We see God's power for us in Christ. He is our king in whom we have God's help in our need. He is the one through whom God says, "I love you, trust in me!" So much does he love and so great is his power that he goes with us through suffering into death.

FRANK L. BENZ
Wartburg Theological Seminary
Dubuque, Iowa

NEW LIVES FOR OLD
Maundy Thursday
Jeremiah 31:31-34

Few things sound as good to most human beings as the chance to begin again. The offer of a new opportunity to make a better start in life, to wipe out tragic or blighted moments of the past, has always been alluring.

Whether it has been an offer made in a fairy tale by an old peddler going through the streets of Baghdad hawking lamps that had genies in them that could grant any wish, or a sales pitch made by a modern charlatan telling us that we can gain a new lease on life by retraining our minds, there always has been a line-up of takers when such an announcement came.

Perhaps it is because it touches this spot in the human heart that the new covenant passage in the prophecy of Jeremiah has had such a hold on me and others. It presents each of us another chance to begin life anew. It is no charlatan nor a figment of some romantic's imagination that is conjuring up a fantasy that cannot be fulfilled. It is the Creator of the world who himself is promising us that despite the failures that we have had in the past, in the face of all the broken promises we have accumulated, regardless of the mess that we have made of our relationships with him and with each other, out of the shambles that have resulted he wants to restore us to wholeness and set us free once again!

The key to that staggering opportunity which flashes through Jeremiah's words like a laser beam, is the figure of God who emerges with forgiveness in his hands. He steps forward into our lives telling us that he is ready to give us a new lease on life simply as a gracious gift. The proclamation and offer are so overwhelming that they may have trouble sinking into our consciousness. Listen to his proffer again:

> Behold, the days are coming, says the Lord, when I will make a *new* covenant . . . not like . . . my covenant which they broke, though I was their husband, says the Lord. But this is the covenant which I will make . . . I will put my law within them, and I will write it upon their hearts; and I will be their God, and they shall be my people . . . and I will *forgive* their *iniquity,* and I will *remember* their *sin no more.*

Eye-popping and incredible though the offer seems, if there is any side of God's character that so many of us so desperately need to know more personally these days, it is just this dimension of his forgiving compassion. For there have been few periods of history when *guilt* has been so overwhelming a burden for so many people as now. It seems to have become a millstone that Americans are not able to cut loose from their necks.

We live in a land heavily weighed down with frustration and despair. It is jam-packed with individuals whose lives have been rubbed raw by the wrongs they have done or the failures they have made. Because of their depression, not only are Americans jumping off so many bridges and taking overdoses of sleeping pills that we now rank third in the world's suicide race, but only God knows how many marriages are broken, how many careers are wrecked, how long the line of alcoholics and drug addicts has grown, because of the pent-up need for forgiveness that we haven't been able to satisfy on our own.

One might wonder why this is so in a society that has some of the best psychiatric care in the world. With all of the analyst's offices in operation, you would think that we would have the freest people on earth. What we have been learning, however, is that psychology and psychiatry have their distinct limitations. They are not the cure-alls for broken lives, nor the saviors that can provide the new tomorrows that we all need at one point or another. Where guilt is based on *irrational illusion*, psychiatry has a role to play. It can help us to understand our need to condemn ourselves and to make mountains out of molehills then use them as weights to crush ourselves and others. Getting to the source of such potential self-destruction can enable us to escape its vicious cycle.

But when guilt has its source *in fact*, in events and experiences where actions were morally wrong and humanly destructive, then explanations, or searching out the roots for those acts, often are of little value. At those junctures of life we don't need to hear *why we did it*, but that in spite of the fact *that we did*, we can be forgiven. At disaster points like that the words:

> I will be their God . . . they shall be my people . . . I will forgive . . . I will remember their sin no more.

are what can transform a hopeless human being into one who sees life as worth living again.

The great miracle of existence is that God is willing to make such an offer to people like us. Whether it is a nation of Hebrews who were destroying themselves with their sins in the sixth century B.C., or people in your city or house or mine who are doing the same things in the twentieth century A.D., it is mind-blowing to see God as so ready to hold out his hands to us again. It seems that nothing we can do to ourselves, each other, or him can make him unwilling to touch hands with us as we are! Nor is there anything that we can do to disguise who we are or what we are, even if we try.

Being who he is, God sees right through the facades that we often erect to shield ourselves from the gaze of others. Because he has this capacity to perceive us as we are, one of the most common symbols for God is that picture of the all-seeing eye. It is a symbol that can be frightening if you think much about it, as Alan Watts has so vividly pointed out.

> I become aware of those eyes watching me right through the back of my head. Eyes that bore implacably into the most tender and disreputable centers of my soul, that soon appear to surround me in all directions, to watch from the outside and from the inside, until everything is just One Eye.
>
> And because there is no brow, no face, I cannot tell what expression that Eye has. It just looks and I can't

stand it! I start running, running in blind panic down the corridors of the temple; but every way I turn I am running straight into that Eye.

I drop to the floor, curl up, shut my eyes and cover my head. Yet that Eye comes at me from deep inside me, vaster than ever, filling all thinkable space. There is no where, no where at all, left to go.

It can be a terrifying symbol of a frightening quality of God, that all-seeing eye and power, can't it? But that capacity of God can be liberating, too. It assures us that he sees all things as they really are, and if this is so there is no need to try and hide. And that realization can be a relief!

Pretense is one of the most strangling aspects of life we all have to deal with so much of the time. We are continually being forced to put on false faces for others in one relationship after another. People may talk about wanting us to be honest with them but we often know that that is not really what they either desire or will tolerate. We know how others truly expect us to operate! We are expected to act brave when we are scared. We are expected to act happy when we are depressed. We are expected to act confident and successful when we have failed. And this kind of role-playing simply wears down and slowly begins to choke us, making us wish to God that we could drop the acts and be ourselves. We long, deep down inside, to stop being hypocritical!

Do you know where that word hypocrite comes from? It had its origin in the Greek theater where the hypocrite was the person who acted out more than one part in a play. As the actor changed characters he put on different masks that symbolized the various persons he was attempting to be, masks that not only gave him a new face but were built to help amplify and project his voice in the days before electronic equipment. The problem with the masks was that they could get stifling. In a long play it was not only difficult to remember the lines that were spoken by the different characters one was playing, but the masks themselves caused the hypocrite difficulty in breathing. At times the masks got so oppressive that the people wearing them would faint because of the effects of the device.

Role-playing, wearing false faces, can be even more killing in real life. It isn't until we can shuck our acts that we ever can really be free. With God, and with very few others, we can throw such shams to the wind. With him, the One who "will be [our] God . . ." who will accept us as "his people," who will "forgive our iniquities," who will "remember our sin no more," we can come as unvarnished human beings, knowing that when we do so he will accept us!

We don't have to try to impress God to be accepted. It isn't our well-roundedness or affluence or grace or successfulness that gain us admittance to him. It is God's goodness, not ours, that opens the way to him for us. In the new covenant promise in the mouth of Jeremiah that fact is made abundantly clear. In the ministry and the life of Jesus it was demonstrated in flesh and blood as he lived out that invitation of his Father again and again.

Jesus, you see, seldom sought out people on the basis of their superior qualifications. He did not go through Galilee rounding up folks who were good to be his friends and followers. Rather than look for *good* people, he looked for sinners and made them good. "I have come," he was to say to those who stood before him on more than one occasion, "not to call the righteous but sinners to repentance."

What he said he lived out with those he called to be his disciples. How completely he lived it out was demonstrated in the Last Supper he shared with his apostles just before his death.

The Gospel for this day describes that event in some of its aspects. Another scriptural account of it is recorded in the eleventh chapter of 1 Corinthians. This version of the event has a sentence embedded in it that shows this amazing character of God in action. It is almost an aside in the text that I had read over hundreds of times until one day it jumped out of the page and overwhelmed me. It is those words . . . "in the night in which he was betrayed [Jesus] took bread" (1 Cor. 11-23).

Jesus did not institute his Supper after some glorious occasion when the disciples had done some heroic or praiseworthy deeds. He did not wait for an evening when good feeling ran high or when the group was in accord and all was joy. No! But on the night when he was preparing for his death, when he knew in advance that those at his table were going to desert him, deny him, blaspheme against him . . . on that night of all nights . . . he lovingly took bread and instituted the sacrament of the new covenant, making a reality that which had long before been promised, in a meal in which love and forgiveness would forever be central.

Are there times when the promises of God for forgiveness, for a new lease on life, for a new chance to begin again, seem aimed at everyone but you? Do they seem like promises that are too good to be true? And does that seem so because you feel that you are not worthy of God's love or that he will not accept you as his person because of what you've done in the past? Then remember these words:

I will make a *new covenant* . . . I will *forgive* . . . I will remember their *sins no more* . . . In the night he was betrayed (Jesus), took bread . . . this cup which is poured out for you is the *new covenant in my blood*. . . .

Those words were not spoken as promises to perfect people then or now. If they were, there would have been none to accept them when they were first uttered or today! They were spoken to sinners, Israelites who had destroyed their nation and themselves in the time of Jeremiah, to self-centered disciples more concerned with their own skins than with the life of the Savior, and for us, *sinners all*, people whose need for forgiveness is so great that we must come face-to-face with God himself, the great All-Seer, the great Lover, the great Forgiver, a great Renewer, and there receive his word of absolution and renewal and the lease for a new start in life.

You can't buy that forgiveness. You can't earn it. You can't ever be good enough to merit it. You can't straighten out your own life so that it is clean and free of blots before God, then come to him on your own terms to claim it. No! You and I are forgiven, renewed, restored, made his people, with our sins forgiven and put aside, and a new bond formed between our Maker and ourselves, only because God, in his unspeakable goodness and compassion reaches out to us as we are, with nothing to commend us, to pull us to his breast and kiss us and make us clean, giving us the gift of new lives for old. Amen.

FRANK H. SEILHAMER
Trinity Lutheran Seminary
Columbus, Ohio

RATE IT R

Good Friday
Isaiah 52:13—53:12

Too Realistic

"There is a fountain filled with blood," we used to sing, but no more. Bad poetry, I believe, it was said. But it is still true.

This imagery is not unlike an R-rated film, rated R because of its violence, violence to the point of obscenity. We may avoid the film, yet we will read Isaiah 52 and 53 with near boredom.

The wrenching violence is like a massive, muscular back spasm that increases in intensity the longer it throbs and twists. The wrenching grows to a turbulence that threatens to exhaust and then destroy its victim. In this instance the violent wrenching does both. The turbulence exhausts and destroys.

It does more.

It humiliates as it destroys.

It disfigures the victim it destroys. His appearance is "marred beyond human semblance." There is "no form or comeliness in him that we should regard him." "No beauty that we should desire him." "He was despised and rejected."

He is the "Thalidomide Child of the Week." Grotesque, gargoyle-like limbs have sprouted, others are truncated, some not there at all, like a laboratory experiment frighteningly come true.

What leprosy was to biblical times, what Hiroshima atomic bomb victims are to our times, so is he in the grandeur of repulsion.

A full-color, wide-screen—perhaps the stark black and white would be better—could not capture the depth and the breadth of that shame.

The piercing, silent cry of the virgin being raped in Ingmar Bergman's, *Virgin Spring,* is something like it. The cries of the wounded, bleeding women in Bergman's *Cries and Whispers* is something like it.

David's poignant, "O Absalom, my son! My son, Absalom! Would God I had died for thee, Absalom, my son! My son!" touches the nerve center. The cries of the Bethlehem mothers traumatized by the slaughter of their innocents is something like it.

Roualt's canvases of Christ try to say it too. Bach's *St. Matthew Passion* catches some of the breadth. "O Sacred Head Now Wounded" by Paul Gerhardt tries to sing the pain into the heart as stanza after stanza grasps at the enormity of that event which divides history into B.C. and A.D.

All of Holocaust is there. And yet there was (is) a debate whether or not the film, *Holocaust,* should be shown, the horror of it all still too large to be believed even by some of its victim/survivors.

After you have seen one episode of *Roots,* you wonder if you can weather the unrelenting pain of a second, and then a third, and a fourth. Further, can you endure one episode of its sequel, and then a second and a third?

One would think that the genius of people to torture people would soon be exhausted. Not so, the resources of cruelty are limitless and orchestrated with all the nuances of a Toscaninni, but the conductors are Hitler, Himmler, Stalin, Eichmann, the man down the street, the good people who bought, sold, worked, and killed slaves, you and I.

"Deep, deeper than we believe, lie the roots of sin; it is in the good that they exist; it is in the good that they thrive and send up sap and produce the black fruit of Hell," writes Charles Williams. Put them all together and we only begin to see through a glass darkly the awesome repulsion that is a crucifixion.

We Made It So

Now to that, add that we put him there. What is so repulsive about it is that *we* put him there! We are that repulsive sight that meets us on the cross. Perhaps we are repulsed by the sight of his crucifixion so we don't have to face the sight of ours.

We put him there. "Surely he has borne our grief and carried our sorrows." "He was wounded for our transgressions, he was bruised for our iniquities." "By oppression and judgment he was taken away." "He shall bear their iniquities." "He bore the sins of many." "All we, like sheep have gone astray, we have turned everyone to his own way."

Many rejoiced when the Western powers left Viet Nam only to have the Vietnamese do it to their neighbors, the Cambodians. Now the mainland Chinese do it to the Vietnamese. We rejoiced as foreign powers withdrew from Africa only to have the Africans do it to the Africans. And in some of the latest skirmishes the Muslims are doing it to the Muslims. As William Coffin reminded us about ourselves, "After all, we are a nation which assassinates presidents." Of course, Isaiah could not have seen or foreseen the cult of the "I" that we celebrate in song and culture. "You owe it to yourself."

"All we, like sheep, have gone astray; we have turned everyone to his own way."

All this pain and suffering we place on him just as we place it all and blame it all on the other. It makes for almost unrelieved suffering. As C. S. Lewis writes of Homer's *The Iliad*, "Here in *The Iliad* there is just suffering. Perhaps this is what was in Goethe's mind when he said, 'The lesson of *The Iliad* is that on this earth we enact Hell. Only the style—the unwearying, unmoved angelic speech of Homer—make it endurable. Without that

The Iliad would be a poem beside which the grimmest modern realism is child's play.'" So, too, it is with the crucifixion.

"He was cut off from the land of the living," like a Martin Luther King. "They (we) made his grave with the wicked, although he had done no violence and there was no deceit in his mouth." In fact, it is often just that absence of violence and deceit that prompts our own. We have difficulty responding routinely to "a lamb that is silent before her shearers and one that opens not its mouth, even while being led to the slaughter." Anything, nothing and everything will prompt us to lay it on the back of another, in this case, the Christ. The very gentleness of the other can be that which invites and provokes our own violence.

So Did God

With all that, there is yet more to say, much more. God put him there. Yes, we put him there. But God put him there, too. "Stricken, smitten of God and afflicted." "The Lord has laid on him the iniquity of us all." "It was the will of the Lord to bruise him; he has put him to grief; he makes him an offering for sin."

God put him there, too. An act of desperation? Perhaps. But what would we do, given the circumstances? To create, then to see the creation distorted, disfigured. What would we do? Cease to love? That is always possible. To continue to love? But how? Angels are equal to some tasks. But not this task. God could have produced a magic universe, made the sins, the sorrows, the griefs, the ignorance, the afflictions, the iniquities, the oppressions, the killing and the maiming, the transgressions disappear by magic. Yes, I suppose he could have done so. But magic, quite plainly, does not seem to have been his way, though some of his helpers past and present have made it appear so.

If we could not take what it took, he very clearly meant to and did. So, "he poured out his soul to death, he was numbered with the transgressors, he bore the sin of many. He was wounded for our transgressions, he was bruised for our iniquities; upon him was the chastisement that make us whole and with his stripes we are healed." "By oppression and judgment he was taken away." "He was oppressed and afflicted." "He was despised and rejected by men," but also by God.

"Crucifixion was an obscene thing," writes Charles Williams. "It was revolting not nearly because of the torture and the degradation, but also because of the disgust; or rather it is revolting to us—I do not know that it was revolting to those who saw it. They were as accustomed to it as our fathers were to burning or castration or we to many years' imprisonment or to the gallows. It was, however, definitely more spectacularly obscene than the gallows; we can hardly in the nature of things, realize it so, and even our best efforts tend to make it a little respectable. But then again, life, as we know it, is obscene; or, to be accurate, it has in it a strong element of obscenity."

He was stretched, he was bled, he was nailed, he was thrust into, but not a bone of him was broken. All by design, not quite ours, yet ours, but certainly by God's design.

So Did He

And by Christ's design, too, let it be known. Despite the attack of people and the neglect of God, and Christ's own innocence, he accepted "the iniquity of us all, yet he opened not his mouth; like a lamb that is led to the slaughter, and like a sheep that before its shearers, open not his mouth." "He makes himself an offering for sin." "He bore the sin of many." Christ agrees with what happens to him, no matter how disagreeable. Startling enough that God should be against him. Even more startling that he should agree that God should be against him if the transgressors are to be dealt with in a godly fashion. In fact, his offering becomes an intercession for the very transgressors who put him on the cross. He shall count many righteous and make many righteous. His reward for all that he has done in his suffering will be to receive those who imposed the suffering. The God who abandoned him on the cross now rewards him in a bizarre way. He gives him those who had no use for him. Is it any wonder that Charles Williams should write, "It is in the gospels that the really terrifying attacks on the Gospel lie."

Fortunately

"Kings shall shut their mouths because of him; for that which was not told them they shall see, and that which they have not heard they shall understand."

That the victim should actively and willingly take up his victimage so that he can reclaim those who victimized him is the strangest response to a stimulus ever recorded. That is perhaps why it is never fully believed, even by those who believe. Say it a thousand times. Sing it a thousand times. Re-run the film again and again. Replay the play again and again. The mystery is not thereby lessened nor more fully grasped. Yet it is said, "He shall be exalted and lifted up."

"Thank God it's Friday!" A tired, apathetic age cries out, apathetic about everything except its own apathy, cries out in a fatigue born largely of indolence and a lack of direction. And the cry is taken up, "Thank God it's Good Friday!" because "it is a tale that is too good *not* to be true" (Frederick Brueckner).

So good, in fact, that someone said, "Write it in Hebrew and in Latin and in Greek."

PAUL W. F. HARMS
Trinity Lutheran Seminary
Columbus, Ohio

THE LORD IS MY STRENGTH AND MY SONG
The Resurrection of Our Lord — Easter Day
Exodus 15:1-11

The great festivals of the church produce the great hymns of the church. Just as Christmas would be unthinkable without its carols, so Easter would not be Easter without its trumpets and exalted sounds: "Jesus Christ is risen today!" "The strife is o'er, the battle done!" "Christ Jesus lay in death's strong bands!"

It has always been so. Our text for today is the great hymn of the exodus: "I will sing to the Lord, for he has triumphed gloriously; the horse and rider he has thrown into the sea." In response to God's great acts, God's people sing. We sing because we must. We could not bring off the victory for ourselves, but God has done it for us. We respond in song, to vent our joy, to praise the name of God, and to let the world hear what he has done.

My Father's God

Who has done this? Who has given us the victory? "My father's God," says the text, "and I will exalt him." We stand in this long line of tradition, in which men and women have recognized the ongoing power of God in their lives, and have sung about it. By combining the song of the exodus with the celebration of Jesus' resurrection the church proclaims that throughout biblical history it is the one God, the Father of Jesus Christ, who has brought life out of death. It is right to do so. John Ylvisaker was correct in taking this exodus hymn, retranslating it for Easter, and setting it to a contemporary melody: "I will sing unto the Lord for he has triumphed gloriously; the grave is empty, won't you come and see?" This God bridges the generations in himself, in his love and majesty. And that is celebrated throughout the Old Testament, in its central event, the exodus, and throughout the New Testament, in its central event, the resurrection. They belong together. That is why my white stole has the exodus symbols of the pillar of cloud and fire on one side and the resurrection symbols of the butterfly and grain on the other. It is the God of our fathers and mothers and theirs before them, back to the empty tomb and beyond that to the joyful group on the banks of the sea, who is our strength and our song.

It has often been noted that the Old Testament has no full-blown doctrine of the resurrection. As a result it has sometimes been thought difficult to find Old Testament Lessons for the Easter season. However, as we read the Old Testament it becomes abundantly clear that over and over again it wants to tell us about a God who brings his people from death to life. Life and death had broad meanings for the people of Israel. Death was the final cessation of breathing, of course, but it was also a power which threatened to force its way into the living of everyday life. Suffering, illness, injustice, captivity, anxiety were deathly threats. They were signs of God's hiddenness which could cut a person off from the life-giving relationship with Yahweh and "lay (him) in the dust of death" (Ps. 22:15).

Full life could only be received and enjoyed through the knowledge and experience of God. "If it had not been the Lord who was on our side," sang Israel in Psalm 124, "if it had not been the Lord who was on our side, when men rose up against us ... then the flood would have swept us away." But, God was with them, so they sang, "We have escaped as a bird from the snare of the fowlers; the snare is broken, and we have escaped." Many of us have had the experience of releasing a trapped bird or animal which otherwise would have been doomed to suffering and death. That picture, says Israel, is a portrait of God, the one who brings his people from death to life.

The greatest celebration of that was at the exodus. A people threatened with extinction under the tyranny of Pharaoh were brought out of Egypt by the mighty hand of a loving God. He who at the beginning had said, "Let there be light!" now said, "Let there be life!"

This God, with his radical inclination toward life, is the Father of Jesus Christ. And the message of Easter, that God has raised his Son from the power of death, has brought life to countless generations of Christians. This God of life, this God of Israel, of Jesus, of our ancestors in the faith, and of our fathers and mothers, this God who is "majestic in holiness, terrible in glorious deeds" (v. 11) is the one we sing about today.

This word of victory calls us to praise and faith, just as it did the disciples on that first Easter morning. The women in the gospel were much like the women in the exodus account. With timbrels and dancing they led the celebration of victory. Our long exodus poem is a response to the short song of Miriam recorded later in the chapter. "Sing to the Lord," she cried, "for he has triumphed gloriously; the horse and rider he has thrown into the sea" (v. 21). And sing they did, Moses and all the people of Israel. And they kept singing, so that the song was passed down, and written down, and has become ours as well.

So also the women of the Easter gospel. Unlike the men, their love had overcome their fear and depression and had brought them to the tomb, where they could be on hand to lead the singing for God's ultimate victory. Like Miriam they spread the word, calling on the men to respond. But, unlike Moses and Israel, the disciples could not. It was too much; their fear and mistrust were too great. It must be an "idle tale."

The point in referring to this is not to criticize the disciples, but, alas, to identify with them. If the joyful chorus of praise of God has been heard in every age, so also has been the crushing doubt of the disciples. It was not new to Israel either. Yes, we have heard the song of Miriam and Moses; yes, we have heard the recitation of your saving acts for our fathers and mothers, but where are you now, when we need you? "Rouse thyself! Why sleepest thou, O Lord? Awake! Do not cast us off for ever!" (Ps. 44:23). Can the wonderful stories be believed? Is this God of my father and my mother my God as well?

My God

The text claims it is true. "This is my God, and I will praise him." But it is not always so easy. I remember seeing the escape from Egypt in a movie by Cecil B. De Mille. The waters of the Red Sea towered over the dry land like mountains of Minnesota snow over a small path of roadway. Can we relate to a God who piles up the waters with a "blast of (his) nostrils"? Can the tomb really have been empty? Where are these great sights and signs in my life?

Even amidst the trumpets and lilies of Easter, we must take these questions seriously if this is to be *our* festival, rather than just a festival of our tradition. Although there would be no faith without that tradition, what finally gives us life is *our* faith, not the faith of our ancestors.

Let us get at the questions in a roundabout way, by looking at the setting of our text in the book of Exodus. To be sure, it speaks of the great God who moves heaven and earth, a God of smoke and fire and terrible deeds, but we would be wrong to visualize a God who is so powerful and so wholly-other that he is beyond the reach of the ordinary Israelite, the ordinary slave, tramping through the mud and straw of Pharaoh's brickyard, muttering his doubts and weeping over the plight of his family. For, according to the Bible, it is precisely those sighs and sorrows which moved God to act.

"The people of Israel groaned under their bondage, and cried out for help, and their cry under bondage came up to God. And God heard their groaning, and God remembered his covenant with Abraham, with Isaac, and with Jacob. . . . Then the Lord said, 'I have seen the affliction of my people who are in Egypt . . . I know their sufferings, and I have come down to deliver them out of the hand of the Egyptians'" (Exod. 2:23-24; 3:7-8).

The amazing gospel of the text is that Yahweh, the God who controls all the forces of the universe and all the flow of history, is a God who can hear and be moved by the cries and prayers of a rag-tag bunch of anonymous slaves.

Did the exodus really look like De Mille's movie? We don't know. Some of the biblical texts make it seem rather like merely a few chariots stuck in the mud in a shallow sea of reeds. But whatever the nature of the event, the nature of God remains the same. He is the one "who sits enthroned on high, but (who) stoops to behold the heavens and the earth . . . (who) takes up the weak out of the dust and lifts up the poor from the ashes" (Ps. 113:5-6, *LBW*).

Over and over again, in the language of the psalms, we meet this kind of God, the one who hears the laments of his people and who has both the power and the will to do something about them. It is this God who answers Jesus' awful lament of Good Friday, "My God, my God, why hast thou forsaken me?" with the victory of life on Easter morning. And it is this God who has spoken, usually softly, rather than with great signs and wonders, to his people over the centuries.

It is, I think, for this reason that we can say: Yes, this is my God. It's true that this resurrection is for history and for salvation and for ever, but finally it is for me. It is *my* life which is restored. It is *my* doubts and fears and sighs which are answered. It is *my* death which is overcome in victory.

The Jewish people of God have passed down this exodus story into our own time. In each generation they too have sung, "This is my God, and I will praise him." As every year, this year too they sat around the tables of the Passover celebration and said, "In every generation each individual is bound to consider himself as if he in his own person had gone forth out of Egypt. For it is written, this is because of what the Eternal did for *me* when I came out of Egypt" (*The Haggadah,* retold by Meyer Levin, Behrman House, 1968, p. 38). From that sense of history has come our insistence on the real presence of God in his word and sacraments, "Do this for the remembrance of me!" This does not mean, "Oh, yes, I remember, God did something once for Israel and for Jesus." It means he is recalled to active presence, here and now, for you and for me.

It is a different day from that of Miriam and the women at the tomb. Our women are in the armies and on the navy's ships, rather than waiting at home to greet the victors with song. But to this age, also, our texts proclaim the message of salvation: God is Lord of history; God is Lord of creation; God is Lord of life and death. He has raised Jesus from the grave and, in that act, he gives *me* new life.

Especially on this Easter day, listen to the words when you receive the bread and wine: "The body of Christ, given for *you!*" "The blood of Christ, shed for *you!*" This is the sign and the wonder for us. This is the parted sea and the empty tomb. And so, we join our voices to those of the heavenly choirs, and the saints in heaven, and the whole church on earth as we sing the Easter songs. "The Lord is my strength and my song, and he has become my salvation; this is my God, and I will praise him, my father's God, and I will exalt him." Amen.

FREDERICK J. GAISER
Luther-Northwestern Seminaries
St. Paul, Minnesota

LET THE FAITHFUL REJOICE IN TRIUMPH
Second Sunday of Easter
Psalm 149

The Psalms are at one and the same time the most familiar and the least familiar of the Scriptures. They are called poetry, but they don't rhyme. They are called hymns, but we don't have the music for them. Many of them sound as though they are the word of an individual to God (which they are). Yet they are included in our Scriptures which we believe to be a Word of God to us!

On these Sundays of Easter when the First Lesson, which is ordinarily a reading from the Old Testament, is a reading from the Acts of the Apostles instead, the Psalms of the Sundays of Easter will be used as texts for the sermons.

For the Second Sunday of Easter it is Psalm 149. This is the version of that psalm that is in the *Lutheran Book of Worship:*

> Hallelujah!
> Sing to the Lord a new song:
>   sing his praise in the congregation of the faithful.
> Let Israel rejoice in his maker;
>   let the children of Zion be joyful in their king.
> Let them praise his name in the dance;
>   let them sing praises to him with timbrel and harp.
> For the Lord takes pleasure in his people
>   and adorns the poor with victory.
> Let the faithful rejoice in triumph;
>   let them be joyful on their beds.
> Let the praises of God be in their throat
>   and a two-edged sword in their hand;
> to wreak vengeance on the nations
>   and punishment on the peoples;
> to bind their kings in chains
>   and their nobles with links of iron;
> to inflict on them the judgment decreed;
>   this is glory for all his faithful people.
> Hallelujah!

This psalm is a hymn and its theme is right in the middle of it:

Let the Faithful Rejoice in Triumph

For those who first used this psalm it was a new song in an old setting. As we use it today it is an old song in a new setting.

A New Song in an Old Setting

"Sing to the Lord a new song; sing his praise in the congregation of the faithful." This is a call for a new song in an old setting.

The call for a new song comes in other psalms as well as this one. Many of the psalms were written to celebrate notable victories or to commemorate some kindness of God. Sometimes it is

115

possible to pinpoint what it is in the history of God's people that is being celebrated. Sometimes we can only guess at what gave rise to a particular psalm. That is the case with this one.

Now that might be very hard on our curiosities but it enhances our use of the psalm. We can use it for situations different from those of the original setting.

What do we know of that setting? That which gave rise to the call for a new song was obviously a victory, a triumph of some sort. It might have been a military victory. It might have been the restoration to the promised land after the captivity.

But whatever sort of triumph it was, this hymn of praise is to celebrate the Maker and Ruler of Israel. It was the insight and the outlook of the ancient people of God that he was with them at all times and in all that happened to them. He was with them to bring them back to himself. He was with them even in judgment. That was the frame of mind, the setting, in which they sang their songs.

The physical setting was in the company of the people of God, "in the congregation of the faithful." That means that this one probably was sung at the temple in Jerusalem. It isn't certain what the expression, "let them be joyful on their beds," means, but it is possible that it is a call to the pilgrim worshipers who were resting in the grounds of the temple at Jerusalem to sing the praise of God even while at rest.

But what about all that vindictiveness in the latter half of this psalm? There have been times in the history of the church when the counsel, "Let the praises of God be in their throat and a two-edged sword in their hand," was used to incite warlike fervor. It was so used in the Thirty Years' War by those in the Catholic camp, and in the Peasants' War by those in the Protestant camp.

God always addresses us where we are. For his ancient people that was in the setting of the promised land which he had bidden them to possess. He spoke to them in that history. The people of God were frequently under attack, and so saw the defense of the land as a participation in the judgment of God. It is difficult to hear in the latter part of this psalm the music of mercy, forgiveness, and reconciliation. And that is more the music of Easter. So what shall we do with this psalm?

An Old Song in a New Setting

For us this is an old song and we can sing it in a new setting. It is still appropriate for the faithful to rejoice in triumph. And the triumph that we celebrate is the resurrection of Jesus Christ from the dead. The triumph that we anticipate is the resurrection of all the faithful. That is the new setting for this old song.

Let the faithful rejoice in triumph in the first victory over the last enemy.

I realize as well as anyone that neither the psalmist nor those people of God in the Old Testament who sang his song had the resurrection in mind. No doubt they did have military enemies and military victories in mind.

It is not unusual to hear military language used in a figurative way in the New Testament. In the Ephesian letter we are urged to "be strong in the Lord and in the strength of his might. Put on the whole armor of God. . . ." That armor is then described in terms of the military garb of the Roman soldier.

In the first Corinthian letter St. Paul uses this kind of language specifically with respect to the resurrection: "Death is swallowed up in victory. O death, where is thy victory? O death, where is thy sting? The sting of death is sin, and the power of sin is the law. But thanks be to God, who gives us the victory through our Lord Jesus Christ."

And so we can take the military language of this old psalm and use it in the new setting of the resurrection to celebrate, to be among the faithful who rejoice in triumph.

What is the triumph in which we rejoice? What is the victory with which we are adorned? What is the pleasure that the Lord takes in his people?

The resurrection of Jesus Christ from the dead is the triumph of truth over falsehood. Jesus said, "I am the truth." To his accusers he said, "Now you seek to kill me, a man who has told you the truth." And they did. The resurrection is the triumph of his truth over falsehood.

The resurrection of Jesus Christ from the dead is the triumph of good over evil. The forces which crucified Jesus were the forces of evil, an unholy and otherwise unlikely coalition. The resurrection is the triumph of good over evil.

The resurrection of Jesus Christ from the dead is the triumph of love over hatred. Hatred killed Jesus. If there were no resurrection then the hatred in the world would have conquered the love of God. The resurrection is the triumph of love over all that hatred can do.

The resurrection of Jesus Christ from the dead is the triumph of life over death. This triumph shows us that death is not the will of God. Paul accurately describes it as "the last enemy." The resurrection of Jesus Christ is but the first victory over that last enemy. Our own final participation in that victory is yet to come.

In that confidence "Let the Faithful Rejoice in Triumph!" Let us rejoice in the victory achieved; triumph of truth over falsehood; triumph of good over evil; triumph of love over hatred; triumph of life over death. We can sing to the Lord a new song, even using the words of an old song, Psalm 149 to do it.

Let us rejoice, too, in the victory anticipated, our own resurrection, for this is the glory of God's faithful people. Hallelujah! Amen.

STANLEY D. SCHNEIDER
St. Paul's Ev. Lutheran Church
Toledo, Ohio

AN EASTER RECITAL
Third Sunday of Easter
Psalm 30

Many of us have attended recitals. My most memorable recital is one in which I, as a youngster, played the piano. I don't remember what I played or how well I played. I probably did not play very well, because I did not practice regularly. What I remember, though, is my bow. It was a very deep bow which brought a laugh from the audience and a blush from me.

Today's psalm is a recital. It has performers, a program and an audience. Specifically, it is "An Easter Recital" that is 1) sung by the thankful, 2) about their restoration, 3) for the Lord.

An Easter Recital Sung by the Thankful

All recitals need performers. This one is no exception. The performers are the thankful. The psalmist is one of the thankful who has been restored. Look at the words he uses to describe himself. He is the lifted up, the brought up, the healed. He is one who cried out, pleaded and was heard. His wailing was turned to dancing and his sackcloth was replaced with joy.

There is nothing illusive or impersonal about his description. He is not imagining his renewal. No, he is one who was going down to the grave with all humanity, whose enemies had a firm grip on him and who would have fallen to them, if left to himself, but who pleaded with God and knew that God restored him.

Like water being drawn from the well, the psalmist sees himself being lifted from the pit. He is among the restored.

We too are among the restored. The revelation of our restoration may not be as spectacular as Saul's conversion in the First Lesson for this day (Acts 9:1-20). We may not encounter a light from heaven or have something like scales fall from our eyes. But God has revealed himself to us through his Word and sacraments. Christ has defeated our enemies. His victory is ours. En route to the grave we have been given life in him. There isn't anything unreal or impersonal about that. We, like the psalmist, are among the restored.

As one of the restored, we can thank God. This we do by joining the recital of the thankful and becoming one of its performers. The psalmist did this. His words testify to it. He begins saying, "I will exalt you, O Lord," and he ends with, "Therefore my heart sings to you without ceasing; O Lord my God, I will give you thanks forever."

The psalmist joined the thankful to exalt the Lord. He became part of their recital. His use of the first person singular should not mislead us into thinking that the recital is his alone. The first person singular in the psalms is used in a corporate sense. The psalmist knew that in order to praise God the congregation had to worship in the sanctuary. To that end he invited God's people to join his thanksgiving, saying, "Sing to the Lord, you servants of his, give thanks for the remembrance of his holiness."

We too join the recital of thanks to God. Without the church and the means of grace given it, any effort to praise him falls short. This is not to say that private devotion as a member of the church is incomplete. But it is to say that any attempt to make worship into an individual matter without the church is heresy. It does not tell the whole truth. Those who perform such an individualistic thanksgiving may discover that it is unacceptable to God.

Thanking God takes action on our part to join his body and to perform its recital. Eugene Brand's book on worship, *The Rite Thing*, has as its first chapter title, "To Be Involved." The title is the preface to the rest of the chapters and he distinguishes between players and spectators at worship. Through the church's worship, we can, if we are willing, perform the Easter recital. Together our responses, hymns and prayers do exalt God. In joining the recital of the thankful, we do what we set out to do, namely, to thank God.

But now what is the recital about? Having identified the performers as the thankful who are among the restored and who thank God, what is the content of their thanksgiving?

An Easter Recital About the Thankful's Restoration

The thankful's recital is about their restoration from God's wrath to his favor. This makes the psalm an Easter recital, because this is what Christ's Easter victory is about. Through Christ the restoration spoken of in the psalm is fulfilled. God remembered his holiness. He dedicated himself to deliver us from his wrath to his favor. The psalm and the church's worship recite this restoration.

The thankful are restored from God's wrath. There isn't always an explanation for God's wrath. Yet, in this psalm we are given a good idea of what incited it. Evidently, the psalmist began to rely heavily on his material wealth. With it he felt secure and thought that he'd never fall or waver. Although he attributed his strength to God, he relied more on what God had given him than on God himself. The gift had replaced the giver. It doesn't take a lot of explanation to see how this violated the First Commandment and ignored what God said about being a jealous God.

The psalmist's disobedience is common today. Many rely on their goods, failing to see them as gifts from God. Jesus' comment, "it is easier for a camel to go through the eye of a needle than for a rich man to enter the kingdom of God" (Matt. 19:24), has been true throughout the ages, including this one.

The manifestation of God's wrath is the same today as when the psalm was written. God is hidden from us and in being hidden from us, we are left to our idols and enemies. The psalmist blamed God for being hidden from him. He writes, "Then you hid your face." I don't know how that happens. Certainly the more we turn from God the less we see his face and our turning may be as responsible as God's hiding. Whatever, when we do incite God's anger by disobeying him, we are left to ourselves.

The result is fear, because we begin to see that what we thought gave security gives very little. Without God there is no security from the natural, political and personal crises that can inflict us. Without his assurance of deliverance from our whims and nature's unpredictability, we are left to wither and die.

God restores us from his wrath which is incited by our disobedience and manifested in his being hidden from us. He restores us to his favor. I suppose that I could say of being in God's favor that it is just the opposite of being in his wrath. That is true, but there is much more, because not only is God present, but he is also a helper, not only can we rely on him, but we can be his servants, not only is there an absence of fear, but there is joy.

Because of God's mercy we are in his favor. Nothing we do warrants it. The psalmist knew that. After his questions, "What profit is there in my blood? Will the dust praise you?" he cries, "O Lord, have mercy on me." God's mercy restores us. He is our helper. As our helper he assures us of his Easter victory and he provides for our needs. Today's gospel (John 21:1-14) records an event in the life of Jesus in which he provided for his disciples and assured them of his resurrection from the dead. That record has served to strengthen our faith.

In God's favor our faith in him is strengthened and we are free to serve him. Depending on what version of the Bible you use, God's thankful people may be called saints or servants. Their lives are marked by kindness and benevolence, goodwill and love, mercy and piety. The same qualities that God used to redeem us, we, as his servants, also may use. In God's favor our reliance on him is restored and he entrusts us to be his servants.

The result is joy instead of fear. Life, not doom, is the forecast, because God's favor is for a lifetime.

The restoration from God's wrath to his favor is what this recital is about. Because of that it is an Easter recital. It praises God for what he has done. It exalts him and declares his faithfulness. It expresses our thanksgiving and is performed for him.

An Easter Recital for the Lord

God is the audience. We know that. To him do the thankful give their praise. For him do they perform. The psalmist did and so do we. There is nothing new about that observation. Yet, it is one that is both rewarding and challenging.

Performing before God is rewarding in that we who are small among the masses are privileged to perform before the one who restored us. That is no small thing. Who has performed before a nobler audience? No one. God is God. There is no other besides him. He is present at our Easter recital.

On the other hand, performing before God is challenging in that we seek to please him and gain his applause. I know of no other way to please God than to be true to him. That is done by being true to what he has restored us to be, his thankful people. In singing the Easter recital with the church, we thank God and he applauds.

Today's psalm is a recital. It is "An Easter Recital" that is 1) sung by the thankful, 2) about their restoration, 3) for the Lord.

It is a recital that pleases God and is given every time his people join in worship. It is one that we, regardless of talent or age, are welcome to be part of, because God has restored us.

> FREDERICK E. HASECKE
> St. Paul's Ev. Lutheran Church
> Toledo, Ohio

BANQUETS IN THE SHADOWS
Fourth Sunday of Easter
Psalm 23

Two facts must be kept in mind whenever we attempt to understand the psalms. Like a pilot, if he is to propel his small plane safely must keep his mind on two things—the instrument panel before him and the sky around him; so if we are to get through a psalm with any accuracy of understanding, we must keep our minds on two facts. One is that the psalms are poetry and not prose, and the other is that this poetry arises out of the experience of the writer and can only be understood in and through experience of the interpreter.

The Psalms Are Poetry

They are symbolic truth. The psalmists picture truth rather than describe it or spell it out in factual language. Thus we must think with the eye when we read and let the words draw pictures in our minds. To interpret a sentence of a psalm literally is to reduce it to absurdity and to deprive it of its grandeur and its warmth. When the Hebrew spoke of, say, the effects of heredity, he spoke poetically as—"If the father be onion and the mother garlic, how can the child have a sweet perfume." Describe that picture in prose and we have a long chapter on how we are limited and determined by heredity. Jesus, the Hebrew, spoke words warmed with generosity and poetry. "This is my body." Chill those words into prose and you have transubstantiation. "I am the good shepherd." Chill those words into prose and we have a cold and wooden dissertation on the general and special providence of God.

The Psalms Are Subjective

The psalmist's pictures of truth arise out of human experience. These magnificent, poetic words are hammered out by tragedy and trauma, and inspired by joy and ecstasy. They are strained through the net of human awareness, bitter and sweet. They are summoned to the printed page from the depths of human emotions. The psalmists wrote not so much what they thought but what they felt. And only if and when we feel the same things can we know of what they spoke. Only the person who is aware of his own depraved nature and the ugly twists in his behavior can understand the poet's anguish when he called "Out of the depths I cry unto Thee, O Lord, Lord hear my voice." Only the one who knows what it is to be emotionally exhausted and bogged down, to be frustrated, to feel failure can understand the cry, "I waited patiently for the Lord, he inclined to me and heard my cry and drew me up from the desolate pit out of the miry bog."

Only the person who has understood how "all things do work for good to those who love God" can understand what the psalmist meant when he looked back over his troubled life and realized that what at the time looked like threatening valleys of shadows were in reality meaningful green pastures. The psalms must be seen as the experience of the writer and understood in the experience of the believer.

The Experience of Banquets

And what is the experience that produced this psalm? Well of course that is open to interpretation, and every interpreter can read the psalm only through one's own experience. If one is living a miserable life full of failure, disappointment and meanness, one's outlook becomes pessimistic toward this life. Then the psalm will be read solely as a promise of goodness to come after death. "Everything will be all right when we get to heaven." I also must interpret the psalm through personal experience. What I see written persuasively here in these beloved lines is that life is a series of continual banquets. And the way to look to the future is to remember life's past banquets, even those we had to eat in haste with shadows, rather than sunlight, falling on the table.

Often it is only the 20/20 vision of hindsight that convinces us of this. Many of the experiences of our lives looked fearful and ominous when we endured them. When we look back, those dreadful valleys of death were really green pastures beside still waters. They were banquets, tables prepared before us in presence of our enemies, goodness and mercy following us all the days of our life. Our life has been guided by a very good shepherd. This psalm probably was not written by a young shepherd boy, as we have supposed. More likely it was composed by an old man looking back over a life of trouble, a life lived in a world of fearful shadows. His life constantly was threatened by death, if not death of the body then of life's essentials: friendships, hopes, ambitions, optimism, joy.

Shadows on the Table

And what is our life? It is mostly grief, if the Old Testament writers are accurate. Job announced, "Man who is born of woman is of few days and full of trouble." Jeremiah lamented, "Why did I come forth from the womb to see toil and sorrow and spend my days in shame?" And a psalmist furthered their complaints, "For my life is spent with sorrow and my years with sighing. My strength fails because of my misery." Psalm 23 echoes this view that life can be a "walk through the valley of the shadow of death." We do live out our lives in the presence of evil and the enemies of our spirit, with threats to everything we most cherish.

Is this miserable, pessimistic, ancient complaint invalidated by modern scientific and psychological progress? Has this ancient wail over life now been discredited? A vibrant young woman was the life of the party one night; playing the piano, leading the singing, full of quick wit and humor. Afterwards she killed herself, leaving a note lamenting, "Nobody really cared." A sensitive man had gone through a personal valley of shadows. His sons had bitterly disappointed him; so had his church. Ill, he was taken to the hospital. His pastor inquired of his doctor, "What is your diagnosis?" The doctor replied, "He has a broken heart!" It seems that suicides and broken hearts are so very common in this century.

Yet the psalmist is not saying here that his verdict on human life is that it is all a dark valley of shadows. He is saying that the event right ahead sometimes, maybe often, looks to be that. Sometimes the experience that we face is ominous, threatening, dangerous. But at a later time when we look back at that trauma, necessity forced us to endure, we see in it a rich occasion of growth and discovery. It was invaluable. We see the joy that was "seeking me through pain" and we "trace the rainbow through the rain."

The Food on the Table

Sometimes the rich banquet of meaning and reward is spread before us right on the floor of the valley of shadows. Suddenly we see as we are engaging in battle with the "enemies" of our soul how inestimably important is this present conflict; how this very painful trouble is essential for our growth and our gaining that needed quality without which our life would be empty and poor. In the midst of this valley, with this shadow falling on us, we have found a banquet for our spirit.

What is the food on which the spirit of a person feeds? Most often people have passed up the entrees to grab only for the junk food and the desserts. We think our soul craves such things as serenity, peace, no opposition, a calm and pleasant life, with a little bit of service and much recreation. But such fare leaves us famished. What nourishes the spirit is something like an act of courage after a personal history of failures of nerve. Or a reconciliation to another person after a time of estrangement. That builds the spirit of a person. The admission of fault—the sudden awareness and confession of damaging others—this is indeed a feast for the spirit; not one of delicacies but surely one of good, nutritious, plain food.

One is forever stronger after acknowledging guilt. And to be forgiven by one whom you have hurt—oh, yes, that is indeed rich food. Even better is to come to the knowledge that God does forgive you for that thing for which you may not have forgiven yourself. Another rich banquet for the spirit is to learn to trust another human being. Ah, that is good food. To trust, when you have rejected other offers to help, claiming independence and self-reliance, never knowing how good and how right it is to let yourself be dependent. To trust and let another person love you. These are some of the banquets which are put before us, and this is the valley of shadows turning into green pastures.

It has happened many times in our history that we have enjoyed the banquet in the very midst of the battles of life. On the eve of disaster those who face death together on the morrow have often found great fellowship and true caring and deep joy in each other so much so that they can say, "Should I die tomorrow, tonight has made my life worthwhile." Bonhoeffer in *Life Together* speaks of such banquets prepared for students illegally studying theology. The Lord's Supper given to the terminally ill often becomes a banquet, as its meaning and communion are intensified by insecurity and fear. Sometimes a mutual struggle casts two strangers together. Risks encountered for each other, hardships borne together and shared dangers weld them together in an enduring friendship and love. Perhaps their relationship is one of those generous and mutually creative kind of which Paul Tournier speaks saying we are fortunate to experience three or four in a lifetime. And it is an established fact of spiritual growth that the eternal qualities a person can, in this life, possess, i.e. faith, hope and love, are given to us by God most often through the experiences of personal failure, confidence-defeating weakness and life-disturbing selfishness. "My grace is sufficient for you, for my power is made perfect in weakness."

"Goodness and mercy shall follow me all the days of my life." That view of one's past and one's future is seen only by a person whose vision has been corrected by faith and maturity. Without mature faith a person's experience has not been characterized by goodness and mercy but rather by misfortune and struggle, or at best by luck and personal fortitude. And without hopeful trust one dare not take a step into the shadows cast upon one's path by the unknown future.

A Word About Trusting

We do long for security in life, for stability and safety. We had hoped that the church would provide us with the still waters of serenity but instead within its walls we hear that we must drink from the churning waters of a life full of risks and insecurities. As Kierkegaard said, "Faith is a turbulent thing." We had hoped that the Bible would tell us of a safe and peaceful path upon which we can walk through our days. Instead on its pages we read of barren deserts, jungles, and wilderness to cross. We read in that sacred book of dangers threatening both body and soul. We read of how our cherished value system taught us by environment and society is turned upside down in reality. It is the wicked who prosper, not the good people. It is God who dies on the cross as a criminal, not the devil. It is healthy saints like Job and Jeremiah, not the pathological nihilists, who agonize over existence, crying out that they wished that they had not been born. It is the people of God, not the worldlings, who are taken into captivity and who watch their sacred, majestic temple destroyed twice, once in each testament. And he who is saved is not he who possesses wisdom and goodness and prosperity but he who trusts, simply trusts.

The essential message of this delicate and beloved masterpiece of the world's literature is the same: life means trusting. Education is to learn to trust. Human existence is full of risks. The path before us is a treacherous one. It leads us over high precipices and alongside cliffs. Sometimes we must scale walls and hack our way through dense jungle. Sometimes we will be exhausted and we will want to quit. He who trusts and goes on will come to the banquet spread before him. He who endures will look back and see the green pastures.

We trust only when we are insecure, when we do not know for

sure whether we are safe. We entrust our bodies to the skill of the physician not when we are healthy and robust, but when disease or injury has taken away from us our security and well-being. We trust the economy when we risk and invest much in it, rather than when we squirrel our funds into a mattress, thus pretending safety. A little child who lets his father throw him up in the air and catch him is not really trusting because he is not aware of danger. But the adult who lets another person stand behind him a couple of paces and lets himself fall backwards into his arms, he is trusting because he is conscious of the risk involved, the insecure position he is in, the element of doubt, the factor of the unknown. We learn to love those for whom we risk and they love us. "Love believes all things," said Paul, but to believe a person sometimes requires some naiveté. When the evidence is to the contrary then to believe is foolish. And to trust that our present illness, mental anguish or other shadow falling across our life will yet reveal an undisclosed banquet—well that is foolish to an extreme.

But only if we do so trust, will we ever find the banquet. To trust in a cross as the source of our salvation is foolishness also. How can something so mean and ugly as a crucifixion ever reveal to us, let alone bring to us, the love of God? And Paul said, "If there is no resurrection, then we are of all men most foolish." There are set before us many experiences of life that will cast on us the shadows of death, many crosses to bear, but in the midst will be the resurrection, the new life, the green pasture, the banquet. We who trust through the shadows will find the banquet.

O. B. FJELSTAD
Grace Lutheran Church
Wenatchee, Washington

SO—SING!

Fifth Sunday of Easter
Psalm 145:1-13

It's the Fifth Sunday of Easter. That doesn't sound terribly exciting. It's hardly the sort of announcement that will bring Easter crowds into the sanctuary. It's probably not what brought you here this morning.

This Sunday used to have an interesting title or subtitle, interesting at least for those who appreciated and understood Latin. It was known as *Cantate*, from the opening (Latin) words of the psalm that formed the Introit. Knowing that bit of information, however, most likely did not bring any more worshipers to church or create any more excitement—unless it was among the choir directors who seized on the name as an occasion for performing cantatas or other special music on this Sunday.

Though the words of Psalm 98, "O sing to the Lord a new song," do not sound the keynote of our worship today, something of the same spirit is reflected in the psalm for the day, Psalm 145. Nowhere in this psalm are we invited or urged to sing. And yet both from the title of the psalm as well as the ancient practice, we know that it is intended to be sung. In fact, singing may be the only appropriate way to give full expression to this text. Merely to speak these exultant and majestic words is likely to generate about the same enthusiasm as Pat Paulson delivering one of his famous newscasts.

At the same time, charity toward those who insist they cannot sing (and perhaps, as well, toward those who would have to listen to them!) keeps us from decreeing—as did a bishop in the early church—that all who refuse to join in singing the psalms ought to be excluded from the community of the faithful! In any event, it is good that the *Lutheran Book of Worship* has restored (at least as an option) the ancient practice of singing the psalms. Since the dawn of history all humankind has given expression to its most intense experiences, both the heights of joy and the depths of sorrow (and a good bit of what lies between), by means of song. And so it is appropriate in this Easter season to give expression to our faith and hope and joy by singing.

A Song of Praise

But what shall we sing? There are songs which each of you might suggest as your favorites, though we might have a little difficulty agreeing on those which are favorites of everyone. There are songs which might express our individual hopes, and there are many that can in one way or another be called religious. That is what I fear sometimes happens on Easter. We bring out our favorites, indulge ourselves for a day, and go home thinking we have celebrated Easter. Our choices certainly reflect the variety of tastes—and occasionally a common taste—in any congregation. But this route to determining what is to be sung too easily ends up with an emphasis on our desires, our tastes, our selves. Then Easter is in danger of being celebrated as *our* event, something we make happen or not happen for the worshiper, depending on how well we have managed to entertain ourselves and others. Here the psalmist, like Ford, has a better idea.

In a very real sense we do not come to church with our songs and there sing them according to our particular mood. The song that the church is called to sing is already given, and we are invited to join in singing it. It is the "new song" which according to the psalms has been placed on human lips. In one sense, at least, we no more choose the songs we sing than we choose the persons with whom we sing them.

One, of course, may choose not to sing that song. One may not feel like singing at all. Or one may not feel like singing it at this particular time, or with these particular people. But in the song the church is given to sing, there is no room for either self-indulgence or self-pity. Self-conscious choice could not be farther from the psalmist's mind as the words of exaltation and praise come pouring out. Obviously there is something to glorify and praise here besides our selves, our feelings, our tastes. What is here celebrated is the greatness and the glory and the goodness and the graciousness of God. It is a song in praise of the majesty of God's sovereignty and mighty acts toward all creation.

The difficulty we frequently have in sustaining our joy and celebration throughout the Easter season may stem from the content and direction of our praise. There are times when our songs seem to be little more than praise of praise itself, or a celebration of celebration. We may have little idea of why we are singing praise or what we are celebrating. (It is a similar kind of misguided religious fervor that insists on singing the *Hallelujah Chorus* in Advent, or even Christmas.) When our own self-interests—however sincere or religious—come to the fore, we end up with a song which is not really new at all, but is very much a part of the old self's praise of itself.

A Ceaseless Song

Those congregations that have trouble sustaining Easter joy even to the Second Sunday of Easter, to say nothing of the Fifth or the rest of the year, might well wonder about the psalmist's enthusiasm for daily and unending praise. There is some indication that this psalm was sung three times a day in the synagogue. Already in the ancient church it was sung daily at the midday meal (because of verse 15: "The eyes of all wait upon thee...").

Throughout much of the history of the church it could literally be said that the song of the church never ceased. The practice of daily hours of prayer and praise assured that somewhere in the world at every moment there were people engaged in singing the song of praise. The song followed the sun in its journey. For reasons which we deem (or excuse as) practical, most of our churches have discontinued daily prayer and lost that sense of universal praise. In fact, most struggle with the problem of getting participation in one midweek service each week—and that during only a limited part of the year, Lent.

Surely the graciousness and goodness of which the psalmist sings cannot be measured by the number of hours we pray or sing in a given week. But just as surely the "wondrous act," the "marvelous work," the "glorious splendor" of the reign begun in the resurrection of Jesus Christ is worthy of ceaseless praise. Or do we honestly think that the grace of God is somehow diminished by too much praise (a claim that is sometimes heard for too frequent participation in the Lord's Supper)? But just as there is "no end to God's greatness," surely there can be no end to the song that sings of that greatness.

A Song of Proclamation

Like all that pertains to the divine nature, the greatness that is the subject of our praise is unsearchable. Our hymns of praise don't penetrate that mystery any more than doctrinal definitions. But in the celebration of God's reign they make it known, they proclaim it. Harvey Cox indicated something of this when he stated: "If God returns we may have to meet him first in the dance before we can define him in the doctrine." The greatness and reign of God is not explained; it is proclaimed. To the church has been given that proclamation as both duty and privilege (or, as one form of the Communion liturgy had it, "our duty and our delight"). The delight may escape us at times or be overpowered by the sense of sheer duty. And yet as we take up the song something of the joy of the new life is to be found in the realization that we are privileged to be a part of the proclamation of God's works from "one generation . . . to another." It is a privilege to be a part of the praise of those who "publish the remembrance of God's great goodness," who speak of "the power and glorious splendor of God's kingdom" to all people. It can be a thrill to "join in the hymn of all creation," to participate in the song by which "faithful servants" and indeed "all God's works" make known the glory and power of God's sovereignty.

But it is also a duty, the sense of duty by which Paul and Barnabas, for instance, carried out a commission to be a "light to the nations," and to "bring salvation to the uttermost parts of the earth." It is the obligation of that commission that does not finally allow us to stand in a neutral corner. It finally does not let us choose whether we will join in the song or not, whether we will choose to sing at all. There is no room for the kind of indifference and non-involvement reflected in the message on a T-shirt: "I'm neither for nor against apathy."

Whether conceived as duty or privilege, the song is to be seen as a part of the answer to the Prayer of the Day in which we ask to be "formed," shaped by that life that makes all things new, including the new possibility of "loving what is commanded" and "desiring what is promised." For, as the Spirit of the risen Christ places the song upon our lips and in our hearts, we are opened to the marvelous grace of God, feeding ourselves on that which we are called to proclaim "to the nations."

That is not a natural response. That's why we sometimes find it so hard to bring ourselves to sing. But it is certainly a response appropriate for those who have been made new through the resurrection of Jesus Christ. One simply cannot view oneself in the light of this new life and still view everyone and everything else in the same old way.

One might, of course, raise a question about the appropriateness of this song. Given the realities of the world which confront us daily and almost everywhere, it may seem most inappropriate to sing and proclaim the "glorious splendor" of God's reign. So long as we remain strangers to one another, alienated from ourselves, and not at home with God's gracious rule, we will not see any occasion for singing this song. Like the complaint of Israel in exile we may protest: "How can we sing the Lord's song in a strange land?"

And yet that is precisely what the church is called to do. Even when the tune itself is strange, and those who worship with us are strangers, we are to sing nevertheless. For it is as we enter into the song proclaiming God's reign that we begin to see ourselves and others in a new and different way. That is because the song does not depend on some affirmation or assertion of ourselves, our accomplishments, or our feelings toward others, but is based on the proclamation of the deed of grace already accomplished in and for the world. And though we may still not feel like singing, we are called to be a part of the message in which faithful, if not willing, obedience may lead us to discover new joys, new meanings of discipleship, and our neighbors in a new light.

All this comes to a specific focus for us in the Lord's Supper. Here the saving presence of God is acknowledged and we thank and praise him for it. Here, though veiled, is to be seen the "glorious splendor of God's majesty." Here is revealed the marvelous work and wondrous act by which we receive life. Here is remembered the great goodness, the kindness, the loving compassion that characterize the manner in which divine power is chiefly shown. And here we witness to the reign of God in our lives as, by our participation, we proclaim the Lord's death until he comes.

That proclamation, along with that of the psalmist, indicates that we belong to the age to come, to a future indicated in the Gospel and which already has broken into the world in the death and resurrection of Christ. To that future ultimately belong all people, all things, all creation. It is the dominion that "endures throughout all ages." ". . . for the kingdom, the power, and the glory are yours, now and forever. Amen."

And that is what the church sings. So—sing!

HAROLD P. KRULL
Glen Cary Lutheran Church
Anoka, Minnesota

THE PRIEST'S EASTER SONG

Sixth Sunday of Easter

Psalm 67

Whether we are gathered together around the Lord's Table on Sunday, or whether we are dispersed in our weekday world, we are about our priestly business of mediating God's presence. We have inherited this mysterious vocation from our father Abraham. Do you remember hearing the Lord tell him, "I will make of you a great nation, and I will bless you, and make your name great, so that you will be a blessing . . . by you all the families of the earth shall be blessed"? Both Peter and Paul confirm our inheritance of this blessing and promise by declaring us to be a kingdom of priests descended spiritually from Abraham. We have been adopted into the family through our baptism into Christ's body and at the same time anointed to a priestly life-style. This life-style calls us outside of ourselves and our meditation and points us to the world that still belongs to God.

Today's responsorial psalm voices our celebration of Easter in terms of our priesthood. It gathers together the fruits of our meditation and expresses them in themes of mediation. We find ourselves in the role of the priest, who sings to his people, who sings to his God, and who sings to the world.

The Priest Sings to His People

Some songs just naturally seem to be addressed to one's own people. They give expression to the joy or the misery of the group. "We Shall Overcome" has become a theme song for people who sing to themselves, because practically no one else will listen. They become reassured of their identity as they sway back and forth, arm in arm. Of course, if the group is large enough, strong enough, loud enough, or persistent enough, other people might listen, and a message might "get out." But the song is primarily being sung for the inspiration and emotion it causes in the singers. Paul Laurence Dunbar, the first black American man of letters to achieve national recognition for his literature, seemed to know about song as an outlet for the soul. In the early days of our century he wrote:

> Because I had loved so deeply,
> Because I had loved so long,
> God in His great compassion
> Gave me the gift of song.

Well, God has given you and me the gift of song, too. We can use the gift to sing to ourselves and the others in our group without being weird and without being ashamed. The people who sang our psalm in ancient Israel may have been singing to themselves because they were happy and grateful for a good harvest: "The earth has yielded its increase; God, our God, has blessed us." We can sing ourselves the same words at Easter, because the earth has yielded the man it could not hold for more than three days; and in him, God, our God, has blessed us! But, you see, when we do that, we're singing to ourselves the story that identifies us as a group, the Good News that we want forever to keep in mind: that Jesus Christ has died for us, and is risen from the dead.

When this song is sung among us we feel intensely personal—the person next to us who sings the same song is our brother and our sister, our father and our mother, to use Jesus' description. We are priests mediating God's presence to each other through our song. Like the people who sing "We Shall Overcome" for a current cause or in remembrance of a cause past, we can sway back and forth, arm in arm, because we know who we are and to whom we belong. The peace that Jesus promises in the Gospel for today seems to envelope us. We feel miraculously or mystically detached from the world that can give us no peace at all. Our priestly song to one another has had its full effect, however, when having discerned God's presence, we feel compelled to address our song to him.

The Priest Sings to God

When the Israelites gathered to sing Psalm 67, they were engaged in an act of worship. That means they believed their song transcended the assembly and ascended to the ears of a God who listens. They had something to tell him, and it was more than just a casual "Praise the Lord." God had blessed them, as he had blessed their fathers before them. They recall this history of blessing by beginning their song with a recitation of Aaron's benediction: "May God be gracious to us and bless us and make his face to shine upon us." Then they fuse or couple the benediction with a prayer that they be used as God's agents to bring his way and saving power to the world. No more priestly a song in Abraham's line can be sung to God than that. The world's needs are laid before God by those who know he has the power to bring about change, blessing, and justice.

When Jesus lived out this role of the priest lifting the world to his Father, he did it out of genuine compassion for those around him. Now, the word compassion may mean more than you might at first imagine. To have compassion really means "to suffer with someone." Out of suffering with humanity Jesus came to know the hurts of our lives and history more than anyone else ever did. He wept because of it and he was angered by it. He used his words and his actions to alleviate it. We, as his body, have no less a priestly task than he did. But do we have the compassion to carry it out? Have we listened to the world's cries, so that our priestly song to God can lift them up to him? Our song really becomes a plea, that we might suffer with the world in order to minister to it! It is just as necessary a stanza in our song as the one that recounts our blessings.

There are some people who sing to God as if their lives were over. They sing to him about the sweet by-and-by, about how wonderful it is to be saved, about how nice a Father he is, and about how good and blessedly assured they are. The song they like to sing never gets to the stanza that says, "And so, God, make me an instrument." Today I hope that each of you takes a look at the songs you've been singing to God, to see whether you think your life is over. If you've only been singing to him about yourself and how nice religion is, then probably we ought to talk about your funeral arrangements. If, on the other hand, your song includes stanzas for the hungry, the imprisoned, the oppressed, and the hurting, then you are serious about being a priest with an Easter song. You are ready to mediate God's presence to the world.

The Priest Sings to the World

Up to this point we have seen that our priestly song is relatively pleasant. Singing among ourselves about our blessings is a safe activity. Singing to God on behalf of ourselves and others is not very dangerous either. But when it comes to singing a priestly song to the world, we might get a little fidgety. The refrain of the psalm, "Let the peoples praise you, O God; let all the peoples praise you," might not be the kind of song the world will take to with enthusiasm. After all, why would a God of justice be praised by a world that promotes injustice? Why would a God of salvation be praised by a world that thrives on destruction? Why would people who feel they can work out all things without help want to praise a God who interferes?

The priest's task of mediating God's presence suddenly takes on the character of a real struggle, a struggle in which God will call "foul" if the priest uses the same weapons the opponent does! If God wanted to do things the way the world does, he would seek the death of the world, and would have enlisted generals instead of priests. He has already shown us how the priest is to engage the enemy in the life, death, and resurrection of his Son. It doesn't seem like a fair fight, does it? But it has worked. That is, if you believe Easter, it has worked! The only way we can choose to mediate God's presence to the world is to sing the song God himself has written. We find that our song to the world is hollow without the cross in our life, just as the cross of the High Priest made the final victory possible. Our songs to the world will probably make sure that the cross is never absent; but just as assuredly, they will end in a victory refrain.

That's why priests of God's presence who sing songs of justice in southern Africa now will not quit singing. They are waiting for the victory they know God's power will bring. It's also why priests who sing songs of equity in economic opportunity for the downtrodden will not quit singing. And it's why priests who sing songs of liberation for the social captives of our era will not quit. This is real Easter hope in songs of struggle. The priest is likely to be shut up by the world, but there will always be another priest to take his place, as long as there is a Christian alive on the earth. The song to the world will not die: that there is a God who saves, who judges the earth, and who guides every nation. The refrain of our psalm, however, is yet to be fulfilled: "Let the peoples praise you, O God; let all the peoples praise you." Maybe one day it will be so. But that's God's business to take care of. Ours is to continue to sing the Easter song, to be faithful priests.

Conclusion

Now we have seen how Psalm 67 is our priestly Easter song, how it has gathered the fruits of meditation to express them in themes of mediation. We know that it gives an accompanying song to each aspect of the priestly life-style to which we were called when we were baptized. It gives us a song to sing to ourselves, a song to sing to God, and a song to sing to the world. It's no wonder that Luther saw in this Psalm 67 an appropriate conclusion to a eucharistic celebration. It's no wonder that he wrote a hymn paraphrase of it (*LBW* 335), so that the whole congregation could express its priestly vocation within the gathered assembly. It's no wonder that we want to sing it as our Easter Psalm today.

RONALD E. C. GRISSOM
Bethel Lutheran Church
Russell, Kentucky

THE CORONATION OF GOD'S KING
The Ascension of Our Lord
Psalm 110

"Crown him with many crowns, the Lamb upon his throne!" The festival of the Ascension is celebrated with hymns and psalms that joyfully proclaim the kingship of Christ and his eternal rule. Having risen victorious over the powers of death and evil he has returned to be with the Father where he lives and reigns to all eternity. Our text this morning, Psalm 110, is one such hymn which the New Testament writers used to celebrate Jesus' ascension. Originally sung at the coronation or anniversary of Israel's Davidic kings, they saw in it a way of celebrating the kingship of Jesus. When we confess in the creed that "he ascended into heaven and is seated at the right hand of the Father," we, too, are using language borrowed from this psalm. But this one phrase invites us to listen to the psalm as a whole as it describes "The Coronation of God's King." The form of the psalm is that of a coronation liturgy which shows us

The King Set Apart by Divine Decree

Picture in your mind's eye the throne room of the palace in Jerusalem with magnificent carved cedar paneling, crowded with a cheering throng who are gathered to celebrate the crowning of a new king. As he comes down the aisle in his ceremonial robes a court prophet steps out to meet him at the foot of the throne. In a loud voice the prophet utters a divine oracle: "The Lord (Yahweh) says to my lord, 'Sit at my right hand until I make your enemies your footstool!'"

A crown is then placed on the king's head and he takes his seat on the throne, assuming his role as God's anointed ruler and protector of God's people. The prophet then takes the royal scepter and offers it to the king with the words: "The Lord sends forth from Zion your mighty scepter. Rule in the midst of your foes!" The scepter, symbol of God's authority, sets the king apart as one with divine authority, one who rules for God.

Next the prophet gestures toward the throng of loyal subjects crowding the throne room and speaks of their allegiance: "Your people will offer themselves freely on the day you lead your host upon the holy mountains." They will gladly follow your king, whom they know to be God's representatives on earth.

Now attention is refocused on the king as the prophet pronounces a second oracle: "The Lord (Yahweh) has sworn and will not change his mind, 'You are a priest forever after the order of Melchizedek.'" Not only is the king to rule the people, he is to be a priestly mediator between them and their God. In this his rule is to be similar to the ancient priest-king of Jerusalem, Melchizedek, whose name means "king of righteousness" and who had bestowed God's blessing upon Abraham in the distant past.

The ceremony ends as the prophet offers the king a sacramental cup of water from the Gihon spring and assures him that the Lord is at his right hand to uphold him and to exercise judgment over the nations.

The King as Mediator of God's Righteousness

While we are not sure of all the details of the coronation ceremony, the psalm does help us to appreciate the deep religious significance of the Davidic kingship in ancient Israel. God had promised David that he would establish a Davidic dynasty and that the ruling king would have such a close relationship with God that he would be called God's son. God would rule through him. This dynasty was to last forever.

The king, then, was the chosen instrument to ensure that God's righteousness and justice would flourish on earth and to serve as the channel of God's blessings for his people. Psalm 72, a prayer for the king, opens with these words:

> Give the king thy justice, O God,
>   and thy righteousness to the royal son!
> May he judge thy people with righteousness,
>   and thy poor with justice!
> Let the mountains bear prosperity for the people,
>   and the hills, in righteousness!
> May he defend the cause of the poor of the people,
>   give deliverance to the needy,
>   and crush the oppressor!

Each king was God's anointed, or messiah, and served as mediator between God and his people. But the language of our psalm goes beyond this. It speaks in terms of universal rule, thus pointing to a sovereignty that far exceeded that of any of Israel's kings.

This picture of kingship is admittedly idealistic. We don't have to look very far in the Old Testament to find that the ideal was never reached. In fact, the opposite was often the case; kings used their position to enrich themselves at the expense of the poor, and injustice, rather than justice, was too often the order of the day. But still the ideal was there, a living hope in the hearts of the people. When Jerusalem was destroyed and kings no longer occupied the throne of David, that hope was transferred to the future—there *would come* a time when God would send his ideal king—a king who would establish a kingdom of peace and righteousness. And it is here that the New Testament writers take up the theme. As they read Psalm 110 they could see

The King as Our Ascended Lord

In the Gospel this morning we read that Jesus, before his ascension into heaven, opened the minds of the disciples to understand the Scriptures, and told them that "everything written about me in the Law of Moses and the prophets and the psalms must be fulfilled." In the light of his death, resurrection and ascension they were enabled to see the Old Testament in a new light. And Psalm 110 was no exception. The ascension can now be seen as the true coronation of God's king! He rules at God's right hand!

One of the earliest confessions of the church is preserved in the words of Peter to Jesus when he said "You are the Christ (the Messiah), son of the living God!" But it was only in the light of the resurrection and ascension that this confession could be fully understood. For during his lifetime Jesus didn't fulfill any of the popular expectations of the Messiah. The people were looking for an earthly king, like David of old, who would secure his kingdom with a mighty display of power, who would throw off the oppressive yoke of Roman rule and re-establish Israel as an independent nation.

But Jesus identified himself with the servant of the Lord, and a suffering servant at that—a servant who would lead no armies, gain no political victories and who had no ambition to sit on an earthly throne. In fact he told his disciples: "Whoever would be great among you must be your servant, and whoever would be first among you must be slave of all." St. Paul writes that he "emptied himself, taking the form of a servant, . . . and being found in human form he humbled himself and became obedient unto death, even death on a cross." Jesus *was* the Messiah, but a suffering Messiah who was wounded for our transgressions and bruised for our iniquities—who died that we might have life.

But the empty tomb turned seeming defeat into victory and sorrow into joy. God's conquest of the powers of sin and death are now seen as a *universal* victory and the basis of our Christian hope. The second lesson reminds us of this when it speaks of the power of God "which he accomplished in Christ when he raised him from the dead and made him sit at his right hand in the heavenly places, far above all rule and authority and power and dominion, and above every name that is named, not only in this age but also in that which is to come; and he has put all things under his feet and has made him the head over all things for the church. . . ."

The coronation psalm is now an expression of Christ's eternal rule at God's right hand. He has been given all authority in heaven and on earth and we, who have been given new life in him, know that his purpose will prevail. For as mediator of God's love and grace he has promised that he will be with us, his subjects, as we engage in making known that love and grace to others. For "God has highly exalted him, and has given him a name that is above every name, that at the name of Jesus every knee should bow . . . and every tongue confess that Jesus is Lord to the glory of God the Father." Long live the King! Amen.

RALPH W. DOERMANN
Trinity Lutheran Seminary
Columbus, Ohio

AN ABSENT PRESENCE

Seventh Sunday of Easter
Psalm 47

A Bit About Preaching

There are many different ways to preach a sermon, and many different ways to describe those differences. Generally, preaching of whatever sort is a mixture of several things. One way to describe one sort of difference is that some preaching is *about* something, while some is a preaching *of* something. While most sermons are mostly one or the other (probably mostly about, that's easier), most are also a combination of both. This sermon is like that—a mixture—and that's important because it makes a difference in how you listen. To start with it's preaching about, near the end it changes.

Images

We live in a world of images—pictures, symbols, signs—images of a reality that is beyond the capacity of our language to describe or the power of our minds to comprehend. At times we make the serious error of mistaking the image for the reality itself and we try to transform it from a dim reflection of reality beyond our competence into a comprehendable reality, and we wallow in an obscure and dingy make-believe world and miss the clarity and color and precision of the reality behind our perceptions.

One of the images we have been given is proclaimed by the name, Emmanuel. That's a Hebrew name, actually a Hebrew sentence; it means "God is with us." The picture created by the name, the image, the idea of God intimately and personally present with his people, is unique to Christianity. Above all else, that presence characterizes and differentiates the Christian faith from other religious experiences and expressions. God is not a distant abstraction, but a present, concrete, personal reality.

Other images support and develop that same reality—the *incarnation*, the image of God in human form and likeness; the *passion*, the image of God's suffering, and submission to the last enemy of humanity, death; the *resurrection*, the image of life reborn and recreated from death; the *church* as the body of Christ, the image of the present, earthly presence of God's Son. Each reflects a different facet of the image of God's gracious and personal presence with his people.

Ascension

Last Wednesday we celebrated our faith in the light of another image, that of God's *absent* presence.

> I believe . . . He ascended into heaven and sitteth on the right hand of God the Father Almighty. . . .

As an image, the ascension points to the enthronement of our Lord which confirms our conviction that Jesus is truly divine, and that the images of his humanity, suffering, death and even resurrection are grounded in his divine nature. The transfiguration, crucifixion, the mocking of our Lord all point in their various ways to the same reality, and the image of the Ascension breaks our expectations of reality. In itself it is an image of absence. Christ has left this earth and returned to the right hand of the Father in heaven. But it is also an image of presence. In the Gospel last Sunday Jesus pointed out that "the Holy Spirit, the Counselor, whom the Father will send in my name, he will teach you all things, and bring to your remembrance all that I have said to you." Christ is absent in his physical being, but God is present in the person of his Holy Spirit.

Scholars tell us that before Jesus was born the people of Israel celebrated the enthronement of God in an annual festival at the temple. The point of the celebration was two-fold: first, to acknowledge God's power and authority as the creator and king of his people, and second, to call attention to his gracious and very personal presence with his people. He was not, as the other gods of the time, an absent God, who lived in heaven and who only came to his people or received their offerings and worship. The God of Israel lived with his people.

The Psalm

The Psalm for today, Psalm 47, is one of the songs sung in connection with the festival of God's enthronement. It speaks of the reality of Israel's experience of her God. God was present with his people. He was victorious over all the nations of the earth. Together with his own chosen people, the rulers of the nations worship him. To be sure, that was not always a visible reality, but it was the reality the Israelites lived in and believed in and celebrated.

Proclamation

For us as well, this Sunday after the Ascension, this Seventh Sunday of Easter, it is a reflection of reality. Our Lord whose resurrection we celebrate each Sunday has been enthroned at the right hand of the Father. He is the King of kings and Lord of lords. He is absent, yet very present.

> He has ascended to the right hand of the Father,
>   yet he is present among us.
> He rules from a heavenly throne,
>   yet his kingdom has come to us.
> He is King of kings and Lord of lords,
>   yet he is our brother, our redeemer and friend.
> He has died and his death is the death of death.
> He lives and we live in him and he in us.
>   He is Emmanuel, God-with-us, our risen and
>   ascended Lord, more present with us in his absence
>   than he would be or could be if he had not ascended.
> We rejoice in his absence ... .
>   his presence ...
>   his absent presence ...

We are led, as Paul and Timothy were, by the Spirit of Jesus. We are one with him, as he is one with the Father. We shall be with him, where he is, to behold his glory and celebrate his presence. All that he is and all that he has done is present in all that we are and have become. God's will is done; his kingdom is come. Not finally, to be sure, but in reality, all the same.

We celebrate the majesty and glory of our King, his power and authority, his grace and compassion, his life and his presence. We proclaim in our lives his presence among us.

> Clap your hands, all you peoples.
> Shout to God with a cry of joy.

> For the Lord Most High is to be feared.
> He is the great King over all the earth.
> > He subdues the peoples under us,
> > > the nations under our feet.
> > He chooses our inheritance for us,
> > > the pride of Jacob whom he loves.
> > > God has gone up with a shout.
> > > The Lord with the sound of the ram's horn.

Sing praises to God, sing praises.
Sing praises to our King, sing praises.
> For God is King of all the earth.

Sing praises with all your skill.
> > God reigns over the nations.
> > God sits on his holy throne.
> > > The nobles of the peoples have gathered
> > > > together with the people of Abraham's God.
> > > The rulers of the earth belong to God,
> > > > and he is highly exalted.

Acclamation

> Christ is Risen. Alleluia!
> > Christ is Ascended. Alleluia!
> > > Christ is King. Alleluia!
> > > > Emmanuel—God is with us.
> > > > > Clap your hands! Amen.

DIEDRIK A. NELSON
Grace Lutheran Church
Watertown, South Dakota

IS FAME THE SPUR?

The Day of Pentecost
Genesis 11:1-9

There is method in the church's madness of selecting the Babel account for use as the Old Testament Lesson on Pentecost Sunday. The intention is that one may inform the other and that a composite meaning might arise from both. Pitted against some current assumptions on the meaning of each, there are not only surprises aplenty along the way—there are shock waves!

It is not unusual to be presented with a Babel treatment such as this:

> The writers whose crude speculations on human origins are embodied in the early chapters of Genesis have given us no hint as to the mode in which they supposed man to have acquired the most important of all the endowments . . . the gift of articulate speech. . . . However, the diversity of languages . . . naturally attracted the attention of the ancient Hebrews, and they explained it by the following tale.
>
> In the early days of the world all mankind spoke the same language. Journeying from the east . . . they came to the great plains of Shinar or Babylonia, and there they settled. They built their houses of bricks, bound together with a mortar of slime. . . . But not content with building themselves a city, they proposed to construct out of the same materials a tower so high that its top should reach to heaven; this they did in order to make a name for themselves, and also to prevent the citizens from being scattered over the face of the whole earth. For when any had wandered from the city and lost his way on the boundless plain, he would look westward and see afar off the outline of the tall tower standing up dark against the bright evening sky, or he would look eastward and behold the top of the tower lit up by the last rays of the setting sun. So he would find his bearings, and guided by the landmark, would retrace his steps homeward. Their scheme was good, but they failed to reckon with the jealousy and power of the Almighty. For while they were building away with all their might and main, God came down from heaven to see the city and the tower which men were raising so fast. The sight displeased him, for he said, "Behold, they are one people, and they have all one language; and this is what they begin to do; and now nothing will be withholden from them which they purpose to do." Apparently he feared that when the tower reached the sky, men would swarm up it and beard him in his den, a thing not to be thought of. So he resolved to nip the great project in the bud. "Go to," said he to himself, or to his heavenly counsellors, "let us go down, and there confound their language, that they may not understand one another's speech." Down he went accordingly and confounded their language and scattered them over the face of all the earth. Therefore they left off to build the city and the tower; and the name of the place was called Babel, that is, Confusion,

because God did there confound the language of all the earth.
(James G. Frazer, *Folklore in the Old Testament*, p. 43.)

Nor is it unusual to be presented with a Pentecost motif like this:

Pentecost was the reverse of Babel with its confusion of tongues, an intensification of the original Pentecost.
(John H. Gerstner, "Acts" in *The Biblical Expositor.*)

To interpret Babel and Pentecost in terms of language commonality or diversity, to suggest that the tower was a threat to God's anonymity and that confusion among people was the way to preserve that anonymity is to miss major points in the biblical record, and, what is worse, it is to reduce the relevance of both accounts for modern readers.

So let's dig!

Initially, this narrative—like the Adam-and-Eve-in-the-garden narrative, or the Cain-and-Abel narrative, or the Noah-and-the-ark narrative—is a commentary on human obtuseness seen in the light of divine correction and care. We must therefore look at the very essence of these texts, particularly this Babel text. What is the writer driving at? What exposé is he making? I think he is saying

Human Actions Are a Tragic Mixture of Creative Ingenuity and Lust for Immortality

Homo faber is a Latin description of human being—we are creatures who build. We fashion pyramids, Foshay Towers, and Sears buildings, monuments to inventive genius and creaturely power.

What motives prompt us to build them?

- Are they erected for strictly utilitarian purposes, or aesthetic ones?
- Are they designed so people will "find their bearings and be able to retrace steps homeward"?
- Are they customed so "we can swarm up and beard God in his den"?

Yes, they may be built for function and/or form; yes, they can be used as landmarks. But is it possible that any group ever really believed that such a structure would transcend earth and enter the heaven of heavens? Luther ventured the opinion that "Men want to climb into the majesty of God." But this is a metaphor. It doesn't mean that they actually thought they could puncture the floor of heaven. God is hardly intimidated by piddling threats to "beard him in his den." Von Rad reminds us, "The statement that the tower should reach to heaven must not be pressed. . . . That men wanted to storm heaven . . . is not said" *(Genesis,* p. 145).

Something more disturbing is at stake, and the writer is fully aware of it. He knows God's concern is respect for his own person and what that should mean in the life of his creatures. He also knows God has endowed humans with creative abilities second only to his own. How can he despise that?

He can't and he doesn't. What is grievous to the Almighty is that instead of using power and ingenuity to his glory, the Babelites "wanted to make a name for themselves!" There you have it. Fame is the spur, self-immortalization the motivating factor; there is no way we can understate this corrupting human passion.

We are, in fact, all Babelites, perpetual builders of cities, towers, skyscrapers, cathedrals, libraries, dormitories, and the like. But when do we ever reflect on what prompts their endowment and dedication?

This Genesis story simply cannot be dismissed as an event from antiquity. It is morally obtuse and evasive to pigeonhole it as "crude speculation on human origin." It is a prototype spanning time and space. It is ancient history, and it is modern history. It is so contemporary that it hurts, and it allows no other conclusion: Within each human personality lies this insatiable lust to be immortalized. Yet, on we go, building towers, redoing cities, creating halls of fame, engraving monuments with names and titles, fashioning bas-reliefs, writing autobiographies, and still not knowing the meaning of *vanitas.*

Over against this is

God's Reaction and Providential Correctives

The writer of the chronicle tells us,

> So the Lord scattered them abroad from there over the face of all the earth, and they left off building the city. Therefore its name was called Babel, because there the Lord confused the language of all the earth . . . (Gen. 11:8-9).

One interesting assessment is that Babel seems to be the only Genesis story not containing an element of providence. The harshness of the eviction of Adam and Eve from Eden is tempered with a word of grace. Cain is given a mark, not to punish him but to protect him. After the flood there is a rainbow to assure people of God's promise that never again would such a calamity descend upon them. But what of Babel? A second von Rad insight is apropos at this point: He sees the Babel story as the termination of primeval history to be followed immediately by sacred and salvific history, beginning with Abraham (ibid., p. 149).

But let us try to handle two troublesome elements before sounding the salvific strain. First, is God's judgment best described as an extrinsic thing, imposed on the situation, or is it an intrinsic thing which arises out of the idolatrous act itself? I believe the latter.

For that reason one can contend that the so-called confusion of tongues emerged from an inner contradiction. When people will not allow God to be God, they will be "... scattered ... in the imagination of their hearts" (Luke 1:51). If you've ever been in a church-building campaign where people would not acknowledge the Lord as the unifying force, you know what self-will and contention and alienation really mean, even as they piously talk about the glory of God.

The broader question, however, is not whether God punished or whether this punishment was extrinsic or intrinsic; but what or who was the unifier? Those people on the plains of Shinar were nudging God out of the center and making this tower their unifying agent. And there it stood, militarily a super-defense, functionally an enhancement of the common life, aesthetically a wonder for all to see. Best of all, it was tangible—something that could be seen, and touched, and properly admired.

History is strewn with such structures — the Kremlin, the Reichstag, the United Nations building. Devotees insist that they be considered expressions of ultimate unity and meaning. That is the heart of Jesus' criticism regarding Solomon's temple. The Jews had invested it with a significance bordering on idolatry and their priests could never tolerate his untimely comments about its impending destruction and the fact that "... the hour is coming when neither on this mountain nor in Jerusalem will you worship the Father" (John 4:21).

But note: He does not represent anti-establishmentism per se; he does not try to force people to the extremes of despising or venerating institutions; he does seek an admission that they are not the end. True unity is not in them. It is in "the one God and Father of us all."

The other troublesome element has to do with language. Some will read the Pentecost account from Acts 2 and flatly state,

"What was distorted at Babel was corrected and restored in Jerusalem on the day of Pentecost."

Well, there is most certainly a relationship between Babel and Pentecost. Something special did happen, but what was it? In my mind the new thing was this: Through the resurrection and ascension of Christ and the gift of the Spirit, people by nature inclined to self-praise, "proclaimed" once again "the mighty works of God." Humanity was getting back on the track! The first commandment was being made operative! The relationship of Pentecost to Babel is not unity of language, but unity of witness. *Who* was proclaimed was essential, not, whether the witnesses used the same words.

The heart of the matter does not center in the gift of articulate speech, or the time when diversity of language appears, or when commonality of language reappears. It is first and foremost a question of what speech is for, and who is to be glorified. Babel should not be exaggerated as a tale about a heaven-piercing tower, and Pentecost should never be reduced to a tale of tongues. Both deal with the elementary question, "Who should be glorified? To whom does immortality belong?"

Now our world has to deal with those who seek immortalization not only by erecting structures, but also by claiming to be the new spiritual elite. They point to healings they have effected, experiences they have had, utterances they can make—not only intelligible but unintelligible—and they warp both texts and make speaking in tongues the prerequisite.

Rarely do they recognize the old, old self-assertion in their drive to effect a new unity, not by tower, but by tongue. Their goal, a new constellation of all who have had similar emotional experiences. To which I would add this footnote: If these spiritualists think they are truly children of Pentecost, they better take another look; and if the church thinks Babel is Aramean history and not American, it better sharpen its critical judgments.

That both narratives are important and inform each other is beyond dispute. But now we must go back to von Rad's point that the grace element and providential correctives lie beyond Babel. It is instructive to find that they start with Abraham. We can insist that they coalesce in Christ. We can rejoice in the fact that they are implemented at Pentecost—but both Babel and Pentecost must find their consummation in another reality, the new Jerusalem of the Apocalypse.

This is what God intends as the end or purpose of history, namely, that in the city of God there are no towers or temples praising people, nor are there individuals seeking to be praised either for their manipulation of the material, or their manifestations of the spiritual.

John writes:

> I saw the holy city, new Jerusalem, coming down out of heaven from God . . . and I heard a great voice from the throne saying, "Behold the dwelling place of God is with men." . . . And I saw no temple in the city, for its temple is the Lord God the Almighty and the Lamb. And the city has no need of sun or moon to shine upon it, for the glory of God is its light, and its lamp is the Lamb.
> (Rev. 21:2-24)

This is the last word on man's sin and God's grace. Neither Babel nor Pentecost is properly focused for us unless we see the new Jerusalem and let that future reality inform our present. Then, under God's Spirit, the old will become new, the old world, the old church, the old human self. Then we will say, ". . . unto the King eternal, immortal, invisible, the only wise God, be honour and glory forever and ever. Amen" (1 Tim. 1:17).

Fame is no longer to be the spur—but faith! And those who believe will be satisfied to find their fullness in him.

WALTER R. WIETZKE
Division for Theological Education and Ministry—ALC
Minneapolis, Minnesota

WHERE SHALL WE FIND WISDOM?

The Holy Trinity—First Sunday after Pentecost
Proverbs 8:22-31

The wall plaque reads, "Too soon old, too late smart." Oh, how it takes time to learn the secrets of life! We spend the better part of our lives, if not the whole of them, learning sensible ways of living. As we learn, we chuckle at the foibles of our youth. How long it takes to catch on to some things!

Ancient Israel experienced this very same thing. In fact, Israel held old age and its wisdom in higher esteem than do we Americans. They made a great deal of wisdom. The hoary heads of the clan collected and reflected on their experiences through the years and passed them on to the next generation. This process grew to become a whole discipline or school of thought. Bible students often term this the "Wisdom School." Our text this morning comes from the wise sages of this Wisdom School. To understand this text better, let us sketch out something of this Wisdom School.

Wisdom in Israel. Three books of the Old Testament come from these sages: Proverbs, Job and Ecclesiastes. Here the wise taught the young that wisdom began with the fear of the Lord. Wisdom came from God. Now God had made wisdom known to Israel in various ways. First, God revealed wisdom through his creation by building the secrets of wisdom and life right into nature. Therefore, you can learn the secrets of life by studying nature. From the ant, for example, one can learn the value of industry, that God requires hard work with a full larder. Nature is also the source of wisdom in Job. God answers Job's deep problems out of a whirlwind, by pointing out the wonders of creation.

The wise did not look to nature alone for wisdom. They also observed the ways of mankind. Since God governed the affairs of men, by observing his governance you could learn God's wisdom. So the sages observed life and then taught the ways that lead to prosperity and happiness. At the same time they urged people to avoid the ways of folly, which God rewards with poverty and shame.

This wisdom was the consuming concern for the wise. They never wearied of teaching and admonishing the next generation, decrying folly and extolling the wisdom God had made known to them. Our text this morning is one of the high-points of their praise of wisdom. The sage wants to claim that wisdom is the greatest thing in the universe, second only to God. Therefore he personifies wisdom, describing it as the very first creature that God created, before any other part of the universe came into being. In fact, wisdom was a craftsman, working beside God during the process of the creation. Listen as wisdom herself speaks. *(Here read the text.)*

What a grand literary device is this personification of wisdom! It testifies eloquently to the overwhelming esteem in which the sages held these secrets of life. Wisdom was nothing less than God's gift to aid ancient Israel to find rich lives, filled with the blessing of God.

Wisdom Today

And where shall we find wisdom in the 20th century? Our era is so very different from that of ancient Israel. We live in a scientific age. No longer is the earth the center of the universe. It is but one planet around one star in a small galaxy among thousands of galaxies ... or are there millions of galaxies out there beyond our sight? In so complex an age can we any longer find wisdom where Israel found it? Remember, Israel said wisdom came from God as people reflected on nature and human affairs.

Christians gave a two-fold answer. Yes! We do find wisdom where Israel found it, namely in God. But there is more to it than that. In these last days God has spoken in his Son, Jesus Christ, and thereby has shown us the full dimensions of his love. Ever since, we Christians read the Old Testament and view the world through Christ-colored glasses. Yes, we find wisdom in God, but he is not only the God of Abraham and Isaac and Jacob. He is the God whom we know and confess as the Triune God, Father, Son and Holy Spirit. On this Trinity Sunday, then, let us reflect on the wisdom which the triune God teaches us.

Wisdom from the Father

We find wisdom for life from God the Father, whom we name Creator and Preserver. Just as the ancient sages, we can discover the secrets of life in the nature the Father has created and in the human affairs which he guides and preserves. The 20th century confronts us with new problems. However, we discover the old truth that God has entrusted creation to mankind and mankind is thus responsible to God. When we pollute the air or the streams beyond a certain point, life dies. When we squander the limited resources of the earth, we run out of the wherewithal to enjoy full lives. We are not total masters, we are responsible. We also discover that life's principles are built into our individual lives. Our bodies need a certain amount of exercise, and if we insist only on sitting and riding, our health suffers. If we abuse ourselves with excessive drugs, nicotine or alcohol, we will pay for it. We are accountable. We could each extend the list. We are accountable, we pay for it if we do not follow the wisdom which the Father would teach us through nature and life.

When we reflect on this, we perceive something more. We are not only accountable to the laws of nature. We are also responsible to our Creator! We are not masters of our own fate. God has placed us each in our own place in this world, and we are each responsible to him. This realization is discomforting to reflect on. For we have not always acted responsibly. In our sin we have grown to be very much in the Creator's debt.

Just what is this Creator like, to whom we are in debt? Is he a benign being, who will not press us in our accountability? Is he after all kindly disposed toward us, in spite of our foibles and failures? Or is he a demanding sort, who will punish us for having been irresponsible and failed? Different people have reflected on nature and life and have drawn differing conclusions. One group points to the bursting power of life in nature and conclude that the Creator is a benign being. See how diseased bodies heal themselves. See how streams cleanse themselves and winds blow away the smog. Each spring brings forth new life. The young grow to replace the dying. But others take a dimmer view. However often one heals, eventually death comes to every creature. Species become extinct. We call the disasters of tornado, flood and famine "acts of God." We can abuse our bodies just so long, and then inexorably, we pay the price. We have every reason to expect the Creator to hold us to account.

This is the wisdom we learn from the Father and Creator: principles for living life successfully, but also the important truth that we are responsible to the Father, for he made us what we are.

Wisdom from the Son

Happily, we also learn wisdom from God the Son, Jesus Christ. This is the glory of these New Testament times. God has spoken anew and clearly in his Son Jesus. In Jesus we see with crystal clarity that the Father from whom he came loves us.

This is Good News! Were we only to look at nature which the Father created, we might well wonder whether he is kindly disposed towards us or not. But in the face of Jesus we see clearly the Father's love. For he sent his own Son. Yes, he gave his Son to the very death for us. As he raised Jesus from the dead, so he raises us from the shambles that we foolishly make of our lives to the joys of life with him. This is the great secret of life, the wisdom we can learn from the Son: God loves us! Note what kind of love this is. It is not a grasping, self-seeking love, that reaches out only to gain benefit for itself. No, this is *redeeming* love. This love is motivated only by need and by the desire to give of itself to help those in need. This is the wisdom the Son teaches, redeeming love.

"Love makes the world go round," they say. Indeed it does! God's redeeming love makes your world and mine go round. When such love is absent, our world goes awry. Redeeming love, that is the secret. To be touched by God's redeeming love in Christ makes life full, gives contentment. For all our failures, for all our foibles, the Father still loves and blesses. He cares for our needs. He gives life anew. In this assurance, our lives are sustained by a deep undergirding joy. What is more, wise to this secret of the universe, we can aspire to reach out to our family and friends with that same redeeming love. This, too, provides a deeply satisfying fullness to life. Of course, it is a lot easier said than done. It is ever so difficult to emulate the redeeming love of the Father and the Son.

Wisdom from the Spirit

Jesus said that when he left he and the Father would send the Holy Spirit. It is helpful when coming upon the word "Spirit" in the Scriptures to substitute the word "Power." For Holy Spirit we do well to substitute "Divine Power." For that is what the Holy Spirit is, nothing less than God's Power working in us, enabling us to live as we ought. Jesus sends us the Divine Power that we need to love as he loved, with a redeeming love that reaches out and gives of itself to help. This is the third great secret of wisdom, God gives us his Holy Spirit, the very power to love. In such loving our lives are enriched and full and blessed. The world does not perceive that giving leads to fulness. But that is one of the secrets of wisdom.

"Too soon old, too late smart." Where will we find wisdom? In the triune God, Father, Son and Holy Spirit. Here we Christians find three great secrets of life, to live in harmony with this creation, remembering that we are accountable to the Creator; to experience the redeeming love of Christ, by which the Creator "makes the world go round"; to be enabled by the Divine Power, the Holy Spirit, to make that redeeming love a way of life by enfolding those about us with a love patterned after Jesus' example.

This is the wisdom we Christians spend a lifetime trying to comprehend and to grow in. Such a lifetime will be a rich, full time, for it will be in the wisdom of the Father, of the Son, and of the Holy Spirit. Amen.

CARL GRAESSER, JR.
Christ Seminary—Seminex
St. Louis, Missouri

GOD IS THE GREATEST

Second Sunday after Pentecost
1 Kings 8: (22-23, 27-30) 41-43

The long years of building are over. The masons' hammers are silenced; the cries of the workmen are stilled. The new temple stands gleaming in stone and cedar and gold above the city. It is time for the dedication. The people gather. They are excited and proud. Solomon clears his throat and begins.

The message we hear as Solomon prays can be summed up in a single phrase: God is the greatest! "O Lord, God of Israel, there is no god like thee" (1 Kings 8:23). God is the greatest—too great to keep in a box—too great to keep at a distance—too great to keep to ourselves.

Too Great to Keep in a Box

The very suggestion that God could be boxed up in a stone temple is offensive to us. It is outrageous. We have a favorite hymn that expresses Solomon's unease over such a thought:

> Not in our temples built with hands
> God, the Almighty, is dwelling:
> High in the heavens his temple stands,
> All earthly temples excelling *(LBW 365 st. 2)*

Whatever Israel's neighbors may have believed about their gods and their temples, Old Testament people were uncomfortable with any attempt to tie God down to some special holy place. His dwelling is beyond this earth we know so well. He says, "Heaven is my throne and earth is my footstool; what is the house which you would build for me?" (Isa. 66:1). "Do I not fill heaven and earth?" (Jer. 24:23).

No, insists Solomon, this temple is only a meeting place, a point of rendezvous between God and his people. We pray here: he listens in heaven. We have not boxed God in with cedar and stone. We could never do so.

But the scandal of taming and domesticating God, of boxing him up, of reducing him to our scale, runs far deeper than any problem of his being contained in a temple. Over and over again we try to remake God in our own image, to shrink him down to our level. We take our own fears and frustrations, our own prejudices and pettiness, our own hopes and fervent dreams. We project them upon a heavenly screen, and we call the reflection our God.

Why should we imagine that, out of all the millions of planets in the universe, God cares only for this one? Why are we so self-centered as to think that, out of all the life-forms and intelligent beings that certainly must populate this galaxy, he cares only about us? Do we pretend that God talks and thinks like a twentieth century American? Do we think his motives and logic are the same as ours?

Sure we do, over and over again. But our God is the greatest, too great to keep boxed up in a temple or a theological formula. "My thoughts are not your thoughts, neither are your ways my ways, says the Lord" (Isa. 55:8).

When all is said, when we consider all we know of God and all we think we understand, we can only confess with Job's friend: "Lo, these are but the outskirts of his ways; and how small a whisper do we hear of him" (Job 26:14).

Too Great to Keep at a Distance

But that is not the whole story at all! If, as Paul told the Athenians, God "does not live in shrines made by man" (Acts 17:24), still the Jerusalem temple was vitally important to Solomon and his people. To them it was not just a piece of monumental architecture; it was a holy and sacred spot concerning which God had promised, "My name shall be there" (v. 29). God's name is understood to rest in the temple as a sort of extension of his own personality. He dwells still in heaven, but somehow he is specially present at that one earthly spot as well. When his people use it as a focus for prayer, he hears them and answers.

The hardest thing to understand about God is not that he is alien and terrifying and distant, but that, in spite of it all, he bothers to make himself so approachable, so available. He is too great to keep at a distance!

He meets his people in a tabernacle of skins, in a temple of stone. He speaks through human prophets. He communicates his Word through human writers.

And then, wonder of wonders, he bridges the impassible galactic gulf between himself and us in an incredible new way. "The Word became flesh and dwelt among us" (John 1:14). God "tabernacled" among us (to bring out the full meaning of the verb in this passage) for one man's lifetime. One man who "spoke of the temple of his body" (John 2:21), a temple to be destroyed and rebuilt in three days' time. God was too great to keep at a distance, and so in place of a stone-dead building he sent us a living flesh and blood temple. God answered Solomon's ancient question, "But will God indeed dwell on the earth?" (v. 27) with an astounding and unexpected yes!

Still today he goes out of his way to be present among us in the most surprisingly ordinary forms: as water mixed with the promise of his Word at the baptismal font, as bread and wine shared by those who love him. Specially present when two or three gather in his name. Specially working now as you hear his Word among my words and make it your own.

God is too great to stay at a distance. He comes near to us because he loves us. To continue the stanza of that favorite hymn:

> Yet he who dwells in heav'n above
> Deigns to abide with us in love (*LBW* 365 st. 2).

His is a love that sticks to the promises he has made, come hell or high water. In Solomon's day he had made a covenant or agreement with Israel as a whole and with David and his descendants in particular. He kept those covenants in love, in spite of rebellion, warfare, exile, and despair. With us as well this great God has made a covenant through his Son, a covenant of baptism and forgiveness. Day after day he draws near to keep it. His Holy Spirit labors with each of us through Word and sacrament, giving each of us insight into God's loving forgiveness and motivating us for the quest for holiness. We praise God for this just as Solomon does:

> O Lord, God of Israel, there is no god like thee, in heaven above or on earth beneath, keeping covenant and showing steadfast love to thy servants who walk before thee with all their heart (v. 23).

Too Great to Keep to Ourselves

The people of Israel knew they were a specially chosen people, but chosen for a special purpose. Way back when God called Abraham to be the father of a great nation, it was for an international purpose: "by you all the families of the earth shall bless themselves." Israel reflected their consciousness of this worldwide mission in its literature, in Psalm and prophecy:

> And many nations shall come, and say:
> "Come let us go up to the mountain of the Lord,
> to the house of the God of Jacob;
> that he may teach us his ways
> and we may walk in his paths" (Micah 4:2).

Thus Solomon's prayer mentions the foreigner too. Many strangers passed through Jerusalem, traders, diplomats, traveling artisans, and some would be attracted to the worship of Israel's unique God. These too could use the temple as focus for prayer, and these too would be heard. Someday, the prayer of Solomon suggests, "all the peoples of the earth may know thy name and fear thee" (vs. 43).

The centurion in today's Gospel was just such a man, a lover of Israel's God to the point where he funded the construction of a synagogue. His prayer was heard by a loving Jesus. Although he considered himself, as a foreigner, unworthy to come beneath the roof of Jesus' house, of him our Lord could say, "not even in Israel have I found such faith" (Luke 7:9).

The surprising love of God is too wonderful to keep to ourselves. It flows out of us to neighbor and friend, to stranger and foreigner. We tell the story to all who will hear, in every language, in every corner of the world. We want them all to hear of God's great name, of his mighty hand and of his outstretched arm (vs. 42).

Our God is too great to keep to ourselves. Today his church is the world's largest multinational corporation, with outlets and branch offices in every country, in almost every city, and in uncounted towns and villages around this shrinking planet. The strangers and foreigners must and will continue to hear God's good news, and many millions more will believe.

Our joyful duty in all this is clear. Gods draws near to the one who is stranger and foreigner to his gospel through us. We are made channels through which the Word of his love is broadcast. The God who is too great to keep at a distance uses us to get as near to others as he can.

God is the greatest. Too infinite to keep in any human box, whether it be temple or theological theory, he is nonetheless too loving to keep his distance but has drawn near to us through Jesus Christ. And this piece of good news is too explosively joyous to keep to ourselves. All must hear, for God commands it.

"Lord God of all nations," we prayed in our collect today, "help us to hear and do what you command, that the darkness may be overcome by the power of your light."

RICHARD D. NELSON
Ferrum College
Ferrum, Virginia

DEATH DEFEATED

Third Sunday after Pentecost
1 Kings 17:17-24

Death had ravaged her home and her life before. She remembered how lonely she had become when death stole her husband, how hard it had been to live on charity. But at least she had her son, someone to love, someone to care for, a reason to live. They made out all right for a while, this widow from Zarephath and her little son. But death stalked them again, hunted them down and had them cornered during the drought. She remembered how she had gone out to gather some firewood to prepare her last bit of food. They might die, but at least it would be together. There was a strange bit of comfort in that.

And then that crazy old man Elijah came into her life. Man of God, he called himself. "Don't worry about food," he said. "God will take care of you." He moved into the little room upstairs. It was good, she remembered. There was food for them all, each day. And it was kind of nice to have a man around the house again. A few of the old gossips whispered when she passed them on the street. But she didn't mind.

And then death came again, slowly squeezing the life from her little boy. She had prayed and prayed, hoped and hoped. After all, that man of God was living in her house. But he got worse, and finally he died.

As she held the still-warm body of her dead son in her arms, her world fell apart. She was overwhelmed with a sense of guilt from her past. The years of lonely, meaningless life ahead of her surrounded her like a shroud.

She looked at Elijah. "Is God punishing me?" she thought, "Man of God, why did you do this to me? Did you come here to remind God of my sins and so cause my son's death?"

"Give the boy to me," Elijah said. He took the boy from her arms and she looked at him carrying her son up the stairs to his room.

The next words she heard were Elijah's: "Look, your son is alive!" Prayer answered. New life for her son and for her. Death defeated. Or was it?

The Last Enemy

"The last enemy to be defeated will be death," St. Paul tells us. And he's right. Death is an enemy. At times it masquerades as a friend. When it takes an old one, long suffering, we say, "My, wasn't it a blessing." But don't be deceived. Paul was right. Death is our enemy. For it haunts us, confronts us with our own finiteness, capriciously reaches into our community and snatches one whom we love from our midst.

After the death of his wife, William Armstrong wrote these words:

> How do you tell your children their mother has died? I cannot tell them separately. They must all come down together. Each day Kip saves a little love, a little energy, a few thank yous to begin the next day. Today Kip will save the broken pieces of his heart. David is a year and a half younger than Kip. He will be seven in six more weeks; he rides harder and sleeps longer. David puts all his love, all his energy, all his thank yous into each day. Today his heart will break and there will be no pieces big enough to save.
>
> Mary, whom the boys fondly call Sis, will be the last to waken. She went with Mommy yesterday to get the invitations for her birthday party. She will be five in seven more days.
>
> They are coming down the stairs, innocently laughing and racing. They are almost at my door . . .

The enemy has struck again. And he seldom comes alone. He brings with him guilt, hopelessness, doubt. The question of the widow in Zarephath is one that is asked in a thousand different ways, but the variations are always on the same theme: "Did you come here to remind God of my sins and so cause my son's death?"

The Haunting Question

In the face of that last enemy, where can we turn? To whom can we go? There is something incomplete about the story of the widow's son being restored to life. It's a beautiful story, to be sure. It could almost end with ". . . and they lived happily ever after." But they didn't. In that instance death took it on the chin, but it wasn't defeated. The widow died, and her son died, and in the face of death this beautiful little story drives us beyond itself. For death still confronts us, and it often brings guilt and despair.

The Surprising Answer

This story drives us beyond the Old Testament to the New, to our question of where to turn in the face of death, "Did you come here to remind God of my sins and so cause my son's death?" To the questions that we struggle with which remind us of the widow's question to Elijah, the surprising answer comes to us from God himself. "The reminder of your sins caused my Son's death."

The Gospel of John says it so well: "For God loved the world so much that he gave his only Son, so that everyone who believes in him may not die but have eternal life. For God did not send his Son into the world to be its judge, but to be its savior" (3:16-17 TEV). Here is the promise of forgiveness, here is the promise of life: in the death and resurrection of Jesus we have been offered the gift of life beyond this life.

In the Meantime

In the meantime, where do we find hope and comfort in the face of the reality of death? I was taught that lesson most poignantly by a little girl named Pamela.

One of the favorite events in my parish ministry would occur when I had finished preaching. My partner would finish the liturgy and I would sneak down the back steps and slip into the preschool Sunday school class. I'd sit on a little red chair and all the kids would crowd around, and we would hug and laugh and sing songs. Then, when we heard the final hymn being sung from the church upstairs, I would run through the basement, robes and stoles trying to keep up with me, up the steps and stand at the door to shake hands. But all the time I had those children and their little "Jesus Loves Me" songs playing "ring-around-the-rosey" in my heart. One of my favorites was Pamela. She was usually shy, but when I came to Sunday school she was always right next to me, even if it meant gently moving a little boy over. One day she whispered in my ear, "My baby brother is one year old today."

Winter, soft new snow, peace on earth, good will to men . . .

"I've got to see him right now," Pamela's mother said to me. "Will you take me there, please?" Her thousand-yard stare briefly focused on me, the doctor nodded his consent, and we walked out of the hospital to my car. Smelling like the fire that had just ravaged her trailer home and her life, blackened by smoke, and looking older than the passage of years could ever make her, she stood in the back room of Wallace More's funeral home looking at the charred body of her one and one-half year old son.

The smell of rich Norwegian egg coffee, hot dishes and warm rolls surrounded us, the gentle rattle of coffee cups and the quiet murmur of friends were our background music as we stood in the corner of the church basement following the funeral. "I'm worried about Pamela," her mother said. "She hasn't talked since the fire." Pamela had been in the trailer with her brother while her mom had taken her dad to work on that cold December morning. The fire had started while the two children were alone.

"Let me take her home for a couple of hours," I said. "You can pick her up when you are done here." On the way home she sat close to me in the car. She didn't say a word, but I think she liked me.

After an hour of silence, I recalled our mornings in Sunday school. "Hey, Pam, do you want to sing with me?" She nodded. "Sit by me on the piano bench. I'll make up the music and you make up the words, OK?" She nodded.

The tune wouldn't make the top forty, but the words to that little song broke my heart: "There was a fire in my trailer. Little brother was screaming. I couldn't get him out . . . There was a fire in my trailer. My little brother was screaming." Tears were running down both our cheeks. "I couldn't get him out."

She sang and sang and sang her little song. Then she leaned over and said, "Let's sing 'Jesus Loves Me.' " We did. "Let's sing it again," she did. We did. "I'm going to play Barbies with Rachel now," she said. She did.

Listen . . . you will hear little songs that will break your heart wherever you turn. Quiet little songs that grow out of the depth of our brokenness. Each of us could sing his own little song that would bring tears to the heart of someone who cares. "There's a fire in my trailer . . ."

We can learn so much from the little ones, Jesus says. Listen to the little ones, for they shall teach you.

"Let's sing 'Jesus Loves Me,' " she said.

There's another little song, a song that tells of him who loves, who listens to our songs, who forgives, who cares. There's a song of one to whom we all belong—Jesus.

"There's a fire in my trailer" . . . "Jesus Loves Me." In these two songs lies the mystery of life: of brokenness and healing, of sin and guilt and grace and love, of darkness and light, of death and life.

For in the midst of all that would destroy, and silence, and leave us hopeless, comes a quiet song of hope and life.

>Yes, Jesus loves me. Yes, Jesus loves me,
>Yes, Jesus loves me. The Bible tells me so.

MARK JERSTAD
Augustana College
Sioux Falls, South Dakota

YOU WOULD BE A NATHAN

Fourth Sunday after Pentecost
2 Samuel 11:26—12:10, 13-15a

You would be a Nathan. You would be a prophet or a prophetess. And what might that mean?

You would be vigilant. You would be ever-watchful concerning matters of justice and morality in the community of faith you are called to serve. "And when the period of mourning was over, David brought Bathsheba to his house and married her."

You would be wise. You would know how to shape the word for that situation, whether by story or parable or proverb or declarative statement, so that it finds its way home into the heart of the hearer. "And Nathan came to David and said to him, 'There were two men in a certain city, the one rich and the other poor.'"

You would be bold. If need be, you would march right up to the revered leaders or sacred cows of your community and let them have a word of judgment right between the eyes. "You're the One!"

You would convey the forgiveness of the Lord. You would bring such a word of assurance and comfort even to those whose sin has wreaked social chaos and all the neighbors are saying, "That's unforgiveable!" And to the repentant David, Nathan said, "The Lord has put away your sin; you shall not die."

You would be a Nathan, with vigilance, wisdom, boldness, and the word of forgiveness.

Vigilance

This entails the proper discernment of the shape of the situation of the people to whom the word is to be addressed. The word of God has to meet the people where they are, or it is a false word. This involves basically keeping your eyes open. Constantly familiarizing yourselves with what's going on around you. In the world at large. In the culture and society of which you and your people are a part. In the often mundane everyday affairs of the life of your community. If you would be a Nathan, it is not enough to sit at home and read the Bible, or devotional literature or theological textbooks, important as they are. You need to get out into the world with both your mind and your body. You need to get out into the lives of the members of your community and discern what is really going on. Lest the word you speak be so general that it relates to no one in particular and convicts few. Then the word of forgiveness will mean little, too.

Wisdom

What resources will you call on to assist you in speaking to that situation? In the face of the complexities of the context, the temptation to take short-cuts is one of the more seductive routes for the person who would minister. Ride with the latest fad: Read a book, learn a system, boil it all down to the ABCs of this or that; or 1-2-3-4, however many, nice, neat, easy on everybody questions that are guaranteed to lead the world into the kingdom of God. Or, take the psycho-intestinal route—grope with the group—discover your potential—I'm OK, You're OK. Or give them 175 mimeographed pages of rules and regulations, all bound between two colorful covers. There's sermons enough there for a year and a half or so. But then the fad begins to fade, and the slogans begin to wear thin, and you begin the frantic search for one more gimmick, just the latest, to carry you through. We have too often abandoned the mystery for a magic that does not work. And a crisis in ministry is not far away.

Or, in response to the situation, you may turn your own feelings loose on people. You may lift up *your* devotion, *your* mountaintop experiences, your heart-trips. You may allow passion to cover up for the fact that you aren't reading anymore. You may be zealous as an easy way to put down those with whom you disagree. You may allow devotion to disguise shoddiness in your truly coming to grips with the issues.

Or, on the other hand, you may intellectualize the faith. You may set up a theological system, and use it to club people who don't have just those answers. Or, you may put your present theological perspective in concrete, refusing to grow or learn or adjust in the light of new understandings, as the Lord's Spirit continues to lead us. You may simply grease and oil your present perceptions, letting that mask the fact that you really aren't doing much thinking about the faith anymore. Or, you may seek to deal with all aspects of ministry by sheer intellect, refusing to recognize that ministry is to the whole person.

The person who would be a minister is not a free agent. You pledge yourselves to the Lord's commission, to stand within a tradition and within a community that is not your own creation. It is not your ministry, it is the Lord's ministry, the ministry of the Word of God, and that means being grounded in a Word outside of yourselves.

You are not called to set out alone with your private faith or the strength of your personality or theology. You are not called on to invent a new message. You have the witness of a community which has gone before and in which you stand. You need to recall all of God's actions on behalf of his people in the past, lifting them up so that God's gracious concern for his world is apparent for all to see. But you also need to shape that witness in such a way that it will speak to people who live in a world so different from that of previous generations. In this task you are to remember that the Word you are called to speak is not your own but the Word of the Lord.

And so, given the ministry of the Word, we would hope for skills. We would hope for creative and imaginative ways of presenting that Word to others. Concern for technique, whether in teaching, preaching, or counseling, is not out of the order, if the center is intact.

And so, given the ministry of the Word, we would hope for passion. The last thing in the world the Gospel needs is dullness. And certainly the antidote to that comes in significant part when you yourself are caught up in the Word and present it in such a way that it has clearly touched the depths of your own life.

And so, given the ministry of the Word, we would hope for theological integrity. In the words of 1 Peter, we are called to give a reason for the hope that is in us. We are not only to transmit the faith, but to contend for the faith. It is not enough now in this place for you simply to find something professionally useful to do, while holding tenaciously to theological formulations learned in childhood. In an increasingly sophisticated and educated church and society, you are called to equip yourselves theologically, so that you might be loyal to the tradition, so that you might clear away false stumbling blocks, so that you might stand straight against the winds of syncretism, and so that you might enable the people of God to think and live theologically, too.

Boldness, Forgiveness

The last two words together: *boldness in judgment; clarity with the word of forgiveness*. To take the title of a recent book, you are called to a ministry which is against the world for the world. There are around us these days those obscurantists or ascetics, who would have us be against the world but not for it. And, on the other side, there are those cultural conformists who would have us be for the world and not against it. For the sake of the world you are to call the world to judgment, so that the word of forgiveness might truly be heard by repentant and believing hearts.

The Christian ministry cannot be defined as helping people through periods of stress, fixing kids, minds, marriages. While not unimportant, by itself or occupying the center, that is a truncated view of the ministry. W. Brueggemann has well said: "Every theology and every ministry which serves primarily to relieve anxiety invites people to accept things as they are. The end result is that we preclude questioning, protest, and civil disobedience." You would be a Nathan. And that means that you are called to deliver that prophetic word, that word that disturbs people, that jars the conscience, that shakes them out of patterns of injustice, immorality and complacency, and strikes deep into the heart. You will have to risk that a David or two, with their contribution, will simply walk out.

And that means focusing in on *God's* continual concern for justice, for life, for peace, for the total well-being of all people. And you are invited to witness to that in word and deed; indeed, to follow God himself into the maelstrom of life, though it means, as it certainly will mean, that you will be a person of sorrows, despised, rejected and continually acquainted with grief.

Above all ministry means bringing the word of God's forgiveness. The basic orientation of ministry must be shaped by that Gospel word. And that means most supremely bearing witness to Jesus Christ. This Jesus Christ was and is God's personal Word to his world and his people, his personal statement that his unconditional love for you will never end. In him God has become involved in the very fabric of your existence. He has entered into the depths of your life, made it his own, and brought you the gift of life and salvation. And ministry means being called to witness to that gracious gift.

How, you might ask, is such a ministry possible? On our own we would only fail. But God has not left us alone. In his word and in the gifts of bread and wine he offers life and strength to those who would be Nathans. And so trust his word, "I forgive you all your sin," and engrave his promise on your hearts: "I will be with you always, to the end of the age."

TERENCE E. FRETHEIM
Luther-Northwestern Seminaries
St. Paul, Minnesota

IN THE PATH OF THE SUFFERING MESSIAH
Fifth Sunday after Pentecost
Zechariah 12:7-10

Popular Notions Concerning Discipleship

What does it entail to be a child of God, to be dedicated to and drawn into God's purposes? This is a question which has been posed by believers from the earliest biblical times down to the present. Early Israelites inquired into signs manifesting their belonging to God's Chosen People, Calvinists sought signs of their election, and on all sides of us today folks are asking, "What does it mean to be a Christian in our complex world?" There are many Christians whose lives give this answer, "It does not mean much at all. A Christian is like any other person." There are others who answer feebly, "The Christian should be a little bit better than others, a bit more honest, a bit more generous, a bit less selfish." Finally, there are those who do not tire of publishing the long glorious list of characteristics which distinguish them as true Christians from the rest of humanity: "A heightened spiritual sense manifested in tongues, an ability to see God's special providence in every minute happening of their lives, and more blessings and prosperity and health than others."

It is the prophetic function of the Word of God in our lives to shatter such trivializing answers, be they of the leveling, the legalistic, or the triumphalistic variety. For God's Word which comes to us in the broad dynamic sweep of Scripture gives its own definition of what it is to be a child of God. It is a definition which is related to God's universal creative and redemptive purposes in the world. Moreover, it is not a definition which came whole cloth out of heaven to Moses on Sinai. As anyone who has been involved in teaching children will understand, God has shown great patience in tutoring a human family toward an understanding of what it means to be called to God's purposes.

Often we see this very unfolding taking place before our eyes in the juxtaposition of Old and New Testament lessons in our lectionary. So it is in the lessons before us today. There is a dramatic development between the throbbing efforts of the seer in Zechariah 12 to peer into God's purposes and the profoundly simple lesson in discipleship given by our Lord to his disciples. It is over this long trajectory of development from Old Testament to a culmination in the New that the Word of God bursts forth into our lives with an arresting message which addresses us with a challenge to discipleship which shakes us free of the trivializing answers we hear around us.

An Old Testament Seer's Vision of the Via Dolorosa
(Zechariah 12:7-10)

The seer in Zechariah is addressing a very troubled congregation. The past century has witnessed the precipitous fall of the nation from the heights of royal splendor under Josiah to the destruction of Jerusalem and the temple, exile, and foundering attempts at restoration amidst bitter inner-community strife. With little visible evidence that God is with his people, the community splits into hostile parties, each claiming a special edge on God's favor, and all presupposing that other nations fit into God's purpose only as objects to be destroyed. Drawing on the image of God as Warrior common at that time, the Seer announces how God will act on behalf of his people: He "will give victory to the tents of Judah first." That is to say, when God comes to deliver, he will not cater to royalty and the gentry, but first he will deliver the common folk of the land of Judah. This involves a turning of the tables on the conception of divine activity which was widespread in that world, namely, that divine purpose and the interests of the king were wedded, and that God was visible when the king manifested his glory. There is an egalitarian thrust here which announces that salvation will come first to the common and the insignificant.

But the manner of God's deliverance receives a second, even more astonishing description: "And I will pour out on the house of David and the inhabitants of Jerusalem a spirit of compassion and supplication, so that, when they look on him whom they have pierced, they shall mourn for him, as one mourns for an only child, and weep bitterly over him, as one weeps over a firstborn." The day of God will bring a shocking recognition: God was present among the people already, but not in the magnificent regalia of the Davidic court, nor in the sacred splendor of the priests, but in the life of a suffering one, one oppressed and pierced and killed by those in positions of power and leadership. The only proper response to this shocking revelation will be mourning and repentance, which will be given to the people as an act of God's grace, as God pours out on the oppressors "a spirit of compassion and supplication."

God, once thought to be manifested in the stunning, glistening splendor of the Warrior King, is here revealed to have been quietly present with the people in the life of a suffering one, pierced by those empowered to lead the people. We do not know precisely who this "pierced one" was, but it is certain that whether an individual person or a group, we have here the living forth of the Suffering Servant described in Isaiah 53: "he was wounded for our transgressions, he was bruised for our iniquities." A flame thus was kindled which burned on through the dark centuries ahead, testifying that God comes not to overpower through the splendor of the mighty, but through suffering to draw to himself the broken in spirit and the pure in heart.

The Suffering Messiah and the Way of the Cross
(Luke 9:18-24)

Frequently during the four centuries before Christ, that flame was nearly snuffed out by powerful voices claiming that the way of suffering was unworthy of the God of the heavens, who would instead surely come in the splendor of heavenly chariots or with the glory of the royal entourage. After thus flickering feebly, in the fullness of time it burst forth with a clarity and an intensity which the powers of darkness could not diminish.

The bearer of that flame addresses a small band of followers in the Gospel lesson. Always confronted by those trying to impose on him the old royal interpretation of what it meant to be the Messiah, Jesus quizzes his disciples. For if they misinterpret who he is, they will miss the mark of defining who they are, and what it means to be a disciple dedicated to God's kingdom. Peter minces no words, "You are the Christ (i.e., Messiah) of God." After centuries of disillusionment, of messianic hopes pinned on one would-be Messiah after the other, only to be dashed to the ground in disappointment, Peter recognized that finally the true Messiah had come who would not disappoint, for he was chosen by God to bear witness to God's purposes, to lead the human family in the path of righteousness.

But lurking in the shadow of the term Messiah was the old notion of regal splendor, so Jesus hastens to give a messianic definition coming out of the Suffering Servant tradition: "The Son of man must suffer many things, and be rejected by the elders and chief priests and scribes, and be killed, and on this third day be raised." And only after the mission of the Messiah has been clarified, that is, only after Jesus teaches clearly how God has chosen to be present among the people, is it possible to dispel false notions of discipleship with a faithful definition: "If anyone would come after me, that person is to deny self and take up his or her cross daily and follow me." This is not the way to personal fame, power and glory. It is the way of self-denial, placing God's purpose first, daily allowing the example of the Suffering Servant of God to strip our lives clean of all that demeans life by binding it to the material comforts and seductive snares of this world.

The example of the Messiah who accepts suffering banishes all trivializing definitions of discipleship. To be a follower of Christ is not simply to do *our* thing in a self-seeking exploration undifferentiated from the life-style of the masses. Neither does discipleship mean being better than others. And most certainly it is not boasting of superior privilege, or holiness. Discipleship is accepting the cross already borne by our Master in the same spirit with which he bore it, the spirit of dedication to God's will and to the well-being of our sisters and brothers in the human family.

Disciples in the Path of the Suffering Messiah

If we define discipleship on the basis of Christ's way of patient, compassionate obedience which eschewed glory and accepted suffering, what manner of life will we lead? It will be a life of compassionate service which derives its strength not from receiving accolades but from worshiping the one true God, meditating on his Word, and joining our fellow servants in receiving God's grace in the Eucharist. We gain strength as well by allowing our notion of discipleship to be modeled after saints rather than the crowd.

Consider, for example, the way in which Martin Luther King Jr. steadily followed the way of the cross. To be sure, in all periods we hear the advocates of a more spectacular way. Remember the late '60s, how one group recommended the bomb as the way God's people should manifest the cause of justice, and how another group idealized the leaders of Hanoi and designated as "pigs" all who would not adopt their way of violent confrontation. Both groups have largely given up on the cause of world justice, the one turning to their personal empires, the other willingly accepting the rewards of the system they had earlier denounced, having since blended drably into the various professions. In those days, as now, little newsreel was given to the quiet, patient, long-suffering peacemakers, working without reward or glory through the complex channels of society and government to enhance the cause of peace and justice in the world.

Very popular still is the way of triumph and glory, modeled not after the suffering Messiah, but the Warrior God who overwhelms all opposition and dazzles people into joining the procession. A church modeling its ministry on this triumphalistic way meets opposition with harsh claims of superiority and exclusivity, measures its success in terms of numbers and monetary strength, marks its chosenness by the signs of special favor, as one religious periodical puts it, "Plenty of health, happiness, success and prosperity."

In the various problems which afflict our society and our world today, there are many who are willing to serve if given adequate publicity, and promised the rewards of prestige and power. Whatever the issue, if it is given the exposure of a cause célèbre, if techniques are used to raise passions, to polarize and antagonize and confront, crowds of followers will not be lacking, for it offers them an opportunity to bask in the warm glow of recognition. But whether the issue be apartheid, hunger, equal rights, ecology, or world peace, little spectacle is visible when the Suffering Messiah's disciples are at work, learning, teaching, raising consciousness, contributing to the point of self-sacrifice, and working at the unpopular point of tension between contending parties in an effort to bring about reconciliation and an enduring justice.

As we seek with our lives to answer the queston of what it involves to be a child of God, and to be drawn into the purposes of our gracious Lord, we begin well by heeding Christ's call: "If anyone would come after me, that person is to deny self and take up his or her cross daily and follow me." When all the dust of demonstrations settles, and the loud rhetoric of the impassioned dies down, our church remains a pretty good context for self-transcending service such as that taught by our Lord. For as recipients of grace, as ones belonging first and finally to God and needing no further legitimization, we are freed from the need for the vain glory given by aroused spectators.

And if the church is a faithful extension of the suffering Christ's body in this world, it will not boast of its privileged status, but humbly accept God's gifts, and then spend them on all who will receive. As we are drawn into the redemptive purposes of a God who entered our lives in the way of patient suffering, let us pray that the spirit of compassion and supplication be poured out on our age anew. May the powerful repent. May the oppressed be empowered. May lines of hostility dividing Jew and Gentile, slave and free, male and female, disappear in a shared oneness in our Lord. And may a faithful church find its life in loosing itself or those in need, sustained by the all-sufficient grace of the most holy and blessed God.

PAUL D. HANSON
Harvard Divinity School
Cambridge, Massachusetts

WHEN GOD BREAKS SILENCE

Sixth Sunday after Pentecost
1 Kings 19:14-21

While the title seems like a contradiction, Paul Simon's song "The Sound of Silence" is as true today as it was when he wrote it in 1964. Its moving and haunting melody sometimes obscures the power of its words of despair and pessimism.

> Hello Darkness, my old Friend.
>   I've come to talk with you again,
> Because a vision softly creeping,
>   Left its seeds while I was sleeping,
> And the vision that was planted in my brain still remains
>   Within the Sound of Silence.

What led to such an encounter with gloom and despair was a vision about the inability of humans to communicate with one another. The words which follow tell that modern relationships take place on such a superficial level that there is no serious understanding of life. What seems prevalent in our day is the commercialism of society, the impersonal quality of life, and devotion to the gods of our own making.

> In restless dreams I walked along narrow streets of cobblestone,
>   'Neath the halo of a street lamp,
>   I turned my collar to the cold and damp
> When my eyes were stabbed by the flash of a neon light
>   That split the night and touched the Sound of Silence.
> And in the naked light I saw ten thousand people, maybe more.
>   People talking without speaking, people hearing without listening,
>   People writing songs that voices never share
> And no one dare disturb the Sound of Silence.

Indeed the song goes on to say that it's foolish to break in with offers of healing, because no one pays any attention.

> "Fools!" said I, "You do not know silence like a cancer grows.
>   Hear my words that I might teach you,
>   Take my arms that I might reach you."
> But my words like silent raindrops fell,
>   And echoed in the wells of silence.

Finally, the vision (and the song) ends with a note of prophetic doom as filth and hustle and inhumanity are publicized by means of graffiti.

And the people bowed and prayed to the neon god they made.
And the sign flashed out its warning in the words that it was forming,
And the sign said "The words of the prophets are written on the subway walls and tenement halls"
And whisper'd in the Sounds of Silence.

No wonder that after such a vision the poet welcomed his old friend Darkness!

The Contagion of Silence

You and I share in the ministry of the Christian church. It's a ministry to other people of laity and clergy alike. It is serving others—and one another too—who experience the "sound of silence" in modern life. It is toil and labor for the sake of bringing meaning to meaninglessness. It is working to replace the adoration of neon gods with the worship of the one true God in whom alone life has meaning.

The superficiality of life in our day can be seen in any daily newspaper. One evening during the past week these items appeared in The Bulletin. The owner of a luncheonette shot and killed a customer who was trying to return a package of unsatisfactory hot dogs. A 36-year-old policeman, a former Marine and one-time boxing champion of the Pacific forces, beat up an 82-year-old man after an auto mishap. A trio of sociologists reported that out of the 47 million couples living together in the United States, about 1.7 million have at some time faced a spouse wielding a weapon. That same evening was aired a show on television about a hockey player who was so aroused by the crowd's cry for blood that he killed his best friend. As he explained it afterward, "That's the way the game is played."

Beyond those which make the headlines and the tube, the superficialities of our own lives—yours and mine—are reflected day in and day out in the things we talk about (and avoid talking about), the neglect of other people's needs, the way we spend our money, and the drives with which we make it. The sounds of silence are apparent as well in the way we go along with the crowds, playing their games, caught up in their obsessions, failing to confront, because it is all too uncomfortable to "disturb the Sound of Silence."

Of course, toiling and laboring and serving without any apparent response gets depressing, even for the most enthusiastic among us. We can all too readily identify with the poet when he says, "But my words like silent raindrops fell, And echoed in the wells of silence."

An Age-Old Problem

Elijah the prophet could identify with that feeling too. His ministry to Israel had as its purpose to help the people distinguish between the Lord Yahweh, God of Israel, and Baal, the god of the Canaanites. He tried everything to make clear that the Lord was not identical to that fertility god Baal. He even had a contest with Baal's prophets on Mount Carmel by which he proved that the Lord, and not Baal, was the God who was alive and powerful.

But even that miracle seemed to "echo in the wells of silence." In fact, as a result of his victory Elijah's life was in danger—thanks to Queen Jezebel. And so the prophet hightailed it to the one place he thought he could be secure: good old Mount Sinai (called Horeb in this story). From childhood he had been taught that Sinai was the place where God was present in a special way. It was on that mountain that God was said to have appeared to Moses when the people came out of the land of Egypt. Why Moses even saw God's back from a cleft in the rock!

And so Elijah arrived at the mountain and spent the night in that very same cave from which Moses once saw God. And the word of the Lord came to him and asked, "What are you doing *here,* Elijah?" And Elijah launched off on a long explanation that he has been so diligent in the Lord's work, toiling night and day, and it just doesn't seem to have much effect. Still the people forsake the covenant, destroy God's altars, and slay his prophets. And, as one feels when everything seems to be going wrong, Elijah added, "I'm the only one you've got left, Lord, and they're after me too. That's why I'm here."

The Lord's response was to make him pay close attention to a demonstration. The Lord sent a fierce wind that sent rocks hurling through the air and smashing in pieces before Elijah's eyes. Then came an earthquake that shook the mountain and split the rock under Elijah's feet. After that a fire raged up out of nowhere, throwing blazing heat and blinding light. And then there followed "the sound of crushed silence."

Could it be that the Lord was suggesting that if you can't beat them, join them? Wind, earthquake, and fire were the ways God showed his presence on the mountain in the past. Besides that, these were the signs for the Canaanites that Baal was present.

But wait! There was wind, earthquake, and fire. But the Lord was *not* in any of them. They were meaningless noises which resulted in "the Sound of Silence." What did all this noise communicate to Elijah? Nothing! When God asked again, "What are you doing *here,* Elijah?" the refugee prophet made exactly the same speech as before. There was no communication at all, and so there followed silence.

The End of Silence

"No one dare disturb the Sound of Silence." God dares! Out of the silence he speaks words that no one, not even Elijah, can misunderstand. "Get out of here, Elijah. Go back where you came from. I've got work for you to do: two kings to anoint, a prophetic successor to yourself to anoint. And get this straight: you're not the only one I've got left; I'll leave seven thousand in Israel. Now move on to where the action is!"

The Sound of Silence was broken by God's audible words. He breaks into time and space in order to carry out his will. And he does it, not by sending Elijah to join them, but to be the agent of his own meaningful and effective word. With this clear word from God, Elijah sets out to accomplish his task. He calls Elisha to be a disciple, and so that man's life takes a drastic change. Elisha leaves the farm and the oxen and his parents, in order to continue the succession of prophets God provides for Israel. This is the way God chooses to make known his will to his people. He commissions some people by his spoken word to affect the lives of others, and the chain goes on and on and on.

Until it reaches even you and me. That's what our ministry is about: to dare to "disturb the Sound of Silence" with the word which God has entrusted to us. For you and me, baptized as sons and daughters of God, that word is the one that became flesh, worked in a carpenter's shop, got calluses on his hands and sawdust all over his clothes, dragged a cross up a hill called Golgotha to die there like a common criminal, and was buried in somebody else's tomb. It isn't chaotic noise but a clear message: the life, death, and resurrection is for you and me and others to make us all his children. And it's a message given to you, as one was given to Elijah, to take to someone else.

But it's a message that flies in the face of the Sound of Silence. And so it might lead you, like Elijah, to feel despair and loneliness in the task and to retreat to the "I'm the only one" attitude. What breaks that silence for you, as for me, is the knowledge and the joy that God has appointed others. When they speak the word of the good news about Jesus Christ, your silence, like Elijah's, is shattered. And then God again sends you back into the thick of things, into "the wells of silence," where most of us live. "The words of the prophets are written on the subway walls and tenement halls, and whisper'd in the Sounds of Silence."

You go back, because God himself has dared to break the silence and meaningless noise with the death of his own Son. And so we have a new song to sing. Sing it clearly so that it makes a difference in someone else's life. Such a difference that others might join in

> Hello Darkness, my former Friend.
> I've come to talk with you again.
> I've heard good news that's brought to end
> Those superficial Sounds of Silence.

FOSTER R. MCCURLEY
Lutheran Theological Seminary
Philadelphia, Pennsylvania

BEGIN AGAIN

Seventh Sunday after Pentecost
Isaiah 66:10-14

Now that the 4th of July is past and summer has settled firmly in for a couple of months, we can take a breather between hay crops to do some reflecting. How are things going? Not just with the crops, the cows, or the resort . . . with everything?

I'm not so certain that they're going at all the way we'd like; things seem sort of messed up. At least my experience is that we—as members of this congregation and community, as well as citizens of this country and world—are very slowly realizing that the miracles and wonders we anticipated for the last quarter of the twentieth century aren't going to materialize. That, instead, we seem to have lost those goals and dreams that one time cemented us together. At the beginning of the 1900s it made sense for people to name magazines with hopeful names like *Christian Century;* to do so now would be nearly impossible.

Even here at home we're disillusioned. Very few people seem satisfied, for example, with our school system. Private schools are springing up in several communities to offer alternatives. At one time we were proud of the work our schools did, glad to offer all the members of our community a chance to improve, to become literate, to obtain a high school diploma.

Now we wonder if school is really an improvement, whether the children of our county can manage the simplest skills, or what meaning a high school diploma has anymore. The dreams of the past haunt our present problems; the future? We are—most of us—too tired to plan for it; it takes less energy to compare disappointments. One dream hasn't materialized; dare we dream again? We won't look ahead.

Choose any part of life today: economy, entertainment, products, politicians, preachers; once we looked for a shiny, bright ending to this century. But now we sit in the desert—inflation, corruption, built-in obsolescence drifting over our proud visions like sand.

We're worn out, disillusioned; our anticipation has overreached our reality. King and Kennedy invited us to climb the mountain, and we've discovered that dreamers are destroyed. Beyond the mountaintop is another range: more inequality, more work, more resistance, more questions. Why not just sit here where we are and look back at where we've been?

After all, nothing escapes. Friendship gets hooked on someone's hurt feelings, and never grows. Romance turns out to have thorns as well as roses, and never matures. Work—whether it's homework or housework or a career—turns out to have its share of drudgery, and is never again that initial adventure. Marriage has its compromises and stand-offs, and sometimes it just plain falls apart.

How Are We Going to Live?

Well, we can't go back to the good old days. This future isn't turning out to be what we expected. So how are we going to live? How are we going to live as people who are sent ahead "into every town and place"—including McKinley and Georgetown—"where Jesus himself (is) about to come"? How are we going to live as people who claim that the defeat of the cross brings victory into our lives? How are we going to live as people who are "in the world, but not of the world"—(who share in the sinfulness of our world, the despair of our age, in the changes and disappointments of school and church, economy and government—and yet live as a people of forgiveness, staking our lives on hope and serving the God who overcomes history)?

Look at Israel. Promised a glorious return to Canaan by Isaiah in Babylon, the people returned to find their temple in ruins, the country impoverished and the people divided. Where were all the nations bowing down to honor them and their God? What happened to the bright vision of a peaceful, secure kingdom with Yahweh enthroned on Zion? Where was the marvelous future *they* anticipated? This present wasn't even as good as exile in Babylon, much less a day to surpass their good old days!

God seemed further away than ever. Ironically, they returned to the temple, but could burn no sacrifices in its rubble. The devout sat stunned, their hopes turned to dust; weary and alone and abandoned. The transgressors shrugged. What did it matter, anyway? God had obviously given up on Israel. If not, where was the rosy dream promised those dried-up women and men who followed Yahweh?

God Answers Israel

God answers them: answers with a chuckle of water for their dry hopes; answers with a full breast to nourish these hungry youngsters. The words pour out of Isaiah: rivers of prosperity; overflowing streams of wealth; abundance; comfort; the invitation to flourish. God answers their dying dreams with "rejoice; be glad; rejoice . . . in joy."

"Give up the futures you had planned. I have a better future for you. I will come closer than Zion; be more than ruler or husband or father. I will hold you close and nourish you. I will be your mother."

God answers those dry, unhappy Israelites with water to wash away their mourning; with a new covenant, with new life. They will become children, God cradling them close. "As one whom his mother comforts, so I will comfort you."

God sweeps away their gritty old lives and makes them children again. The disappointed dreams of the faithful fall away; they shrink to the soft-skinned hopefulness of babies; God's babies—hopeful little ones to be nursed, and carried on her hip; to be played with; to comfort; to "flourish like the grass."

They came home to start where they had left off. But God intended that they begin all over again.

God's Answer to Us

In order to live as bearer's of God's name in this world we must begin again. Just like Israel, returning home worn out by exile, we are offered God's new start: to be brought to life through God's labor pains, nursed by God, carried, comforted, even enjoyed by her.

God answers *our* disappointment with a chuckle of water: with baptism to wash away the old; with this cool washing and a scrub to strip off the dust of defeat and death. Then, like Mom setting out milk and cookies, God puts bread and wine into our newly cleaned hands. We begin again, little kids in God's house: washed and full of hope, hungry but fed.

How Near?

Jesus sent out the seventy in pairs to proclaim to "every town and place where he himself was about to come," that "the kingdom of heaven has come near you." This is how near: the one we confess in the Nicene Creed to be the "giver of life," the one who claimed "I am the way, the truth, and the life," bends over those who wear the sign of the cross to nourish them with life.

The kingdom of heaven has come near enough for your weariness and hurts to be eased by this eternal mother; has come near enough for you to "drink deeply with delight" and be nourished in God's warmth.

People all around us still need to hear how close God comes with life for us. On a wall in a McDonald's a year ago I read an exchange that went something like: "Jesus is so wonderful; I can't wait to be with him." . . . "Well, if he's so great why don't you Christians kill yourself so you can be with him?" "Because I have to witness to the people who haven't heard about him, then I can die and go home."

That last answer, while more or less correct, seemed to miss an important point. I couldn't resist adding one more comment to the series. So I wrote below the last remark, "I came that they may have *life,* and have it abundantly" (John 10:10).

Near. With life. We must begin again. So we don't have to fear the future. We don't have to worry that it might be difficult. Policies and practices, in fact, will probably continue to change. Friendships will sometimes wither; romances sometimes hurt us; dreams will disappoint us.

But hopelessness has no power over us. We are the "begun again" people, "daily drowning the old self in repentance." God delights in life. Hurting, bruised by falling against evil, crying over disappointment, even dying—God hugs us, rocks us, comforts us. We have the promise of God that "the hand of the LORD is with his servants, and his indignation is against his enemies."

Why? We are born out of God's labor pains in the noontime darkness over Golgotha, we are nursed, carried, and comforted so that we might have a share in life. We are children to rejoice in the work of our God, proclaimers of the nearness, born to "sow to the Spirit . . . ," to "walk by (God's) rule . . . ," to begin again, swimming in the overflowing stream of God's nearness.

JOYCE D. SANDBERG
Trinity and Georgetown Lutheran Churches
Cumberland, Wisconsin

GOD'S GIFT—A NEW HEART

Eighth Sunday after Pentecost
Deuteronomy 30:9-14

Our Text in the Canon?

Was the text you just heard unfamiliar? If so, that's not surprising. Lutherans are not overly fond of Deuteronomy. Most of us, most of the time, prefer reading from the Apostle Paul. And, even when we read other parts of the Bible than Paul's we tend to do so with glasses supplied by him.

The sermon you are about to hear, however, is based on the text just read from Deuteronomy. Initially, I had reservations about that, such as you may still have. But, to begin thinking more positively, consider this: things could be worse. The Inter-Lutheran Commission on Worship could have selected today's lesson from Leviticus, or I could have chosen a free text from James. If anything, we tend to like those books even less than Deuteronomy.

Yes, in our circles, Deuteronomy seems to have a bad reputation. The reason is that it is supposed to teach so much punishment for so much sin, so much blessing for so many good works. And Lutheran theology takes a dim view of reward for good works, if not of punishment for sin.

But, if we think we are off to a bad start with a text from Deuteronomy, it is at least one from the Bible, the Holy Scripture. Whether the book teaches a wrong view of reward and punishment needs first to be examined before we make that assumption. Perhaps, we should reserve judgment until we see what it has to say to us. Maybe the wisdom of the church in accepting this book into the Bible will be vindicated.

Which Is the Key Verse of the Text?

As with any sermon, this one began with work in the study. One of the chief questions to answer was: which is the key verse or idea in the text? You only heard the text read once, so it is unfair to ask you what the key is. Instead, let me suggest that the key seems to revolve, of all things, around the little Hebrew word pronounced *kēy*. This *kēy* means "for, that or because," and it occurs no less than four times in verses 9-11 of Chapter 30. Strangely, the Revised Standard Version translates two of these *kēys* one way, and two another. But, if we translate all four of them identically as "because," note what we get! "Because the LORD will return to you ... because you will listen to his voice ... because you will return to the LORD your God ... because this commandment is not too difficult for you."

What are we to do about the four "becauses"? How do they relate to each other? Which is the main one? Or to put it in the Hebrew: which is the real *kēy* statement? Which of the four? After much searching, I finally concluded that it lies, as key matters so often do, in none of them. Instead, it lies outside the assigned text. There in verse six it reads: "The LORD your God will circumcise your heart." Here is the key idea of the thirtieth chapter of Deuteronomy. But, far beyond that, it is a key promise of God to all Israel for the future. Both Jeremiah and Ezekiel also promise this new, circumcised heart as God's great gift to Israel in the new era. And, since God's promises are fulfilled in Christ, a circumcised heart should also be found in every Christian. So, our search for the key to the text has led us to a major theme of Old Testament, of New Testament, and of our own lives.

Deuteronomy is now spared the onus of teaching some great heresy. By retranslating the four Hebrew *kēys* as "because," the main message becomes relevant as well as orthodox. The writer of this chapter did not make the mistake of building a towering superstructure on a foundation of human achievement. God's promise and our hope for the future are not dependent upon our doing enough to win God's blessing. The future is assured because of God's act of giving us new hearts.

Our relationship to God begins and is fulfilled when he circumcises, not our foreskins, but our hearts. The covenant sign that you have a relationship with God is a circumcised heart, and that is God's act, not yours. God, not we, initiated and accomplished that. God, not we, radically changed our motives, our hearts, and gave us a new nature. Then, after God has done that, anything is possible. Before that, or without that, nothing good can take place, at least not between us and God.

It was so also in ancient Israel. Then they celebrated an annual festival of covenant renewal. During their fall New Year's celebration they thanked God for choosing them and for entering into a special relationship with them. They renewed that old covenant in ceremonies which had the effect, the purpose, of bringing every generation to Mount Sinai. There they promised to love and to obey God. But, they soon learned that their hearts and wills were not good enough to do that. They needed to be remade. They tried to serve God with their whole heart, mind, soul and strength, but it did not happen. There was something wrong inside the mind, the heart, the will. The strength to do right was not there. And so, Jeremiah, Ezekiel, and Deuteronomy promised, that too God will do. That too, God will give—a new heart, circumcised and soft rather than uncircumcised and hard.

Do you have such a heart, such a spirit within you? If you are in Christ, are a Christian, yes! In Christ it is not just a future hope. It is a present possession. It is the gift God gave you at your baptism. It is the present power of God in you, his Holy Spirit. What Deuteronomy could only envision as a future hope, is yours in Christ and now.

What Is Our Response?

In some sermons and in some Bible passages we would now be at the end of the tale, but not so today or in Deuteronomy. God gives the gift of the circumcised heart for a purpose. The covenant is a relationship between two persons. God's acts are much more impressive, much more important than our acts, but our acts are not unimportant. Deuteronomy expects Israel to use those circumcised hearts in the service and love of God. So did our patron saint, Martin Luther. He spoke of our baptism as a drowning from which a new person daily arises to walk before God.

The circumcised heart is a great and wonderful gift. But, like many of God's best gifts, it is not intended to be put on the shelf and admired. It is intended for use, for life, for work, for service to God and to our fellow humans. That is what Deuteronomy asks us to do. It calls us to daily repentance, to turn back to God, to a life of obedience and of love to God. We are to walk God's paths with those new, circumcised hearts, just like a person with an ill heart corrected by surgery must be out exercising the restored, rebuilt heart. Without a beating, working heart you die, unless you are on a heart-lung machine, and then you are unconscious, not serving anybody.

Heart circumcision, like heart surgery, may be painful in giving that new lease on life. But its purpose is to give us a new heart for our daily walk with God. In Christ, you have a new heart, oriented away from self toward God. You have an organ which has new powers for unselfish service. It should also be gifted with a new knowledge of God and a new motivation of love and thankfulness to him.

Deuteronomy supposes that the words of this book will be on your lips and in your hearts. We will not now check up to see if this, in fact, is so, but it is a fine idea. We speak of learning something by heart, for words which have been committed to memory. Words of promise and hope, words of commitment and decision, words of love and service to God from a rebuilt heart—all this can be committed to memory and be nearby when you most need it. God has given you a new heart which can store up for future use, just such treasures.

Beyond that, we in Christ have that word more powerfully present with us than Deuteronomy ever suspected possible. The Word of God, Christ, has become flesh and dwelt among us. The gift of God's Holy Spirit has been given, not just to a few but to each of us when we received that circumcised heart, that new life in baptism.

Whether memorized or on a printed page, or through the presence of Christ or the Holy Spirit, what is the purpose of this new heart? Private enjoyment? Yes, of course, I hope your relationship to God gives you joy. But, Deuteronomy has some other things in mind too. That book is not intended for a shelf of sacred relics. It is a practical book for everyday life out in the world, for tomorrow and every day of this coming week. Your circumcised heart and the Holy Spirit go with you wherever you go. They empower you for a life of devoted service to God and to others.

So, as Deuteronomy did, I exhort you to take a look at the great gift God has given you! Recognize that new heart for what it is—a vital organ full of new life. Don't just sit in an easy chair and listen to it beat. Be out in the world where people are in need of your service, and where God has sent you to live. Find ways of strengthening that gift by exercising and working it. If you don't, the gift will not accomplish what it was sent to do. The world will not be richer for the gift, as God intended it to be. Instead of growing stronger, your new heart will grow weaker, and finally be useless to you and to anyone else.

What is asked here is not impossible. It is a task to perform in God's strength, using God's gift of a new heart. One doesn't have to wait until heaven or the next world to begin doing something that really counts, something that by human strength is impossible. This work is intended for here and now. So, no more of the typical Lutheran heresy that the service of God in the here and now is an impossible endeavor. If it were in our own strength, yes, but it isn't. It is to be done by using God's good gift of a circumcised heart. You don't have to wait for heaven until you cross the river of death for that. It is possible here. It is to be done now. God gave you that gift of a new heart to use in his service.

What Is God's Response to Our Response?

Again, many texts and sermons might end here, but not Deuteronomy or this one. We must speak not only of our obedient response to God's gift, but of God's response to our response. God does not sit off somewhere fifty million miles away unperturbed by our offenses and unmoved by our love. Long before Jesus' parable, Deuteronomy showed us a waiting father who loves his prodigal son, Israel, in the far country and longs for his return. The repentance and the obedience of God's people are a joy to him. And he, in turn, takes pleasure in giving a whole array of gifts to his children. They are not such primary gifts as the new, circumcised heart, but they are not unimportant either. For lack of them many of the people of the world live in misery and suffering.

For example, possessing and living in a bountiful land is a great gift. When someone conquers and takes away the homes and land of a people it is a sad day. Bitterness and longing for return, like Israel in Babylonian exile, are the result of such dispossession. Or, if drought moves in and parches the land and its crops, as is now happening on the fringes of the Sahara, that too is a horrible thing to endure. Locust hordes and plant diseases plague the fields of further millions of the world's hungry. Deuteronomy also spoke to a world which viewed childlessness as a great curse. He must have known others whose daily work was a chore and a drudge, rather than a blessing. We should know, then, that every blessing of family, field and factory, of table, shelter and friendship should be counted as a gift of God. Deuteronomy ranks them lower than the circumcised heart with which we serve and love God. But they are God's gifts and, whether we agree or not, they are God's response to our love and obedience.

A wrong reading of Deuteronomy makes of him a legalist—so much blessing for so many good works. A right reading shows us a warm-hearted preacher concerned that God's people bring joy to God. Have we not lost something with our "worm" theology and our constant wallowing in our sinful state? Our preoccupation with our evil, fallen nature? Why not live our lives following the key from Deuteronomy 30? God has circumcised our hearts, and having new hearts, we naturally and willingly live a new life. We know that will please the One who gave the gift. We have God's gift of word and sign and presence and power. Things really are different, now that he has circumcised our hearts. We are not the old people we once were. We have new strength, new zest, new courage, a new lease on life. It is based on a new relationship which God himself gave us as his gift in Christ. Let us use that gift and bring some joy to God who made us and loves us.

WENDELL W. FRERICHS
Luther-Northwestern Seminaries
St. Paul, Minnesota

AN OLD PROMISE MADE GOOD

Ninth Sunday after Pentecost
Genesis 18:1-10a (10b-14)

Our text today relates the amusing story of God in human form visiting the ancient patriarch Abraham and his wife Sarah —what shall we do with it? If it is to be anything more than an entertaining tale, it might speak to us of the virtue of hospitality. "For thereby some have entertained angels unawares" (Heb. 13:2). Or we might see here encouragement to serve people in need or to use our resources to love and help our neighbor. That would be as if we served Christ himself. And so we should.

Still, we should not neglect the message in this story: God himself comes to be our guest. If we mean what we say in our prayer before meals, "Come, Lord Jesus, be our Guest," we should be willing to learn what it means to receive him into our dwelling and to have him present with us. We should take God's visit seriously. For, as today's lesson points out, he not only comes to partake, but he also promises and gives. His presence and promise invite us to live as people who believe he is with us and who await the fulfillment of his promise.

God, the Guest Makes the Promise

What strikes us as amusing in this story is the sudden activity that explodes in Abraham's household at the unexpected appearance of the wayfarers. A delightful story. One moment Abraham is enjoying a siesta. The next moment he is offering his guests some shade and a bite to eat before they continue on. But then Sarah is asked to bake what would amount to a week's supply of bread, and Abraham dashes out to select one of his very best calves to be butchered for an ox roast. Then with milk and cheese —in no time at all—he spreads before his guests a meal fit for a king!

The story suggests that Abraham probably didn't realize as yet the importance of his guests or the reason for their visit. Therefore, we may be puzzled at his eagerness to serve these strangers in this extravagant fashion. We can readily understand why Martha would take such pains to serve Jesus. He was someone very special and a dear friend. Actually, in those times it was customary to extend such hospitality to strangers. Abraham, himself, was probably welcomed like this on his extensive travels.

But before Abraham's guests went on their way, something happened which indicated that they were not ordinary travelers. They asked about Sarah. "She's inside," said Abraham. Their spokesman said, "In spring I will come back, and Sarah, your wife, shall have a son!" The men had come not just to partake of Abraham's generosity, but to promise and to give. Surely by now Abraham and his wife perceived that it was the Lord who had come to their home. The promise had a familiar ring to it. Abraham must have related to Sarah how God had appeared to him recently and elaborated on an old promise. This promise he had first heard as a young man, and it had reverberated in his hearing ever since. "I will make of you a great nation" (12:2); "I will make your descendants as the dust of the earth" (13:16); "Look toward the heaven and number the stars . . . so shall your descendants be" (15:5); and again, "You shall be the father of a multitude of nations" (17:4).

Promises! Promises?

What sort of response should one make to such a promise? At first Abraham believed. But if we follow the lengthy saga of Abraham, we too may be ready to join in laughing with Sarah, even if we recognize that this promise is a solemn word from God. How much time should we reasonably allow God to make good on his promise before we stop waiting and start laughing? Abraham was by now a hundred years old, and Sarah was ninety. All this time, every reasonable expectation of a meaningful fulfillment of any part of the promise had been disappointed. Still the promises didn't stop! This very day Sarah could see and hear their guest saying it all again. But of this she was sure: her body and her person could not accommodate the provisions of the blessing. "I'm far too old myself to become part of this living hope." So, too, thought Zacharias, the father of John the Baptist. Mary likewise knew that God must do the impossible if she was to become the mother of the Savior. Jeremiah was sure God had betrayed him, and Elijah wanted to die because he despaired that the Lord would ever redeem Israel from her troubles.

What shall we do with the promise? We may laugh with Sarah at the absurdity of God's offer to her. But what about us? What, if anything, is God promising us? Has he spoken any promise for our future which we have been able to hear, absurd *or* reasonable? Has God guaranteed us health, security, or happiness? He certainly hasn't promised us significant wealth or honor. Can we have any assurance that the proceeds of our long labors will be here to sustain us in our old age or that we will have friends and family to comfort us in our infirmities? If indeed we are witnessing the devaluation of our securities and experiencing the eroding of our natural resources and national prestige, if we must lament the lack of pride in traditional values and loss of commitment to family, home, church, where is the promise? If the future holds uncertainty, it does hold the certainty that we shall age and die. There is the certainty also that children will be born, that the sun will rise and set, that the seasons will turn. But where in all this is the promise?

God's Promise—His Presence

The patience of Abraham and Sarah had run out, and apparently for good reason. So now the repetition of the promise with the new specification, "Sarah will have a son; you now have only a very short time to wait," seemed like a bitter joke. But it is in this very insistence, even though it was no longer met with belief, that we see another, and perhaps the most important, aspect of the promise. God is always with Abraham. He keeps reminding him of his presence. God picked out the place he was to live. He protected him and Sarah from danger and from enemies. He gave him wealth. He made his covenant with him and even gave him a new name. The story of Abraham is *not* one of unfulfilled hope. It is an account of God's continued presence, protection, and promise.

Nevertheless, the most dramatic feature of the promise was still the pledge to present Abraham and Sarah with a son. And the fulfillment after the long wait emphasized the power and grace of God. Where is the evidence of God's grace when Sarah said to Abraham, "Have a son for me by Hagar"? For the son of this union, Ishmael, was not the child of the promise. What Sarah and Abraham did not succeed in doing with all their contriving, God did. He kept his promise. He did it even when Sarah's ability to have a child, humanly speaking, was impossible. Now God's presence and promise was clear.

God's Presence—Our Response

God's promise, his presence, may not be so dramatic for us, yet he has given it to us. He has protected us and has given us a new identity and has covenanted with us at our Baptism that all the gifts of life and of his Spirit will be ours for ever. And we have received again and again assurance of forgiveness and salvation. So he promises his presence. To be sure, he is already with us!

When we pray, "Come, Lord Jesus!" we are really saying that we acknowledge and accept this gift of his presence. We are saying that we believe he is with us. There is little danger that we will deliberately close our hearts and homes to God. We wouldn't think of laughing at his promises or disdaining his gifts. But the scene that follows our "Come, Lord Jesus!" may be one of discord. There can be trouble in just putting food on the table. There is the high cost of meat and produce, the frequent aggravation of getting back and forth from the market, the lack of imagination and joy in preparing meals. The food we eat may not be all to our liking. If we should like it, we may be told that it really isn't good for our health.

We often use the "Come, Lord Jesus!" time to express dissatisfaction with our lot in life, or the bad treatment we received during the day, or our unhappiness over the behavior of the children. Conversation at meals is usually a reflection of how we feel about living. And if our anger or impatience is sounded, this can become the occasion for saying no to God's presence and promise just as effectively as if we said no to God by overindulgence in food and drink or by laughing at his offer to be with us.

So it is a fact that we must deal with impatience, anger, and frustration. Even the Colossians must be encouraged to live according to the reality of "Christ in you" (1:27). Their striving to attain maturity in Christ can be undermined if distracted by the hostilities and evil works from which they had been redeemed. Continuation in faith and the hope of the gospel, then, describes what their response to God's presence is to be.

The Evidence of His Presence

So for us, as for Abraham and Sarah and the Colossians, the time of waiting is an extended moment to be filled with hope rather than despair, to be nurtured by faith rather than unbelief. And the longer we must wait, the stronger the fiber of our faith is to become, and the more profound will be the impact of God's fulfillment. The prayer of the day speaks to this interval of waiting and growth. It asks for bread. The request includes our desire for spiritual food. That loaf of bread which came from the store or which mother baked, that tasty but rather ordinary stuff, represents the answer to both aspects of our petition. Bread can fill you, or if you're still growing, it can "build strong bodies twelve ways." What is more important, this bread speaks of God's care, it reveals his concern and presence during the long wait. The prayer for bread is a prayer for his presence, but since he is already with us, it is also a prayer for his Spirit that we may become more fully convinced of his presence and promise, and that we may be thankful.

God does deliver what he promises. As he delivered to Abraham and Sarah a son, Isaac, at the moment when the impact would be greatest, so he delivered his own Son, Jesus, as he had long promised, at the right time. Meanwhile, he provided the bread and the word that sustained his people through the wilderness of waiting, the hunger of temptation, the laughter of unbelief, the weeping of fear and despair, the nights of unproductivity and exile.

Our Confession of His Promise

"Is anything too hard for the Lord?" When the Lord faces us with this stern and challenging question, his displeasure, his frustration at our slowness to believe is mixed with pity and kindness. The question admits only the answer "No!" Once more our lives and persons are made, by our own admission, to depend on his care and his promises. This is the final confession of Abraham and Sarah. Elijah and Jeremiah, Mary and the disciples who waited in Jerusalem for the Spirit, and we, too, must confess, "No! Nothing is too hard for the Lord." And with the Apostle we are confident, that "he who began a good work in us is able to complete it at the day of Jesus Christ," when we shall experience fully his presence as the final fulfillment of his promise.

HERBERT C. SPOMER
Lutheran Theological Seminary
Gettysburg, Pennsylvania

HIDDEN IN A PRAYER

Tenth Sunday after Pentecost
Genesis 18:20-32

You can learn by listening in. That's also true about listening in on someone's prayer. Even in the Sunday prayer of the church you learn who's sick or getting married. And naturally in that kind of listening in there is a lot to be learned between the lines, from what isn't said in so many words. That's especially true in this conversation—or prayer—between Abraham and God here in this text. Something important about each partner is disclosed here as hidden in a prayer. What we find disclosed about God is

The Mercy of a Gracious God

That mercy is so great that God *wants to share his plan.* Actually the whole affair happens a bit awkwardly. These mysterious visitors who had come to see Abraham are about to leave, when a final bit of conversation takes place. God wants to renew his promise to his faithful servant Abraham, but God also reveals that he is on his way to Sodom. Now everybody knows that Sodom is the worst place on earth. That makes the mood of the whole conversation rather ominous. God begins by thinking to himself, "Shall I hide from Abraham what I am about to do, seeing that Abraham shall become a great and mighty nation, and all the nations of the earth shall bless themselves by him?" No, God decides not to conceal his purpose from Abraham. He wants to share his plan, and so he announces the investigation that he is going to undertake about Sodom and Gomorrah.

But then God, although the conversation is finished, just stands there waiting around. Actually this line was so offensive to the Jewish transmitters of the Scriptures that they simply could not permit it to stand, because it made it seem as though Abraham was in charge. They turned it around so that it read, "Abraham still stood before the Lord," when actually the original wording had been, "God still stood before Abraham." You've probably had the experience, I'm sure, of having finished a conversation with somebody, only to discover that they don't go away. They just stand there. That kind of a moment makes you wonder if you've forgotten something. You tend to think to yourself, "Was I supposed to invite them to dinner?" When we come to this awkward pause in these verses, we can't help wondering what is it that God is waiting for? What is it that he wants? He *wants to end his anger!*

But why doesn't he just end it? Does he want to be coaxed? No, he wants to talk about it; and he wants Abraham to take the initiative in that conversation! That can only be because he wants Abraham, and through Abraham all of his people—even us, to understand, to understand how God feels about what he is about to do. He's about to do something drastic, to destroy Sodom. An investigation which winds up with a decision to do something drastic can be charged with emotion. My wife and I once took our two sons to an ear-nose-and-throat expert to ask whether their tonsils had to be removed. This doctor turned out to have the absolute minimum as regards bedside manner, for he simply looked into each child's mouth and then spoke in each case the same three words: "Gotta come out." Well, in the case of tonsils that wasn't too serious a matter. But could you imagine an eye doctor examining your son's eye with a view to surgery, and then delivering himself of those same three, stark words: "Gotta come out." It would be utterly inconceivable that someone could come to a decision like that without more feelings being involved. A doctor would have to want to share more gently with you his feelings in the case of something as serious as removing an eye. Here, as God is about to destroy Sodom, he wants us to find the mercy of a gracious God hidden in a prayer.

What he wants is this. He *wants to love without limit*. That, and that alone, is the point of the declining number of people for which it might be possible that the city of Sodom could be spared. Sometimes people are reminded when they read this text of bargaining at a garage sale. But actually there is considerable difference. At a garage sale trying to get a bargain on a lamp that you want always winds up with reaching the point of firm resistance. You may bargain all you want, but once you get down to $5.00 you find that's as low as you can get the seller to go. Amazingly in this story there is no such point of firm resistance. None at all! Abraham moves gently from 50 to 45 and then to 40. Then he goes more boldly to 30 to 20 and to 10. All along God shows no resistance whatsoever. The price goes lower, and God just goes along with each proposal. I cannot help thinking: Suppose Abraham had gone further? Suppose he had said, "What if there were only five people found there who were righteous?" Suppose he had gone so far as to say, "What if there were only one?" That would seem to be the rock bottom, but actually it is not. Suppose Abraham had said, "What if there were none?" Would not God, of course, have to destroy the city if there were none who were righteous? Well, in the first chapter of John's Gospel we hear that Jesus came to his own and his own received him not. All 12 of his apostles fled and left him alone. How many righteous were there there? How many righteous people are there here in this congregation? I guess that depends on what righteous means. How does one get to be righteous? How else, but by forgiveness, by the mercy of a gracious God. All of us are evidence that God wants to love without limit.

But there is something disclosed about the other party in this conversation as hidden in a prayer. There is disclosed not just the mercy of a gracious God, but also

The Mission of a Serious People

By a serious people I don't mean those who can never smile, who can never appreciate a joke. I mean instead those who take God seriously, those who are *serious about the promise God gives*. Through Abraham's family God had promised a blessing for the world. But Abraham had no family! He had no child, and Sarah was too old to have one. At that point, the verses before this text tell how the Lord and these mysterious visitors brought the news to Abraham and his wife Sarah that she was to have a child next spring. That promise was so absurd that Sarah laughed out loud.

In addition to that, the possibility of sparing Sodom is even more absurd. Spare Sodom? You've got to be kidding. When God announces an investigation of Sodom and Gomorrah "to see whether they have done altogether according to the outcry which has come to me," there is no suspense whatsoever. It's like the housewife who asks, "Do you remember the time I baked biscuits without using baking powder?" There's no suspense involved here. Everybody knows that biscuits without baking powder is a recipe for homemade poker chips. But Abraham took God's promise seriously, even for Sodom! The mission of a serious people is revealed as hidden in this prayer. Abraham heard God's promise and took it to mean everyone. Therefore, he prayed for Sodom.

That prayer leads us to be *serious about the purpose behind us*. Through Abraham God created a people, and that's who we are. We are God's people, and our purpose is still blessing. Christ was sent as the instrument of blessing. The Second Lesson speaks of how in Christ God brought us from death to life. It also speaks about us being buried with Christ in baptism. We are called to be a part of Christ! We are his body! As we pray in the eucharistic prayer, we who are his body ask that we may indeed be his body in the world. Myriad examples of what that means crowd in upon us. Certainly God's people can be the instrument of blessing by leading others to find a peaceful way for school desegregation to happen in every community. Surely God's people can be the instrument of blessing by leading the world to a way of life characterized by peace instead of war. And the list goes on! The family of God, like every family, has a purpose beyond itself. Just to survive is not a big enough reason for our existence as God's people. We have to be serious about the purpose behind us.

And that means *serious about the consequences for ourselves*. We are not called simply to pray for others; we are called to a life committed to serving others. This is after all what ministry means. We are a church called to minister, to serve. The point of our existence as a church is measured not by the number of members on our roll, and not by the amount of money in our budget. Instead we are measured by the question, "Is ministry happening here?" The kind of life that takes that question seriously is the kind of life that takes our mission seriously, to live a life in Christ's pattern, to hear his call, "Come after me," and then to come!

When in our Sunday worship we share in the bread and wine, we know that this is a sharing in Jesus' dying, his body and blood. That makes it a serious business. But because we also know that this body and blood were given and shed for us, that makes it also a gracious business. All of that is hidden in a prayer, hidden in this conversation of Abraham and God. There is hidden there the mercy of a gracious God and the mission of a serious people. But those same things are also hidden in the prayer in today's Gospel, the Lord's Prayer. All of it is hidden in the very first two words of that prayer, "Our Father." The only reason that we can call God "Our Father" is because Jesus made us his brothers and sisters, and that is the mercy of a gracious God. But as the brothers and sisters of Jesus we have a pattern for what is to be our family life-style in God's family, and that is the mission of a serious people.

RONALD M. HALS
Trinity Lutheran Seminary
Columbus, Ohio

THE GRACEFUL POINT OF VIEW

Eleventh Sunday after Pentecost
Ecclesiastes 1:2; 2:18-26

St. Luke's Gospel tells the story about Jesus that began when one day, as happened to this well-known young rabbi, a huge crowd of people had gathered around him. Perhaps they came to listen to his wonderful stories and his enthralling words; probably some came to be healed and cured; still others however seem to have skulked after him, looking for what he might say that could be used against him. On this particular occasion someone asked him for help: "Teacher, bid my brother divide the inheritance with me." Did he really need help with the inheritance? Was it another trap set for Jesus, to lure him into saying something that ran counter to the numerous Jewish laws on inheritance or that would anger and disappoint people with similar inheritance problems or anxieties? We'll never know the man's reason for going to the Teacher. But Jesus replied with a memorable rebuff—"Man, who made me a judge or divider over you?"—and with a parable that has gained wide recognition over the centuries. It was the man's point of view that Jesus regarded as the real problem, and which he rebuked.

The Sorrow of Seeking Satisfaction

"The world is so full of a number of things, I'm sure we should all be as happy as kings," wrote Robert Louis Stevenson in a charming nursery rhyme. But if the world of creation is indeed so rich and bountiful, why are so many people unhappy? In the example before us a man was at odds with his brother about an inheritance. This is not an uncommon problem, but perhaps one upon which his happiness depended, and so he came hoping for a solution from the Master. After all the word was out that this Jesus could do wonderful things and solve all sorts of problems, the first century equivalent to the modern automobile bumper sticker, "Jesus Is the Answer." So Jesus' reply may have confused him, telling him that for this kind of question he (Jesus) was not the answer!

Instead Jesus told a parable about a rich man who, on the way to expanding his wealth and consolidating his possessions, decides to build even larger barns. To put it in modern terms, with this new capital investment he can increase storage capacity, take better advantage of fluctuating prices, perhaps even stabilize his cash flow, and improve his already positive financial picture. This does not sound like a bad deal! This man appears to be no different from millions of strivers in our own generation. His life is rather satisfying, it seems to him anyway, and he is managing to get out of life more or less what he wants. With expansive self-congratulation he tells himself, "Now you have made it; you've laid away plenty for the future—a hedge against inflation and a sound investment (a binding contract for adequate wage and retirement benefit scale increases might be the idea in a different context). Enjoy it now, and take it easy!" But that night he dies; God calls him, death takes away everything that he has so carefully planned and worked so hard for, and he faces his Maker instead of his secured future. The agony of brotherly quarrels, the long years of estate-building—all of it rendered futile by death overnight! A sorrowful story indeed.

Ecclesiastes' Personal Problems

The book of Ecclesiastes wrestled bitterly with these very same painful questions and disappointments, and our Lord may have had this Old Testament document in mind that day. This small book, resting quietly after Proverbs and before the well-known books of Isaiah and the other prophets, does not often draw our attention. It is not a book of splendid pronouncements, powerful denunciations, or sweeping historical claims. Instead, it argues out, rather tediously too in places, certain problems of understanding life. But remarkably they are the very questions that Jesus raised.

The author of Ecclesiastes had tried everything in his search for satisfaction and contentment in life. He had gone the route of garnering great wealth and gratifying every urge and desire. He had immersed himself in knowledge and wisdom, in hopes of being satisfied by at least knowing the answers to life's important questions. But these strenuous efforts had produced no lasting effect. His quest ended in frustration; he had not found lasting value or peace from this wealth or wisdom, and he finally concluded that there is no ultimate meaning behind such things, and that getting them is just vanity and emptiness. "Vanity of vanities, all is vanity!"

We know this feeling from our own experience too. The Harrisons work carefully in life, building an estate, and then the estate is consumed by taxes and wasted by carelessness or incompetent heirs. Ed and Emma Johnson invest money and dreams in the children's education and future, but the children don't appreciate their chance, and one child dies tragically and cannot use it. Julia White works hard, not enjoying life much now, in order to have the means for enjoyment later when she is older, but illness or early death destroy the hope for a happy old age. These things happen every day, says Ecclesiastes, and demonstrate how futile and vain are such hopes and plans.

Even more discouraging to Ecclesiastes was the fact that people are not dealt with equally or according to evident merit. God seems to let good people suffer and permits the wicked and ungodly to prosper. Sometimes the luckiest or most successful person is also the most unscrupulous. This person's success is very exasperating to us. Some people seem blessed with every gift and good fortune; others come into this world so limited and handicapped that physical and spiritual survival demands a heroic effort. God does not treat his creatures on the basis of comparable fairness, but on a one-to-one basis, on what the sovereign loving Creator and Provider will do for each of his creatures.

For Ecclesiastes, the sharpest problem of all lay in the specter of death. Just as for the rich fool, it upsets human plans and wrenches away any control or guarantees for a pleasant future. There are cases where death is longed for and prayed for, and comes as blessed release from torment. But when it comes by surprise, untimely, prematurely, tragically, it seems to make a mockery of the worldly point of view that looks for order and fairness in the structure of creation, and that provides a place for human planning and control of final destiny.

Surrendering Control

Ecclesiastes weighed the issues around this worldly point of view and made a bold claim that is close to the Gospel. "Give up trying to control your destiny," he said. "Anything that you can seem to control is unstable. It will fail you and disappoint you. It will break, or turn sour. There is something far better, but it really means adopting a whole new point of view, a graceful point of view. Its slogan is, 'It's better to receive than to take,' and it is a way of living by grace, receiving grace."

This message is not good news to the person with the new barns. It is bad news for those who put their plans before God's grace.

We are all encouraged to believe that, whether in business or private life or even in the church, "we plan to fail if we fail to plan." Planning is a way of guiding and controlling the future; it is a means of governing what happens, and is supposed to eliminate surprises as much as possible. It has become a modern way of life. But, says Ecclesiastes, for all the obvious benefit that planning provides for daily life, God simply doesn't allow it to stand as the last word for us. Human efforts to keep control of human destiny and to rule out God's grace are all puny in the light of his great power. Our best-laid plans fall through, and in the end death snatches away the shreds of planning and controlling to which we desperately cling. At death we fall, once and for all, into the hands of God's grace.

Accepting God's Grace and Gifts

The life which rests in God is freed to be surprised by grace; it is open to his plans and his will. Rather than declare to God what is adequate or fair reward or security, it is willing to be accepted and approved by him, and rests upon what he gives. Rather than demand explanations from him, it accepts the reasons he supplies. With this graceful point of view in Ecclesiastes we know a deeper, livelier joy from what he gives us; we can praise and thank him in every time and place. When death comes, we accept it too; we do not always have reasons and answers, but we seek to ask the right questions.

We discover the extent to which we receive his grace day by day, in simple and complex ways. What is good for us comes from his hand, not always just because we ask for it, and often even without our knowledge: "for apart from him who can eat or who can have enjoyment?" (2:25) "Whatever your hand finds to do, do it with your might," Ecclesiastes says later in the book. "Eat your bread with enjoyment, and drink your wine with a merry heart; for God has already approved what you do." We do not always get to enjoy what we plan, but we can relish his benefits to us, and enjoy his approval.

We do not need an explanation for why the wicked prosper. We do not insist on clarification amid the sorrow of untimely death. There is no need for great schemes that unravel the mysteries of life. We have given up our sovereignty, and accepted God's control.

Living Gracefully

When Albert Schweitzer decided to go to equatorial Africa, to devote his life there, he passed up the security of several promising careers in Europe. A brilliant musician, Bach expert, and organist, and an established theologian, he might have "nailed down" numerous guarantees for his future, securing a position, and establishing himself. Instead he felt a call to study medicine and go to Africa. Friends and acquaintances thought that he was being foolish. Taking the obvious risks was serious enough; but he was also disregarding his "opportunities" and throwing away a great future. He, however, felt a call, felt God had put something into his hand that he should accept and do, and believed that this style of life and new point of view should guide him.

He was an example of living gracefully. Not grimly, with a morbid intention to sacrifice oneself; not smugly, determined to enjoy having made such a sacrifice. Not sorrowfully, saddened by the security which is given up. And not carelessly and irresponsibly, refusing to apply forethought and care and even the planning of which we are capable to what God has given. This is a joyful way of life, happy in what God chooses to give; a responsible way, careful to plan and use what he bestows; a rich way, able to eat and drink and take pleasure in his benefits.

The Gospel comes to us, asking us to let go of a worldly point of view. It brings us the assurance of God's arbitrary, personal love—love shed upon each of us as he sees fit. It thrills us with the promise of great joy which is ours as we accept God's gifts. For this joy there is no need for barns or inheritances, for special pleasures or wisdom; for this joy we only need to believe God's word of love and promise, to accept his mercy, and to hold fast to his claim upon us.

WESLEY J. FUERST
Lutheran School of Theology
Chicago, Illinois

IS ANYONE ELSE UP THERE?

Twelfth Sunday after Pentecost
Genesis 15:1-6

The story is told of a man who had the misfortune of stumbling over a cliff. As luck would have it, however, he did not plunge to his death, but rather hung precariously from a tree limb jutting out from the otherwise barren rock wall. As he clung tightly to that limb, the man looked down to see that his fall would have meant certain death. Further sizing up his situation, he looked up to see that there was no possibility of scaling the smooth face of the cliff. As the seriousness of his predicament dawned upon him, and in a last-ditch attempt to save himself, he cried out to God. He looked far above the face of the cliff to the skies, and loudly called out, "Is anyone up there?" and following up his question with a plea, he continued, "If there's a God in heaven, show yourself to me now! Get me out of this mess, and I'll do anything that you ask!"

A deep baritone voice boomed in reply from heaven (God is, after all, supposed to sound like Charlton Heston!). "Yes, I'm here," affirmed the Lord, "and if you wish to be saved from your terrible predicament, all you need do is have faith. Simply let go of that branch, and let yourself fall, for I will catch you in my hand, and no harm will come to you at all!"

The man looked down once again, down what seemed endless miles into the bottom of the ravine. He paused, reviewed his situation thoughtfully, and eventually turned his gaze into the heavens once again. At last he drew a deep breath, and yelled back, "Is anyone else up there?"

A Punch of Reality

Perhaps you, too, have wondered in a time of trial, "Is anyone up there?" At the tragic death of a loved one, in the face of the senseless violence all around us or even as you, like the man in that story, found yourself in an extremely difficult situation, then it was that you may have caught yourself wondering, "Is anyone really up there?" And when God's response was not immediately forthcoming or seemed to call for more than you could muster, then it was that you may have been even further tempted to wonder, "Is anyone else up there?" For it is in just such a fashion that the world is intent upon expressing its faith!

Yes, that story belies much about the nature of our faith. While fully intended to be humorous, that story packs a punch of stern reality for us all, and in several different ways.

First, it reminds us that the only time we feel the need to call upon the Lord is in the midst of a crisis. We delay our worship until we are hanging on the cliffside; a time when God's help is not only desirable, but necessary.

Second, our cry for help usually sounds very much like we are trying to strike a bargain with God, a bargain of which we, of course, are the chief beneficiaries. "Bail me out of this mess, Lord, and I'll do anything you ask in return!" we say; a promise, by the way, which is forgotten almost as quickly as it is made.

Third, when the type of answer or action we had in mind is not forthcoming, we immediately begin to consider our options. Perhaps, we think, God is not the answer to all our problems at all. Perhaps we ought to be looking elsewhere for rescue from the various dilemmas of our lives. In that case, anyone and anything will do just so long as we are instantly gratified. But finally, that humorous little anecdote actually undermines an appropriate understanding of faith. To ask "Is anyone up there?" or in a last-ditch attempt to save ourselves, "Is anyone else up there?" is really to miss the point of what faith is all about!

A Clue in Abraham

But today, in the man Abraham, our forefather according to the flesh, we have a clue and an example of what real faith is all about! Yet it is more by what Abraham did not do than by what he did that we learn about the true nature of faith for our own lives. Abraham did not express his faith in the usual fashion of this world, but as a gift from God. Abraham did not express his faith as a last-minute cry for crisis intervention from God, but as an ongoing relationship with one who would do what he had promised. Neither did he attempt to drive a hard bargain with God, though he certainly quibbled over the ultimate fulfillment of their agreement. Nor did he finally turn from God to consider more promising options; the word of the Lord was his only alternative. In other words, Abraham's faith was far more than a last-ditch attempt to save himself, much more than any one man could muster. It was rather all a gift, as much a gift as God's promise to him of a land, a great nation, a blessing and even of a son to come.

What a bargain! Here was a bargain far better than anyone could ever negotiate. God gave Abraham a good deal! Abraham got something for nothing; the kind of deal a consumer society is constantly seeking. Why? Because he was a man who had "the assurance of things hoped for, the conviction of things not seen." He was a man with a vision, enough vision to begin numbering the stars in heaven as the Lord suggested. As Abraham did so, he did not pause to reflect on the question of whether or not anyone was really up there. Nor did he wonder, in light of the fact that he did not yet have an heir, whether anyone else was up there. No, but rather the Lord caused it to dawn upon him in the course of his stargazing that here was one whom he might fear, love and trust to do what he had promised. So it was that "he believed the Lord; and (the Lord) reckoned it to him as righteousness." God, by his own action, would soon make Abraham right!

God, by his own action, is making us right, by the fulfilled promise of a land, a great nation, a blessing and even of a Son who has come and gone and will come again! In the meantime, however, Abraham is busy teaching us much about what faith is and is not. Faith is no momentary emergency measure, to be resorted to only in times of greatest need. Rather it is the attachment of God upon our hearts and minds and souls in such a way that we will fear, love and trust him to do what he has promised, no matter what. Neither is faith something which involves plea-bargaining or collective-bargaining or any other kind of bargaining. "You scratch my back, and I'll scratch yours" has no place in our relationship to God. Yet that, in fact, is precisely what faith is all about: a relationship, a relationship between father and son, mother and daughter, which never doubts for a moment the absolute reliability of our loyalty to one another. After all, we're family! Nor finally is faith considering the alternatives, gravitating toward whoever or whatever will produce the best results. No, but faith is rather sticking with God through thick and thin just as he, all down through human history, has stuck with us through thick and thin. In short, faith is never having to ask, "Is anyone else up there?"

Abraham, the Visionary

Abraham enjoyed a relationship with the Lord which few of us have known since. In some ways, Abraham wasn't much of a visionary, passing off his wife as his sister down Egypt way. "That's bigamy," he may have quipped. In other ways, however, Abraham shared the same foresight which most visionaries possess. He left the comforts of Ur on the word and promises of a relatively unknown God. Heaven knows why he wanted to leave such a convenient address behind; and he really had no reason to believe that a desert journey might result in anything more than an aversion to sand, let alone the fact that he might be the beginnings of a great nation in a land where he would be greatly blessed and possess a great name to boot. Yet as all true visionaries, he possessed one vital characteristic; faith, the faith which is only God's to give, the faith which is certain, despite all odds, that this God will do what he has promised. Abraham simply sensed the presence of this God, a God with whom he might quibble, yet ultimately a God whom he might recognize as a greater visionary than himself.

When I read the stories concerning Abraham in the book of Genesis, I can't help but be reminded of a comedy sketch done by Bill Cosby some years ago. It's a favorite amongst the Luther

Leaguers and confirmation students of our parish. While it is a take-off on a conversation between God and Noah as he was instructed to build the ark, it could serve as well as a take-off on the several encounters between God and Abraham. As Cosby has it, God spoke to Noah as he was involved in some routine carpentry around the house, improving his rec room and such. Suddenly, out of the blue, God calls Noah by name. "Who is it?" Noah wonders.

"It's the Lord!", comes the reply.

"Right!" shoots back Noah in mock assent, and as God unfolds his mission for Noah, Noah responds with all kinds of questions. "Where are you?" "What do you want? . . . I've been good!" "Who is this really?" "What's going on?" "How come you want me to do all these weird things?" Finally, in Cosby's humorous re-creation of the scene, Noah wonders, "Am I on Candid Camera?"

This is a re-creation, only for the sake of comedy, and we ought to take it as such. Yet we may be tempted by such a humorous treatment of the story of Noah, or even the stories of Abraham, to assume that these biblical characters possessed the same degree of inquisitiveness that we do, that they had a total lack of vision as we most often do. It was not so! For while they may have posed their own kinds of questions, they did not wonder about the who, where, what why, and how of God. Least of all, I suppose, did they wonder if they were being caught in the unseen eye of Candid Camera! They had few doubts, indeed they were quite confident, that someone was up there. That someone was Yahweh, the God of their fathers, in the process of becoming the God of Noah and Abraham, of Isaac and Jacob and Joseph, but finally of you and me. We share the vision of Abraham when we refuse to question whether or not anyone is really up there!

Abraham's Loss of Vision

Yet more often in our day and age, we share Abraham's loss of vision. Abraham wondered, according to today's Old Testament text, how he might become a great nation in a land where he would be greatly blessed with a great name to boot, and all this without the benefit of an heir. The perils of parenthood just didn't seem to be in the wind for Abraham and Sarah. We can understand Abraham's concern; after all, it's fairly difficult to hand on the family farm when there's no one to hand it on to. So it was for Abraham, as it is so often for us, of great concern that the estate not end up in the wrong hands. Not many of us would be overjoyed at the prospect of signing over the farm or ranch to one of the hands prior to our death. Yet such fears, for Abraham at least, were soon shown by God to be unfounded.

Abraham had lost his vision, but not his faith, for this one solitary moment. His faith, of course, was still tied up in his "conviction of things not seen." In other words, he was fully confident that someone was really up there, someone who was listening to his concerns. His loss of vision, however, had to do with a lapse in his "assurance of things hoped for." To put it another way, he wasn't quite sure what that someone up there was up to. Would God fulfill his promises or not?

We may regain this vision along with Abraham. Few of us actually wonder, "Is anyone up there?" That is, few of us really question the existence of God. On the other hand, however, like Abraham, we may begin to question when and how God is going to act. Yet in this sense, we are one up on Abraham! Abraham could only trust that this God would do what he had promised, that he would give him a son and heir in the future. We have the advantage of a God who has already acted in the past, giving us a son, his Son, of whom we have been made heirs. Therein lay the difference between Abraham and ourselves. Abraham believed in what he could not see, while we often find it difficult to believe what God has already shown us. So it is, ignoring God's great act in the sending of his Son, we begin to wonder, "Is anyone else up there?"

Abraham's Vision Restored

God restored Abraham's vision in an innovative way. He made a stargazer out of him, and likened his offspring to the number of stars in the sky. It was enough! Abraham "believed the Lord; and (the Lord) reckoned it to him as righteousness." Modern day stargazers are having their vision restored in much the same fashion. A syndicated columnist writes that astronomy professors are returning to theories in keeping with the biblical accounts of creation. He further points out that science has always been just another form of religious faith anyway. Thus, as the astronomers gaze at the stars through their telescopes, they are receiving an increasing vision of the God who has been there all along. What they have seen has apparently been enough to convince them that someone is really up there!

In a similar way, we may have our vision restored with this one subtle difference. Unlike Abraham, unlike those modern day astronomers, we are called by God not to be stargazers, but rather to be cross-gazers. Then we will realize the magnitude of God's sacrifice for us. Then we will know the "anyone" up there is a somebody; somebody designated to go to the grave ahead of us that he might overcome death with "the assurance of things hoped for," somebody called Jesus Christ. Then our faith in God will find its necessity, not in crisis intervention nor in our bargaining position nor in our consideration of other alternatives, but precisely in the realization (as we perhaps stare off into space with Abraham, but even more as we experience the effects of Christ's cross) that there is no other alternative. Then we, like Abraham, will believe the Lord; and the Lord will reckon it to us as righteousness.

A young boy, upon returning from Sunday school, was asked what he had learned. "Well, Mom," he began, "our teacher told us about how God sent Moses behind the enemy lines to rescue the Israelites from the Egyptians, how they built a pontoon bridge when they got to the Red Sea, about the Egyptian tanks chasing them, and how Moses radioed to headquarters for back-up air strikes."

"Bobby!" the boy's mother cried, "Is that really how your teacher told the story?"

"Not exactly," admitted the boy, "but if I told it her way, you'd never believe it!"

We, too, have a Teacher who has a story to tell, a story which needn't be exaggerated to be believed. It is the story of Someone, and nobody else, who went up there on the cross that we might live. It was enough; you'd better believe it! Amen.

ROLF NESTINGEN
Keene Lutheran Parish
Keene, North Dakota

THE WORD TO SHATTER DREAMS

Thirteenth Sunday after Pentecost
Jeremiah 23:23-29

They had a dream.

It was a good dream, a pleasant dream about salvation and deliverance. It was the kind of dream God's people always like to hear—especially when they're in trouble.

The problem was the way they shared their dream. It wasn't like Martin Luther King Jr. who told his dream as a dream and never pretended it was anything else. No, the false prophets of ancient Judah were telling their dream as a special revelation from God—the Word of the Lord, they said. But that was a lie.

At the time, however, there was a word from the Lord, spoken by another prophet, Jeremiah. It was a word which stood in stark contrast to the dream. Jeremiah's word was more like a nightmare; it was a harsh word, an unpleasant word about judgment and destruction. It was the kind of word God's people never like to hear. But it was the truth.

The word that God spoke—that God still speaks—is always a word to expose and judge the lies which false prophets delight to tell and which God's people delight to hear. God speaks the word to shatter dreams.

The word to shatter dreams is

A Confession about God's Presence

"Do I not fill heaven and earth?"

God is with us, but God is also removed from us; God is close by, but God is also far away; God, is in our midst, but he fills the whole universe. The word never confesses a God who is completely localized, who becomes so involved with one segment of his creation that he ceases to be Lord of the rest. The word of the text challenges that deluded assumption of the false prophets: "Am I a God at hand and not a God afar off? . . . can a man hide himself so that I cannot see him? . . . Do I not fill heaven and earth?"

Did these prophets actually imagine that the Lord didn't see through their dreams or hear their lies? Did they really search for secret places, which were supposedly hidden from God, to share their fantasies? Or as seems more probable, in their preoccupation with dreams, did they merely ignore God's awareness of their activity?

Whatever the case, the obvious answer to Jeremiah's rhetorical questions, the true confession that God is both here and everywhere, brought with it a shattering conclusion: "I have heard." The dreamers were indeed noticed. They could not hide themselves from the God of Israel, the God of the word.

Nor could their dreams be hidden. The content of those dreams betrayed the same mistaken impression about God: that he could not see, or did not choose to see, the sin of his people. The dreams omitted any reference to the corrupt leadership, the oppression of the poor by the rich, the ritualized worship which were all so prevalent in Jerusalem. The dreams could perceive the threatening Babylonian army only as an unrighteous intruder which God surely would destroy, rather than as an instrument of his judgment which could not be successfully opposed. But the Lord who saw and heard the sin of the false prophets also saw and heard the sin of a false people. Both stood under his wrath, and neither could be hidden by a dream.

"Do I not fill heaven and earth? . . ." The questions are still appropriate; in fact, they may be more urgent today. After all, in our enlarged understanding of the universe, does God still look—or even care to look—in every nook and cranny of this tiny planet? It hardly seems reasonable, but even today the Word confesses no other Lord than the one who calls galaxies out by name, who is aware of a sparrow falling, who is both seeking Shepherd and King of creation.

Yet it's still the hallmark of those who claim extraordinary revelations from that Lord to ignore the wider confession of his presence. Sometimes, as in the text, it's overt deception. Charlatans and frauds who seek wealth, popularity or personal gain in telling their "dreams" or "messages from the Lord" never seem to understand that the Lord has also heard them and seen through their lies. Sometimes it's simply a matter of pious, but wishful, thinking. Sincere believers who feel they've been given a special word from God frequently fail to test that word—to see whether or not it's consistent with the way God has worked all along among his people or in his world. Dreams and revelations which in any way limit God's presence to the here and now and close at hand are worthless. He remains a God afar off as well as a God at hand, and God's people must always confess his remoteness as well as his closeness.

The word to shatter dreams is a confession about his presence and

A Reminder for His People

". . . who think to make my people forget my name . . ."

Through the ages from their beginning God had given his people a continual reminder of whose they were and where they had been. The reminder, too, was in the word which God spoke—specifically, the reminder was God's own name which had been proclaimed to Moses and then through Moses to all of Israel.

The name was Yahweh, he who is, or he who causes to be—who knows for sure?—a name whose meaning concealed as much as it revealed. But more important than the precise meaning of the name was the history which the name suggested:

"I am Yahweh your God, who brought you out of the land of Egypt, out of the house of bondage ..."

Or the attributes which accompanied the name and spelled out the relationship between God and his people:

"The Lord Yahweh, a God merciful and gracious, slow to anger, and abounding in steadfast love and faithfulness ..."

It was God's name which bound Israel together in good times and bad, which gave the nation its reason for being, which destined God's people for a future yet undiscovered. More than once, however, God's people forgot his name for the name of other gods. These gods were no gods, but they had easier and less demanding names like Baal which false prophets uttered glibly. God kept trying, though, to call back his people through the prophets *he* sent. And whenever those prophets spoke the word, they reminded the people once more: "Thus says Yahweh. ..."

Jeremiah faced a more difficult situation. The false prophets in his day were speaking not in the name of another god, but in the name of Yahweh: "who prophesy lies in my name ... the deceit of their own heart." The false prophets were speaking in God's name but ironically their purpose was to make God's people forget his name. By preaching dreams they were actually focusing attention on themselves.

For us, the name has been extended by a further unraveling of God's word:

Jesus Christ, crucified and risen ...

The Holy Spirit, the Lord, the giver of life ...

Every time a sermon is begun, or the water is poured, or the bread is broken there's a new reminder from the word as name:

"Grace to you and peace from God our Father and the Lord Jesus Christ ..."

"... in the name of the Father and of the Son and of the Holy Spirit. Amen."

"In the night in which he was betrayed, our Lord Jesus took bread ..."

To be sure, other voices today still speak God's name not as a reminder of him, but to call attention to themselves:

"The Lord told *me* ... "

"He spoke to *me* in a dream ..."

But dreams which profane God's name by making his people forget are always doomed. The name is a reminder from that word which shatters dreams.

The word to shatter dreams: a confession about God's presence, a reminder for God's people,

An Expression of God's Power

"Is not my word like fire . . ."

Wishing won't make it so; neither will dreaming. The people of God wished otherwise. They longed for the dreams of the false prophets to come true. For that matter, so did Jeremiah. "Amen!" he would later say to one of his adversaries, "may the Lord make the words which you have prophesied come true." But even the best of dreams is powerless. It cannot make itself happen.

That kind of power lies in the word alone. The word truly expresses God's power. As prophets like Jeremiah proclaimed the word, the events they described were set in motion. With each "Thus says Yahweh . . ." the match was lit, and the hammer bore down on the rocks. The word of God was nothing to trifle with; and those who spoke it faithfully often got burned in the conflagration or crushed by the blow.

To spread the fire of the word Jeremiah suffered ridicule, rejection and hatred. He was abandoned by his friends; and at some awful moments, it seemed, abandoned by God himself. To cast fire upon the earth Jesus, God's personal word, would have to suffer a baptism by fire on a cross. There he would be ridiculed, rejected, hated, abandoned by his friends; and for one awful moment, it seemed, abandoned by God himself. For only in that event could all the old words of promise and hope, faithfulness and truth, forgiveness and life, witness and mission reach their full potential.

But the power which the word expressed didn't end on the cross; it flared up more brilliantly than ever three days later. And on Pentecost it was distributed not just to prophets but to the whole church: fire from Jerusalem to the end of the earth, to the close of the age.

Neither the power of the word nor the risk involved in declaring it has diminished through the centuries. While in our struggle, we have not yet resisted to the point of shedding our blood, that always remains a possibility. Ridicule, rejection, hatred—those who would follow in the path of a prophet, in the path of their Lord, in the path of a cross had better reckon seriously with that kind of price. And abandonment too—abandonment by friends, by members of one's own family, and sometimes, it seems, by God himself. Such is the continuing power that the word of God expresses.

Dreamers about God have it made in every age. Glory and acclaim and popularity attend them as they relate by word of mouth or mass media their private visions. God, however, still speaks through his word, the word of his prophets and his Son and his church, the confessing word, the reminding word, the powerful word, the word to break rock and shatter every dream.

DAVID B. KAPLAN
St. Martin Lutheran Church
North Tonawanda, New York

A VISION OF GOD'S UNIVERSAL GLORY
Fourteenth Sunday after Pentecost
Isaiah 66:18-23

One of the Proverbs (29:18a) can be translated: "Where there is no vision, the people perish" (or "are cut off"). These words were true when they were first spoken and they are equally true today. Often we get so tied up in the day-to-day routine, in the minutiae of getting through another week, that we lose any sense of the meaning of life. The same thing happens in the church: pastors and people become so involved in the "nuts and bolts" of running a congregation that they tend to lose sight of the real reason for the church's existence. Our text this morning addresses this issue as it presents us with *A Vision of God's Universal Glory*.

Both in the biblical accounts and in the history of the church there are many instances where those who claim to be God's people try to place limits on him. Jonah tried to tell God that he should be merciful to the Hebrew people but not to the people of Nineveh; we often assume that he should be concerned about us but that he should judge our enemies. The vision before us, however, is a strong reminder that

God's Concern Is for All People

Picture the situation at the time these words were first spoken. Small groups of people had straggled back to Jerusalem from their exile in Babylon. On their arrival they were confronted by heaps of ruins: the temple destroyed, city walls torn down, nothing but rubble everywhere. And to make things worse, all of their efforts to begin rebuilding had been fiercely opposed by neighboring peoples. It was a far cry from the bright picture which had inspired them in Babylon: God triumphantly leading his captive people to freedom across a transformed wilderness, back to a glorified Jerusalem! Little wonder that hope dimmed and zeal diminished. It was only with the constant encouragement of their leaders that the temple, or a poor copy of it, had been rebuilt and after many more years the walls of the city repaired.

The people then saw as their task the preservation of their identity as people of God. The earlier prophets had interpreted the fall of the temple and the city as God's judgment on a faithless people, and they wanted to be sure this didn't happen again. Under Nehemiah and Ezra strict rules were set up and enforced. Priests had to be able to trace their geneology all the way back through Zadok to Aaron; the rest of the people had to be born of Jewish parents in order to be part of the covenant community. Marriage with non-Jews was forbidden and those who had married aliens in the past were forced to renounce spouses and children or they themselves would face expulsion. Laws concerning sabbath observance and temple worship were spelled out in great detail. "Faithfulness" became almost synonymous with ritual and ceremonial purity. The kingdom of God was thought to be made up of those who were good enough and pure enough to win God's approval.

It is at this point that the prophet's vision confronts and contradicts this limited view of who God's people are. God himself speaks: "I am coming to gather *all* nations and tongues; and they shall come and see my glory. And I will set a sign among them!" Representatives from among them will go out to all the world: to Spain, Africa, Turkey, Greece and to the "coastlands afar off," declaring God's glory among the nations. Then the great procession will begin From the ends of the earth they come—in chariots, on horses, mules, camels, by whatever means of transportation is available, converging on the holy city to worship the Lord. Some of these "foreigners" will be consecrated as priests and Levites and will serve him. In God's good time "all flesh" will worship before him!

In this beautiful vision there is no room for any kind of exclusiveness. There is no place for special claims on God's goodness and grace based on birth or religious purity. His love is for *all*.

Those who try to resist this universal love may well find that they are excluding themselves from the kingdom.

The vision thus helps us to understand

The Reason for Christ's Coming

In the Gospel message of God's sending his Son, the vision begins to be reality. The reason for his coming, John reminds us, is so that *"whoever* believes in him should not perish but have eternal life." Luke shows us the aged Simeon, standing in the temple with the baby Jesus in his arms, praising God with the words, ". . . mine eyes have seen thy salvation which thou hast prepared in the presence of all peoples, a light for revelation to the Gentiles, and for glory to thy people Israel."

When Jesus proclaimed that "the kingdom of God is at hand," he directed his message not only to the "righteous" but to all people. He viewed his ministry as the servant's task of proclaiming good news to the poor, release to the captives, the recovery of sight to the blind and liberty for the oppressed. The Pharisees and other religious leaders condemned him because he ate and drank with publicans and sinners, but this did not bother him at all, and he bluntly stated that outcasts were much closer to the kingdom of heaven than were their self-righteous accusers.

In the Gospel this morning Jesus is asked about those who will be saved. He answers with a parable about a householder who shuts the door and will not permit the self-righteous to enter, even though they cry out, "We ate and drank in your presence and you taught in our streets!" Instead "many will come from east and west and from north and south and sit at table in the kingdom of God. Some are last who will be first and some are first who will be last."

The prophetic vision speaks of a sign that God will place among the nations, but it does not say what that sign will be. From the New Testament perspective we can confidently state that that sign is the cross. It is a sign that breaks down all barriers in that it proclaims that God's love is for all. "You are my witnesses," says the living Lord to his followers, and he sends them out to make disciples of all nations. No longer is there to be any distinction, for "there is neither Jew nor Greek, there is neither slave nor free, there is neither male nor female for all are one in Christ Jesus our Lord." Filled with his Spirit, the envoys of the Gospel go forth to proclaim God's glory among the nations: from

Jerusalem to Judea, Samaria and the ends of the earth—even as far as the United States of America.

And now that vision of God's universal glory confronts us as

A Reminder of Our Mission.

We desperately need to see and heed this vision. For we, like others in the past, are constantly tempted to try to limit God. Many of us have come to the comfortable conclusion that our God is interested primarily in white, middle-class Americans. He is *our* God and it is his duty to support and uphold us and "the American way of life," even if that means the impoverishment of the rest of the world. *Our* comfort and well-being take precedence over the basic subsistence needs of others. Somehow we have deluded ourselves into thinking that it's okay for others to starve so that we can enjoy our high standard of living. Because we *deserve* God's favor. Haven't we been faithful to him?

But the prophet's vision breaks through our complacency. It exposes our selfishness and self-righteousness for what it really is—an affront to God and his universal purpose. It reminds us that we who have the privilege of being God's people also have the *responsibility* to proclaim that grace to others by word and deed. We dare not think that we have a monopoly on God. His concern is for everyone, and we are called to live as witnesses to that truth. This means that as God's people our task is to fight against every form of prejudice, to participate in breaking down the barriers that separate class from class, race from race, and nation from nation, even if that involves a good deal of personal sacrifice. Our mission begins in the congregation and in the community, but it dare not be limited to that—it extends to the whole world.

But the vision also assures us that the eventual outcome is in *God's* hands, not our own. *He* is the one who will bring it to completion. No matter how discouraging the circumstances may be, no matter how helpless we may feel, the vision of God's universal glory stands before us as a constant reminder that his purposes are sure—they will not fail. In his own time all nations will see his glory and all flesh will worship before him. It is *that* vision which gives meaning to our faith and provides hope for the future. Keep it before you! Amen.

RALPH W. DOERMANN
Trinity Lutheran Seminary
Columbus, Ohio

AN OLD SICKNESS: "GET-AHEAD-ITIS"
Fifteenth Sunday after Pentecost
Proverbs 25:6-7

When I read the text for today I remembered my student days and how I whiled away some boring lectures by reading the Book of Proverbs. I had a terrible problem though, because I had to suppress my urge to snicker or laugh out loud or cry as I recognized myself and my fellow human beings described by the proverbs. Now I am a professor myself and I have committed my share of boring lectures, but I have given my students useful advice: in case of boredom, turn to the Book of Proverbs.

Few people could be so unfeeling or dense as not to appreciate the truth which is so eloquently expressed in the proverbs. For example: "A fool takes no pleasure in understanding, but only in expressing his opinion" (18:2); "A rebuke goes deeper into a man of understanding than a hundred blows into a fool" (17:10); "Hatred stirs up strife, but love covers all offenses" (19:12); "Like a gold ring in a swine's snout is a beautiful woman without discretion" (11:22); "The getting of treasures by a lying tongue is a fleeting vapor and a snare of death" (21:6); "Righteousness exalts a nation, but sin is a reproach to any people" (14:34). Most areas of human life are touched by the proverbs and they hardly need an explanation in spite of the fact that they come to use from an oriental culture which thrived thousands of years ago.

Not Just Another Advice Column

One may rightly ask how this collection of wise sayings differs from the advice columns of today, such as Ann Landers or Dear Abby which we see printed in newspapers and magazines. In some respects there is no difference. Both dispense advice which is based on astute observation of what is advantageous and life-giving and what is not. Both realize that wise behavior is not a natural endowment, but that humans are born with the capacity to learn. Both are an appeal to reason, to the conscience and to a person's desire to gain knowledge and to live a fully satisfied and meaningful life, in spite of the chaos lurking inside and around us.

The claim is made that one *can* learn to live wisely, that there is an order to be discovered and that one can conquer chaos. Observation will soon teach us that it is much easier to pull a rope than to push it. The wise will use such an observation and find joy, peace and competence. The fools will continue to push the rope and find life frustrating and meaningless and remain incompetent. The wise men of Israel went a step further than merely dispensing advice. They saw in the truth of their observations how the will of God takes on concrete forms in everyday life.

There were mainly three groups of leaders in the ancient Israelite community: the priests, the prophets, and the wise men. The priests gathered together the history of the relationship of God with his people and expressed it in five books, Genesis, Exodus, Leviticus, Numbers, and Deuteronomy. The Greek term for this collection is Pentateuch, but the best descriptive terms is the Hebrew word Torah, which means teaching, instruction or guideline. It is unfortunate that the word Torah was then translated into Greek as *nomos* and then into English as Law. The word Law has connotations which the word Torah does not. The Torah is a welcome guideline which enables the people of God to live in a way which is faithful and true to the will of God at all times and in all places. It covers the liturgical and ethical ideals of Israel. The prophets, on the other hand, filled with the word and spirit of God, challenged, warned, cajoled, and also comforted the people in the name of God. Their work was collected and thus we have the prophetic books of the Bible.

The wise men had neither the authority of the priests nor that of the prophets. They could not say: "Thus says the Lord!" The wise simply taught what they themselves had found to be true and right. Throughout the Bible one finds their concerns expressed, but the books of Proverbs, Job, Qoheleth, Song of Songs, and several psalms, apparently stem exclusively from them. They accepted the wisdom and the proverbs of other countries, e.g., Egypt, Babylonia, Canaan, and they coined their own proverbs on the basis of their own observation of the rules of life. The validity of their instructions and teaching was seen in the fact that it was always in harmony with the Torah and prophecy. Therefore it was accepted by the people of God as a part of Scripture and an expression of the will and concern of God for his people and the world.

It is this close connection with the will of God which makes the advice column in the Bible different from today's advice columns. The wise men translated the precepts of the Torah and the challenges of the prophets into concrete and specific terms which were applicable to everyday life, or what we call secular life. They knew that nothing exists as an end in itself, but only as an expression of God's will. Everything created may be used either in compliance with the will of God and therefore for the benefit of humankind and the world, or in disobedience of God's will and therefore for the destruction of people and the earth.

The wise men warned that even wisdom, taken as an end in itself, accomplishes nothing. They knew that the inherent danger of wisdom, of know-how, is the false sense of security it can provide for what appears to be mastery of human destiny. They knew that there is something ultimately wise in realizing that even wisdom is in the end futile and powerless to bring about lasting enjoyment, peace, beauty, competence, and a purpose of life. They summarized this conviction by stating: "The fear of the Lord (i.e., the awe, reverence, and piety before God) is the beginning of knowledge" (1:7). The true foundation of wisdom is found in the knowledge of what it means to be a creature in relationship and conversation with the creator.

The Text and "Get-Ahead-Itis"

The advice given in the text today is straightforward and readily understandable: "Do not put yourself forward in the king's presence or stand in the place of the great; for it is better to be told, 'Come up here,' than to be put lower in the presence of the prince." The Hebrew word which is translated "do not put yourself forward" could also mean "do not glorify yourself, or make yourself out to be more than you are." Although the advice is given to officials of a king, we have no trouble recognizing here a response to our own constant desire to get ahead, our pretention to be more than what we actually are and can be.

Just think for a moment of the last time you fell victim to this desire. I am sure that many of us also know the searing pain of humiliation, which accompanies the disclosure of the fact that we tried to bite off more than we could chew. We live in a culture which heightens the bad and unhealthy effects of a sickness one might label "get-ahead-itis." We are constantly urged to prove that we are better, stronger, wiser, sexier, richer, more intelligent, etc., than others. Our desire to get ahead is shrewdly exploited by advertising.

One particularly crass example of "get-ahead-itis" I found in a newspaper article entitled "Vanity gets a lift from back door plastic surgeons." The first two paragraphs read: "Having a face-lift, formerly the exclusive option of the very rich and very famous, has become a popular cosmetic tool in the last decade. And Betty Ford's successful and highly publicized face-lift last year made cosmetic surgery more of a booming business than ever. Removing wrinkles has, in fact, become the 'in' thing. Princess Luciana Pignatelli, who sometimes speaks for the Beautiful People has proclaimed that anyone who needs a face-lift and doesn't get one is a 'slob.' " Well, what do you think? There may be nothing wrong with a face-lift, but surely to call someone a "slob" if one does not get one reveals a very shallow existence. Even without the guidance of the teachers of wisdom in the Bible or any other advice column of today it should be easy to realize the foolishness of such an attitude and statement.

"Get-Ahead-Itis" among the Followers of Jesus

Some of the ugliest forms of "get-ahead-itis" can be found among the followers of Jesus, not only during his lifetime but also throughout the centuries. Is it not reasonable to expect a different behavior from Christians? The jockeying for position and status affected even Jesus' disciples. In Matthew 20:20-28 we read that the sons of Zebedee, employing the help of their mother, asked Jesus for the two most prestigious positions of power in Jesus' kingdom, namely, to sit at his right hand and at his left. But although they were willing to suffer, Jesus told them point blank that even the most dedicated sacrifice, even death, in the work of God's kingdom does not *entitle* to privilege and status. They were told that what counts in the kingdom of God is not status but service to the best of one's ability: "Whoever would be great among you must be your servant, and whoever would be first among you must be your slave; even as the Son of man came not to be served but to serve, and to give his life as a ransom for many" (vv. 26-28).

This age-old desire for power and to be a master instead of a servant, to give orders instead of obeying the orders and life-giving rules and regulations which are given to us from nature and God, is always with us. Can we conquer it? The ancient poem in Genesis 3 describes the painful truth that we are all tempted to be more than we are, to "achieve" a status which is "higher" than we occupy. In a word, we are dissatisfied to be "merely human" and we want to be God. We do not want to be creatures but the Creator himself. We stand in front of the tree of temptation to be more than we are and we are tempted to disobey God's loving advice and warning not to eat of the fruit of this tree. But its fruit promises us physical strength, beauty, and, most important, wisdom, a wisdom equal only to God's. We bite into the forbidden fruit and realize immediately that we were tricked and that we have become less than we were. We are overcome by shame, fear, and a desire to hide from one another and from God. Our relationship with one another and with God become defensive and defiant and ugly.

Jesus and "Get-Ahead-Itis"

But as Christians we have no need to despair. We turn to Jesus for help and advice. His advice is clear: if you want to get ahead, in a way that really counts and is pleasing to God, then become a servant, even a slave. Improve your abilities as much as you can, of course, but use all of them according to the intention and will of God. Should such a life-style cost you your life, so be it.

In the Gospel for today, Jesus made excellent use of the Old Testament Lesson and his punchline drives home the same point as the proverb: "For every one who exalts himself will be humbled, and he who humbles himself will be exalted" (Luke 14:11). Jesus' whole life is an example and advice to us. He resisted the temptation to get ahead the way we usually want to get ahead. In the temptation story (Luke 4:1-13; Matt. 4:1-11; Mark 1:12-13) the gospel writers tell us that he resisted the pressure to enlist economic, political, and even religious power to accomplish his mission. He chose to be obedient to the will of God and to be a servant and healer. The message of the temptation story is clear: if Jesus, our brother and fellow human being, could resist temptation and live according to the will of God, so can we, with the help of God.

A Little Victory Over "Get-Ahead-Itis"

Recently I stood in line at a bank and someone tried to get ahead of me. I usually am very angry at such pushy people. I do not know what came over me, when this person pushed ahead of me, but I gave him room and simply said: "What is better, to get ahead or to get along?" The person looked at me, stepped back, thought a moment, and replied: "You said a mouthful!" We both looked at each other and bathed in the glow of recognition that in the hustle and bustle of life it is possible to fulfill the will of God.

I hope that this sermon was not too boring. Maybe some of you have already taken my advice and have turned to read the Book of Proverbs. If not, it might be a good idea when you get home. A proverb a day will keep temptation away. The advice of the wise and the example of our Lord Jesus is indeed an excellent medicine against "get-ahead-itis," but will we take it?

WALTER L. MICHEL
Lutheran School of Theology
Chicago, Illinois

WISDOM AND LIFE

Sixteenth Sunday after Pentecost
Proverbs 9:8-12

Most of us, deep inside ourselves, desire the good life. We constantly seek the key to successful and abundant living. We want happiness and health, wisdom and wealth. We earnestly strive for the necessary knowledge and skills that will enable us to make it big in our world.

Our culture feeds our voracious appetite for the good life. Our educational system seems primarily concerned to teach skills that enable us to earn more money. Advertising constantly excites us with images of the successful person and all of the good things surrounding that person. Certain religious groups fuel the desire for abundant living by promising "if you love God enough he will reward you with material prosperity and abundant living." The current concern for the self is a heightened manifestation of this quest for the good life. Current wisdom says that the desire of our life and age is for success and abundance. To be wise is to have the good life.

Recently I had the opportunity to hear another wisdom. I had a conversation with a student in his final year of study in a Lutheran seminary in East Germany. He spoke of life in images and desires much different from our own culture. He shared what living as a Christian, and particularly a Christian pastor, was like in East Germany. He spoke of little money, opposition to the church from the government, and the possibility of persecution. Yet he also passionately shared how he desired to remain in East Germany and become a minister of the gospel with and among his own people.

The image of life this young man presented was an image of poverty, persecution, and pain. His vision was to become a voice crying out for all the voiceless people of his land. He hoped to be the strength for the weak and the defender for the defenseless. He understood very clearly that he might possibly be imprisoned for his ministry and work. Yet he impressed me as a very wise young man. To be wise means the risk of imprisonment and even death for him.

Here are two pictures of wisdom in our contemporary world. The one seeking the good life. The other seeking the life that seems not so good. Yet how often our own cultural search for making it turns to ashes in our mouths. How the boredom and dullness seem to need escape. Yet the young German student conveyed excitement and vitality, even enthusiasm, for his very considered choice of life.

Biblical Picture of Wisdom

Two similar pictures of wisdom are found in the ninth chapter of Proverbs. Proverbs 9:1-6 paints the picture of dame wisdom's inviting people to eat at her banquet table. To accept her invitation is to enter into life. Proverbs 9:13-18 paints the picture of dame folly's inviting people to eat at her banquet table. To accept her invitation is to enter into death. Between these two invitations—one to life and the other to death—stands our text. The text speaks of the wise person, the person who would reject dame folly's invitation and readily accept that of dame wisdom to feast at her banquet of life.

The heart of our text is found in verse 10:

> The fear of the Lord is the beginning of wisdom,
> and the knowledge of the Holy One is insight.

Wisdom is not generated in and of ourselves. In biblical faith wisdom begins with knowledge of God. The wise person is the one who fears the Lord. Fear is not primarily a psychological terror, but rather it is something that is expressed in the actuality of living. Fear of the Lord means for the wisdom teachers obedience to the divine will in the context of everyday life. Fear of the Lord is confidence and trust in God who creates the world and who continues to sustain it.

The confidence and obedience to God is the beginning of wisdom. Fear of the Lord leads to wisdom. The same insight occurs in the Gospel for this day. Jesus is on his way to Jerusalem to die on the cross. He speaks to the crowds who follow him on that path. They have followed him, but he warns them to be wise, to know the cost of following him. He speaks two stories that portray wisdom and calls his followers to act wisely. Luke proclaims that in Jesus God is bringing his kingdom near. In Jesus God has fully made himself known to human beings. In obedience, in following Jesus is the beginning of wisdom for us. And for the New Testament writers following Jesus means being obedient unto death, following him all the way to the cross.

Wise Living Today

The young German seminarian with whom I talked in East Germany was wise. He had made a conscious decision in his life to be obedient to God in Christ Jesus. He had counted the cost of his discipleship. He knew what the price that must be paid is for ministering to and for people in his own land. He fears the Lord because God has come to him in his baptism and loved him into relationship with himself. His obedience may lead him to suffering and pain, to imprisonment and perhaps even to death. Yet, in the view of biblical faith his choice is the acceptance of the invitation of dame wisdom to eat at her banquet table of life.

Many of us in our deepest selves desire the good life. But is that desire, that seeking after making it in this world, wise living? Where does God enter into our thinking and planning as we strive for success and wealth? The voracious appetite that our culture has for more and more goods in order to live the good life, where is there any thought for fellow human beings? The constant striving for fame and wealth, where is the concern for being servant people to those who do not have the necessary essentials for living as human beings? In the idea of some that God will reward those who love him enough, where is the understanding that in Jesus the Christ suffering, self-sacrifice, and even death have become the marks of discipleship?

The fear of the Lord is the beginning of wisdom. God has shown himself to us in the life of ancient Israel and in the life of Jesus of Nazareth. The image of God given to us is one of a loving, caring, suffering and dying nation and person. There is no image of successfully making it in the world with fame and fortune. God shows himself to us as the eternal weakling who stands beside and with the poor, the despised, the outcast, the losers of life. God has come into our world, and he keeps coming to us, always as the drooping and dying figure on the cross.

But the good news of the gospel is that precisely in the weakness of dying and losing is the strength and power of God made manifest. There is no success orientation in the gospel. There is no desire for fame and fortune. God promises only that life with him will never be dull and boring. God promises only that he can be trusted and followed obediently, even unto death. That is the fear of the Lord that is the beginning of wisdom.

Then what does that say to us in the deepest quests of our hearts for the good life? God says to us that the gifts we have been given can now be used on behalf of and for the sake of others. The skills and knowledge that we have can now be turned from self-seeking gain toward service of and care for other persons. The concern for ourselves can now be set loose to work in our world and life for justice and equality for others.

Wisdom that grows from the fear of the Lord permeates all of life. The decisions that we make in every area of our life are affected by our confidence and trust in God, if we are wise people. The way we organize ourselves and our lives in day-to-day existence displays our wisdom or our folly. The fool says in his heart, "There is no God." The wise person fears the Lord and grows wiser still, even to following the Lord into death. This is the wisdom of the disciple of Jesus the Christ. We have been baptized into his death and resurrection and committed ourselves to follow him. Have we counted the cost? Have we feared the Lord and thus begun to be wiser still?

THOMAS E. RIDENHOUR
Lutheran Theological Seminary
Gettysburg, Pennsylvania

HOW MANY GOLDEN CALVES HAVE YOU MADE THIS WEEK?

Seventeenth Sunday after Pentecost
Exodus 32:7-14

If you have been reading the newspapers recently, you know that the news does not look very cheery. The economic outlook: Recession at best. A stringent national budget, yet still with a budget deficit. A frightening balance of trade deficit with our international trading partners. The world outlook: Fighting in Cambodia, Iran, Northern Ireland, Lebanon. Russia and China with troops massed on their common border arguing over Southeast Asia. Strategic arms limitation talks creeping along while both sides increase their armament. We could go on to stories here at home: Corruption in county and city politics. Four murders in one day with no indication of rhyme or reason. It's in these kinds of situations that we sometimes begin to lose our bearings, and, like Israel at the foot of the mountain, begin to grow restless and make golden calves.

How many golden calves have you made this week? I'm sure you think that is a pretty strange question, because you immediately reply, "honestly I haven't made a single one. I couldn't afford the price of the gold in the first place." Literally that's true—no golden calves—not a single one. Yet, in this kind of situation, where the delay seems long, the news seems dismal, and when we look up toward the mountain where God is supposed to be, all we see are thick clouds and darkness; we too, each in our own way, just like ancient Israel, begin to make our golden calves.

We're always looking out for something we can see that will protect us. How can we best invest our money as a hedge against inflation? What can we do to take advantage of all the loopholes in the tax laws? Or how can we protect ourselves from this world in which we live? And we begin to erect barriers between ourselves and God, to shield ourselves from any uncertainty.

Contrasts and Surprises

But let's look at the story again—with God and Moses up on the mountaintop and the people of Israel down below. It's a very familiar story. It's a story of contrasts and surprises. The people with Aaron, the chief priest and Moses' brother, as their leader are at the foot of the mountain. They had been there forty days and forty nights—and that's an interminably long time when you're waiting. While at the top of the mountain Moses is in deep meditation with God. The top of the mountain is serene and calm as Moses receives God's instruction.

In the valley below the people are disturbed and restless. Where has Moses gone? Has he brought us from Egypt into this desert and deserted us? What has become of this strange man? This Moses? And so the restlessness turns to frenzied activity as Israel seeks her own gods—someone—something—to protect her from the uncertainty—something to look at, to see, to feel, to touch. They decide to construct a solid, permanent image—something present, comfortable. Not off somewhere in those clouds on the mountain—fearful and fearsome. But something to be present at all times. Visible. Comfortable. And so in their anxiety the people begin to build an idol—a golden calf.

Your People

And on the mountain God speaks to Moses telling what *your* people had done and what God will do in response. That little pronoun *your*—we miss those little words sometimes—is our first clue as to how God views what is going on down in the valley. They are no longer his people, for they have turned away from him. They have refused to be his people, so he addresses Moses: "What are *your* people doing down there? What are *your* people doing that *you* brought up from the land of Egypt?" Just a few chapters earlier in Exodus 20, we read: "I am the Lord your God, who brought you out of the land of Egypt, out of the house of bondage." But now they are Moses' people, and Moses has brought them out of Egypt. And remember that the very next verse of Chapter 20 says: "You shall have no other gods before me. You shall not make for yourself a graven image. . . . " That's exactly what the people have done. And that special relationship with God is broken. We are reminded of it by that one little pronoun, *your*.

God's response reflects the brokenness of the relationship. God's people in their folly have made themselves Moses' people. For Israel's God is a just God. He has called his people to be his own and promised to be their God. But now they have lost their nerve. They have built their own god. They have deserted God, and so he calls them *your* people. They have refused to be God's people and they must suffer the consequences. The little pronoun, your, gives us the first clue of what happens to our relationship to God when we begin to make golden calves—to set up gods of our own construction—to set up barriers between ourselves and God.

And then we get a second hint. God will raise up a new people for himself—not the children of Abraham, and Isaac, and Jacob—but the children of Moses. For now God turns to Moses, and makes to Moses the very same promise that he made to Abraham, to Isaac, and to Jacob. If these people at the foot of the mountain —these descendants of Abraham—refuse to be God's people— then God will make of Moses a new people of God. He says to Moses: "I will make you a great people."

Moses' Response

This promise of God gives Moses just the opening he has been waiting for. He picks God up on just these two points: Whose people are these who have made a golden calf? And to whom does the promise made by God belong?

Moses' response begins to give us a little pattern—a little insight into how we may approach God through Jesus Christ. And how God, too, will forgive us when we begin to make golden calves for ourselves. Notice how Moses approaches God. First, Moses reminds God that these are indeed God's people in spite of what they have done. He begins just that way. He does not say, "Oh, no, Lord! These are not *my* people." And he does not say, "Oh, but God, you are the God of these people." But when he addresses God, he says, "Why does thy wrath burn hot against *thy* people?" And it's that little pronoun again. And Moses begins to remind God of what God has done for these people. He does not apologize or make excuses; rather he looks firmly and directly at what God has done—not what the people have done.

And he reminds God, once again, that in spite of what the people have done, they are indeed the same people that *God* called out of Egypt. Just as they were God's people then because of what God had done; so now they are still God's people because of what God had done and in spite of what *they* had done. He had called them out of Egypt—not because they were so fine and so great—but because he loved them. That's why he called this mixed multitude, this rabble, out of Egypt. And Moses reminds God that these are still those same people in spite of what they have done—in spite of the golden calf they have made.

Then Moses also picks up that second clue that God has given to him. And he reminds God that these people are indeed the descendants of Abraham, Isaac, and Jacob. They are the fulfillment of God's promise to the Fathers. "I will multiply your descendants as the stars of heaven, and all this land that I have promised I will give to your descendants, and they shall inherit it forever." So says God to Abraham. And Moses reminds God that this promise belongs to God—no matter what the people may do—how they may run after other gods—God's promise still stands. And we begin to see something of the heartbreak of God that finds its culmination in the cross of Jesus, the Christ. And something of the pain that our golden calves bring to God.

Our Golden Calves

And so, too, for us, when we make our golden calves and we begin to feel that we have been cut off from God. Or we begin to put the barriers up. Jesus Christ comes to tear those barriers down. To destroy those golden calves that we construct. To re-establish that relationship with God once again—and again. Not because of what we have done, but in spite of what we have done—in spite of the golden calves we construct—the ways we forget God's care, concern, protection and try to construct our own. It is God who really gives the protection. And this is what Moses speaks with God about on the mountain and also with the people in the valley. Moses goes back down the mountain and reminds the people when there are long delays, when things don't seem to be going well, when God seems far away and we become restless, then we are reminded to look once again at what God has done for us—to look again at God's promises to us. For it is in these things that we will find our God, our salvation, our protection—not in the golden calves that we erect for ourselves.

Justice and Love

This passage reminds us that God will remain true and faithful to his promises. And so even when we fall short of God's demand for absolute loyalty and devotion, the gap between God's justice and our sin is bridged by God's love—not by anything that we can do. We cannot build ourselves up to the level demanded by God. But rather as he did to Israel through the mediation of Moses when Israel made golden calves so through the life, and death, and resurrection, of Jesus Christ he comes to us with love and forgiveness when we deserve wrath and justice.

And true, the world in which we now live often looks scary, as we hear the international news, the economic news, the local news. We are often fearful. But the answer is not in making our own golden calves—trying to erect our own protective barriers to ward off the uncertainties of the times. We don't always hear and see clearly God's message. When we look up at the mountain we see only cloud and darkness. When the delay seems long, we, like Israel, become restless and fearful. Then Jesus reminds us of God's promises and what God has done for us in the past. And, most important, we are reminded that God does not desert us even when we begin to make golden calves to take his place. He still cares for each of us with his love and his forgiveness.

JAMES S. AULL
Lutheran Theological Southern Seminary
Columbia, South Carolina

QUICK PROFIT AT A HIGH COST

Eighteenth Sunday after Pentecost
Amos 8:4-7

A few years ago I was involved in a team conducting a congregational study in one of the more affluent suburbs in our country. The problems mirrored in the congregation were the problems of the larger community. One of the lay persons made the observation that the trouble with the people in this community was that they had champagne appetites and beer billfolds. Their tastes were beyond their resources to underwrite them.

I think this statement is an accurate description of modern society. We have expensive tastes and a life-style that is continually outstripping our resources to underwrite them. We also want our gratifications now while they are obtainable. There seems to be too much lack of confidence in the future to postpone our rewards for a later time. Inflation may cut deeper into our resources. We have worked hard. We need our recreation, we have earned our rewards. We deserve the good life that has been promised us.

But something must go so that we can bring our resources more in line with our expectations. Oil, gas and energy resources? No. Consumer protective legislation? Yes, if it interferes with cost. The later model cars and houses? No. Environmental protections? If need be, yes. Pay raises? Certainly not. Occupational health and safety standards for people working in dangerous vocations? Yes, if they increase prices. Recreation and vacations? No. Armaments and defense spending? We had better not. Charity, welfare? Certainly. We have worked for our share, why can't they?

Perhaps I am being too simplistic. But you listen to radio and television, you read the newspapers. Is it not true that the social causes instigated in previous decades to improve our environment, working conditions for laboring people, protect us from consumer frauds, and efforts to help the minorities and the poor are now under angry attack. We are discovering that our economic resources are under a heavy strain to correct these ills in our social fabric at the same time as maintaining an ever-increasing standard of living.

Our value system is reflected in our budgets more so than in our professed ideals. I am afraid that some of our budgeted goals speak louder than we care to admit. But before we join those that cry out "down with American capitalistic society" perhaps we had better look deeper into what is a human issue not simply a national or economic issue. Let us look at our text which deals with some of the same issues in another time and another place.

A Style of Living That Made the Prophet Amos Livid

The little country of Israel, in about 800 B.C., was living in a time of prosperity. It was a time of peace. Business was good. There were summer homes and winter homes. There was ease and security. Food and drink were plentiful. The people were crowding the religious sanctuaries for their festivals and observations. However, things were not good for everyone.

The little people living on the land or forced off the land for slavelike servitude did not share in the good life. They were seen as a source of increased profit. They were crassly exploited by false weights and measurements, impure grain and food products.

The words Amos uses to describe the action against the poor and needy literally mean to crush, to trample, to crash into ruins. But it did mean quick profit. The little people were in no position to defend themselves. Their wretched conditions forced them to subsist on whatever would come into their hands.

On the other hand people were very religious. They filled the sanctuaries but their religion was without ethics. It stopped short of seeing and hearing people suffering hardships in the midst of affluence. It stopped short of seeing and hearing and being sensitive to the hurts of the little people that were being exploited to maintain standards of living of the more prosperous. Even their formal religious observances, though supported with affluence, were under criticism. They took too much time away from the business of gaining more profits. The little people living from hand to mouth from day to day, who were not in a position to take in the religious festivals, were the objects of this greed.

The prophet is livid at this callous injustice against those not strong enough to look out for themselves. He proclaims, "The end has come upon my people Israel." "The Lord has sworn by the pride of Jacob: 'surely I will not forgive any of their deeds.'" He reminds them that they have obtained quick profits at high cost.

Why Was the Prophet So Severe in His Judgment?

We could say that Amos was a country boy who came to the city and was offended by the luxurious living he discovered. We could say he too was one of the little people living on the land who was angry at the exploitation leveled against himself and others of his kind. We could say that he had a strong sense of justice that he saw violated. A sense of justice born on the sparse slopes where he tended his sheep and nursed his vineyards. We would be right in all of these assessments.

Amos was a man of justice. People of justice are outraged when they see other men and women oppressed and exploited by others for selfish gain.

But we must take one step further. Amos sees the people of Israel as a people redeemed by a God who by grace lifted them out of their poverty to be his own people. They had forgotten their roots as redeemed of God and were exploiting other human beings as if they were not recipients of God's grace themselves.

Amos also sees them insulting God their creator who is a God who remembers and loves the poor and needy. He is a God who asks his people to reflect his image of them in the world. The covenant theology of Exodus and Deuteronomy is filled with exhortations to remember the poor with compassion. The Psalms, their prayer book, speaks over and over again of God as remembering the poor and the needy. The prophet Isaiah, picking up this same theme at a later time, not only denounces those who oppress the poor. He also identifies the messianic age as the age when God's redemption will come to the poor and needy. The honor of God the creator is insulted by the very peoples who are to reflect his image to the world about them.

Amos takes it one step further. He sees the greedy exploitation of their fellow men the visible symptoms of a society rotten to the core and no longer even able to sustain itself as a people among the nations.

And it happened. They obtained their profits at a high cost. The affluent exploiters of their fellow countrymen were carried off in slavery by the armies of the Assyrians.

A Message for Our Day

Does the wisdom of the ages proclaimed by Amos 800 years B.C. have anything to say to us in our day with our advanced technologies and complex economics? I feel it does. We are caught between an ever expanding expectation of the good life we feel we want and deserve and our resources to underwrite it. But we are not simply dealing with economic formulas or technological message. It is a human issue as well.

We can obtain quick profits at a high cost if we allow ourselves to be dehumanized to the point that we are willing to get quick profits at the expense of our fellow humans.

Who are these less fortunate? Who are the poor and needy? Who are the little people? Perhaps it is all relative? Perhaps it is only a matter of degree? I suspect that each of us has to ask the question who are the less fortunate who are dependent on us or our society, directly or indirectly for sustenance? We all to one degree or another are in a position to be helpful or hurtful to those men and women who are dependent on us. This is true as individuals, as a society. These are our opportunities to reflect God's grace.

Our sense of justice as human beings needs to reach out to all people of good will, religious and irreligious, to find a base to build quality life that need not sacrifice the less fortunate members of our society for the more fortunate.

We dare not stop here. I am speaking to you as women and men baptized into Jesus Christ who as such are part of the people of God of all ages. You have been adopted by God's grace and you are called to honor his name and reflect his image in this world. Our God is a God of compassion on the poor and needy. He stepped into this world becoming one of the poor and needy. We reflect his image in our attitudes and deeds toward the poor and needy. The ideal society God is struggling to usher in is an age in which the poor and needy will be exalted and remembered.

He called us to be a salt and a leaven in our society to spend ourselves, to preserve, if possible, our society. We may not be able to legislate laws to stop the rapid movements to disenfranchise the less fortunate among us. But we are called upon to be a salt and a leaven. We can be a voice calling out in the wilderness for the justice of a holy God. This will not be less costly. This will have no quick profits but it is our calling regardless of cost.

We are God's people. Let us be certain whereof we receive our values. We are a part of a long and great tradition of people called and redeemed by a holy God who loves the poor and needy. We dare not choose quick profits to nurture an ever increasing appetite. To honor the name of our compassionate God in word and deed is our calling in our day as in the day of Amos. As it was in the day of our Lord Jesus Christ and as it will be when he steps on the stage to usher in his kingdom.

RICHARD D. VANGERUD
Luther-Northwestern Seminaries
St. Paul, Minnesota

RICH MAN, POOR MAN

Nineteenth Sunday after Pentecost
Amos 6:1-7

It was a game we used to play as children. Maybe you remember it. Recite the rhyme as you counted the buttons on your shirt, your jacket, your trousers:

> Rich man, poor man, beggar man, thief;
> Doctor, lawyer, merchant, chief.

The last button then offered a prediction of your future vocation. Or, if I remember rightly from those pre-women's-liberation days, if you were girl, it indicated what sort of man you would marry one day.

Rich man, poor man . . . This old rhyme recognizes some of the fundamental structures of human society. There will always be, one suspects, rich and poor, doctors and lawyers, beggars and thieves. The texts for this Sunday focus on the first two of these classes: the rich, and the poor.

The Rich

The Old Testament Lesson presents us with a word from Amos. We don't know much about that prophet. But we do know that he was a layman, a cattleman or rancher, who never made the clergy roster. Somehow, God had got hold of him one time and directed him to go to Israel and deliver a message. He was commissioned as God's messenger, God's prophet.

So, one day, Amos went to Israel. As he approached one of the cities where there was a place for worship, he could hear the singing and he could see the smoke from the sacrifices going up into the clear sky. Then Amos, fired by God's Spirit, interrupted the activity with the word he had been directed to deliver:

> I hate, I despise your feasts (says the Lord)
>   and I don't like the smell of your solemn assemblies
>   [that's a literal translation of the Hebrew]
> Even though you offer me your burnt offerings and
>   cereal offerings,
>   I will not accept them,
> and the peace offerings of your fatted beasts
>   I will not look upon.
> Take away from me the noise of your songs,
>   to the melody of your harps I will not listen.
>   (5:21-23)

"God doesn't like what's going on in your churches," this farmer said. "He doesn't like the smell, the sight, or the sound of the whole business!" And no one, we may be sure, shook his hand after the services and said, "Your message warmed my heart this morning, pastor!"

But why should God reject what was going on in these Israelite places of worship? We find the clue in the text for this Sunday. Here the prophet is speaking to a group of comfortable middle-class people. He begins his words by saying woe, and we need to have a bit of background on what the cry of woe meant in the ancient world.

I used to walk past a church building each day on my way to work. And every so often, I would notice many cars and a long, black hearse by the back door. Then I would hear the bell ring, indicating that a funeral was in progress. (My mother once told me that when she was a girl, the church bells in her town would toll the age of the one who had died. What excitement when an 80- or 90-year-old went to be with the Lord!) But that sound of the bell was a reminder that one day there would be a funeral, and only one person would not go back home again, and that would be me!

The cry of woe was the funeral bell at the time of Amos. Professional mourners would go about the city, crying, "woe, woe," in this way announcing a death. And now Amos addressed these people with a "woe," saying to them, "I'm announcing a funeral, and the funeral is your own!" Listen to his words, once again:

> Woe to those who lie upon beds of ivory,
>   and stretch themselves upon their couches,
> and eat lambs from the flock,
>   and calves from the midst of the stall;
> who sing idle songs to the sound of the harp . . .
> who drink wine in bowls,
>   and anoint themselves with the finest oils,
>   but are not grieved over the ruin of Joseph!

These were a people lounging in luxury, enjoying the sounds of the latest music and the tastes of the finest wines. Amos, who had just announced that God rejected their worship, now adds that God rejects their amusement as well! But why? What was wrong?

The Poor

Think for a moment about those people to whom Amos was speaking. Who were they? They were Israel, God's own special people. And they had received some great things from their God. Amos reminded them of that. "Remember," said he, "that God brought you out of bondage in Egypt, led you through the wilderness, and then gave you this beautiful and bountiful land!" (2:9f.; 3:1f.).

Indeed, God had given them much. And now they enjoyed a prosperity that their ancestors would never have imagined possible. Houses were being built and vineyards were being planted (5:11). Some, in fact, were decorated with expensive ivory. There were a good many who maintained separate residences for the summer and the winter (3:15). The economy was solid. The merchants were busy and, we discover, dutifully closed their stores on the Sabbath (8:5).

Yes, God had given them much. But then what was wrong? The prophet tells us that they were "not grieved over the ruin of

Joseph." They were, in other words, affluent, but unconcerned about the ruin of Joseph or Israel, their nation. As we listen to a few more words from Amos, the picture becomes more clear.

We discover that there were others in Israel for whom these were not good times at all. These were the widows, the poor and the needy. They were trampled upon (2:7), oppressed (4:1), and when they brought their complaints to the courts, dishonest judges accepted bribes so that their cases never got on the dockets (5:12). These were the poor. And when they made purchases downtown, during the week, they were cheated by those same businessmen who piously sang hymns and said prayers at worship on the Sabbath!

These citizens, you see, had made a split, between religion and life. They had a "Sabbath religion." They were faithful about going to worship, paying their pledges, and offering the proper sacrifices. But when they left the church, they left their religion behind. "Business is business, you know!" There must have been some who were honest enough in their business. They may have been honest, and they had become affluent, but this affluence was coupled with an unconcern about the ruin of their nation.

And here this ancient text begins to speak to us. We, too, are a people who have received much from God. He has delivered us, not from bondage in Egypt, but from the bondage of sin, death, and the devil, through the death and resurrection of Jesus Christ. We, too, enjoy a life our ancestors could not have imagined, in this beautiful and bountiful land.

But do we know what it is to make a split between religion and life? Do we know what it is to sing the hymns and pray the prayers on Sunday, and then on Monday—well, "business is business, you know!" Most of us would never think of cheating a poor man or woman. We enjoy the good life which we believe we have earned. We may listen to the latest music, drink the finest wines and lounge in quadraphonic affluence. But could it be that we have not even noticed the widow, the orphan, the poor in our midst? That we are not grieved over the ruin of our nation? Could it be that we who have received so much from a gracious God have been affluent, but unconcerned?

Rich Man, Poor Man

Rich man, poor man . . . That rhyme does catch some of the basic facts of life. The New Testament speaks a good deal about the rich and the poor, too. In fact, at its center is the story of one who was rich, but became voluntarily poor: "For you know the grace of our Lord Jesus Christ, that though he was rich, yet for your sake he became poor, so that by his poverty you might become rich" (2 Cor. 8:9). Jesus was well acquainted with both the rich and the poor. He also had a good many dealings with beggars, and his life ended on a cross between two thieves.

He once told the story which was read as the Gospel for today. There was that rich man who was "clothed in purple and fine linen" and who "feasted sumptuously every day." He sounds very much like those people that Amos was speaking about! But then there was Lazarus, the poor beggar. And it wasn't that the rich man hated Lazarus. Nor did he cheat him, or beat him. It was just that he had never even noticed Lazarus, the needy one, on his doorstep. He was affluent, and unconcerned.

We are called to watch for Lazarus. We have received so much good from the God whom we worship. But the Epistle warns us that the good things that we have may cause problems for us.

> There is great gain in godliness with contentment . . . if we have food and clothing, with these we shall be content . . . For the love of money is the root of all evils; it is through this craving that some have wandered away from the faith.

We are called to watch for Lazarus on our doorstep. Who is Lazarus? Perhaps the lonely widow, who lives just down the block and who is worried about her future. Perhaps the young boy or girl in the neighborhood who would make a fine college student, but who doesn't have the money to get there. Maybe the new family down the block, whose children face a different kind of poverty, that of having no friends.

These texts call us to lift our eyes from our color TVs, to turn down the volume of our stereos, and to look and listen for the hurts of those in our neighborhood and our nation. When we begin to work at healing and helping those hurts, then we may also hear the voice of another, who told us that when we have done something for one of the least of these his people, we have done something for him.

JAMES LIMBURG
Luther-Northwestern Seminaries
St. Paul, Minnesota

HOW TO LIVE IN THE MIDST OF TROUBLE

Twentieth Sunday after Pentecost
Habakkuk 1:1-3; 2:1-4

Anna asked Fynn, "Does Mister God love us truly?" "Sure thing," Fynn answered; "Mister God loves everything." "Oh," she said, "Well then, why does he let things get hurt and dead?" Her voice sounded as if she felt she had betrayed a sacred trust, but the question had been thought and it had to be spoken. "I don't know," Fynn replied. "There's a great many things about Mister God that we don't know about." "Well then," she continued, "if we don't know many things about Mister God, how do we know he loves us?" (*Mister God, This Is Anna*, p. 26).

Every generation encounters pain and struggles to find the reason why. Why does evil seem to run rampant in a world which we believe was created and is ruled by a good God? Why do the righteous so often suffer while the wicked flourish and live in prosperity? Or, we hear the issue raised in more personal terms: Why has this happened to me? What have I done to deserve this? Why doesn't God do something?

In a small and obscure part of the Old Testament, tucked away somewhere in the middle of the minor prophets, is one who raises and sharpens just such questions, though he doesn't answer them on an intellectual level. He lived six hundred years before the birth of Jesus at the time when the country of Judah was on the brink of disaster. Habakkuk was his name. Of the outward circumstances of his life we know nothing. But here was a man with a soul sensitive to hurt, yet firm in his faith in a God both powerful and good.

Habakkuk lived in a dying nation. In 600 B.C., the little kingdom of Judah had thirteen more years to live, but the death pangs had already set in. Judah was a captive nation, barely surviving by paying a yearly, heavy tribute to Assyria, its overlord. Then, for a while, Egypt moved in to take control of Judah until finally the great Chaldean Nebuchadnezzar added Judah to his empire.

Habakkuk's book was produced in the midst of all that. We see it first as a response to all the turmoil, terror, and tragedy of those years. Yet the prophet spoke with a kind of liturgical poetry as though to give his words a universal appeal so that they might speak with a peculiar directness time after time to those of other ages and places who find themselves in deep trouble. We discover that this prophet is helpfully pastoral, giving a word from the Lord on *how to live in the midst of trouble*. Four cues are provided.

Acknowledge the Reality of Evil

This first point is implicit in Habakkuk's action. Habakkuk lived at a time when violence, oppression, and injustice prevailed and strife, contention, and wrangling were rampant throughout Judah. He refused to close his eyes and to pretend that it was not so. God's Law, the constitution of the nation, the heart and soul of Judah's political, religious, and social life was neglected. The few righteous people remaining were so hedged in and restrained by the wicked as to nullify all their efforts to reestablish the authority of God's Law. Judicial decisions were perverted, the judges disregarding the justice or injustice of the cause, as they invariably favored the "right people," their own cliques.

"If God is good and God is all, therefore all is good and evil does not really exist." So reasoned Mary Baker Eddy, the founder of Christian Science. But the Bible never reasoned that way. It insists that evil is not merely an appearance, illusion, or delusion; it is horribly real. It cannot be denied or wished away but must be dealt with in life. Habakkuk begins with the cry of an anguished human being who sees suffering and injustice all around him and, by acknowledging the reality of those evils, refuses to be mockingly cheerful or falsely optimistic.

Nor can we deal realistically with the ills of our day and the maladies of our nation until we acknowledge our twisted values, our neglected duties, our willful pride. As a nation, not unlike Judah, we put our trust in armaments and alliances. Blatant examples reveal that our judicial system by no means guarantees equity. Voices calling for sanity in the nurturing of the earth's limited resources get lost in the cries for bigger and better technological achievements. Prophets of our day are charging that the signs of the decline of American democracy, indeed of Western civilization, have been clearly visible for at least 60 years, and that present problems and crises merely manifest the acceleration of that decline. Signs of alienation, the high incidence of social disruption, the alarming rate of mental illness, increasing tolerance of hedonism, growing religious cultism, and spiraling economic inflation are all historic indicators of revolutionary change. The discerning eye notes that changes are seldom unmixed blessings. It seeks to acknowledge and ferret out the reality of evil in all of life as a first step to living triumphantly in the midst of trouble.

Take Your Complaints to God

Look who's doing the complaining about the evils all about! In contrast with Amos, Micah, or Isaiah, there's a seeming role-reversal in regard to Habakkuk's relationship to God. Here the initiative lies with the prophet, for it is he who is discontented and impatient, while God is the one being questioned. If the Lord is the Ruler of history, why can invaders sweep like a wild avalanche over the world, destroying all patterns of meaning and defying the most elementary human justice?

For a long time Habakkuk had cried to God, "Violence! Oppression!" Yet the Lord, who had chosen Canaan as his land and Judah as his people, had not "saved," had sent no relief to his oppressed children. Iniquity prevailed while the Lord seemingly moved not so much as a finger to punish the evildoers and deliver his oppressed people. Is God complacent? Is he satisfied that such grievances go unrequited? Had God forgotten that in his land his glory was to dwell, mercy and truth were to meet together (Ps. 85:9-13)? Had he lost his power to establish law and order in his land? Why did he not answer the prophet's prolonged cries? Why had he not done anything to make it once more a holy land, and Judah a holy people? Why?

Habakkuk's talk with God may seem rather startling to those who do not know the Bible and who think that persons of faith never speak to God in such a bold way. It seems to many that the way of faith is to wait in patience and silence for God's redemption from trouble. But in the Scriptures we find that it is not unbelief but the strength of one's faith that forces one to ask of God, "How long?" After all, he taught us that his way is a way of justice and righteousness. It is he who has promised us redemption. It is his word that makes us hunger and thirst after righteousness. So if we truly believe the Gospel which has taught us that God is sovereign and righteous, and our Savior, then we must ask, "Why?" and, "How long?"

"The soul of the wounded cries for help; yet God pays no attention to their prayer." That passage from Job 24:12 is surely one of the most terrible statements to be found anywhere in the Bible, and yet, on the human level, isn't that the way it really seems to be, far too much of the time? We say to people in the name of our faith, "God is good, God is just, God is love, God cares for you, God will help if you turn to him," and they *do* turn to him in prayer; they plead for help. But some still die in pain from disease, some are left widows or orphans, some lose their jobs and can't find others, some lose everything by storm or accident, some cannot fight the power of evil and are crushed beneath it.

If we are to be of any help to those who have been crushed by the tragedies of life, I believe that we must cry out, with those victims and with Job and Jeremiah and Habakkuk, Why? and How long? Pain and oppression and injustice are all about, and it is not enough just to say to one suffering that "Christ is the answer." We need to cry with them first and plead with God a bit.

I wonder. Should there not be in our public worship some liturgies such as those in Habakkuk and the psalms of lament? Christian worship so often tends to be all triumph, all good news. Even the confession of sin is not a very awesome experience because we know the assurance of pardon is coming; it's right there next in the green book! Has the Christian community eliminated the need, which Judah recognized so clearly, to lay all the failures and evils of this life very openly before God himself and ask him, as a believing, worshiping community, why and how long?

It has been said that often those who question God's justice are to a great extent indulging in self-pity. That may be true in many cases and we need to beware of falling into that trap; yet that possibility ought not to keep us from any and all serious questionings of God. The danger lurking on the other side is that we become guilty of that "weak resignation to the evils we deplore" of which Harry Emerson Fosdick wrote in his hymn, "God of Grace and God of Glory." And that weak resignation has been known to masquerade under the name of faith.

God is by no means displeased with those who question him. Indeed, perhaps we reveal the depth of our faith that God really does intend to keep his promises when we come to him to ask him how long it will be before we see the fulfillment.

Listen, Even When God's Answer Seems Unsatisfying

God does not answer the prophet's "Why?" Nor does he tell him the reason for delaying his answer so long. The Lord is the sovereign "I Am That I Am." He owes no apology and no explanation of the whys and wherefores of his ways and actions to anyone. Habakkuk knew that, and yet he hoped to receive some instruction that would make him less doubtful, unsettled, and perplexed. Before the preacher can properly teach, he must be sure of his ground. If he could find no answer to his own complaint, how could he hope to answer the same or similar charges raised by the people?

Habakkuk himself cannot answer the questions his reason raises. He has tried until he is at wit's end. Now he will quietly wait to see what God will say to him.

In answer to Habakkuk's prayer of complaint, he is told to write something which came to him from the Lord in a vision. He was to write it in large, clear letters and put it on public display so that even people rushing on their way to work or business or worship or play or sin might read it.

In response to Habakkuk's question "How long?" God says of his promised salvation, "It will surely come, it will not delay." And yet his words seem to contradict themselves. It is hastening but it awaits its time. It will not delay but it seems slow and we must wait for it. In these, at first puzzling words, is to be found God's way of assuring us that there is indeed an answer and that he *will* give it—that he will act on behalf of his people and does not forsake them—but that this can come only in his own good time. At this point we are frankly left with a mystery, because we cannot calculate the time; we do not understand why the time is not now. Only God knows that. And that is where faith comes in.

Hang On in Faithfulness

God assures us that our waiting *will* come to an end—that we do not wait in vain. And he tells us how we can get through that time. He calls upon us to hang on and not give up when there is no explainable reason why we shouldn't. The righteous are they who remain faithful to their God precisely during those times when faith doesn't make sense. When it does not seem reasonable to believe in a good God, when God's justice and mercy are eclipsed, when the righteous do not get rewarded for their goodness—precisely then as in no other time do they prove their righteousness by continuing to be faithful. But this is a promise, as well. He has not just left us on our own, as though hanging in through thick and thin would be a tribute to our courage in the face of a seemingly absent deity. God assures us that in just such hard times the one who remains faithful shall know God's best gift of life. We shall live and not merely exist through it all; we shall not be defeated by the worst that this world can bring. We who have faith in God and are faithful to him will be justified by the life he gives us.

Such faith and faithfulness can be kindled from generation to generation—from grandmother Lois to mother Eunice to son Timothy, as our Epistle declares.

Such a life of faith and faithfulness is our duty as our Gospel reminds; we have been called to it. It does not answer all our questions about evil in God's good world, but we discover that we are able to live in a world where evil exists and not be beaten by it. We discover that we are summoned from speculation to action, from questioning to conduct, from brooding to duty.

Examples of the times when faithfulness is needed and of those who have found the faith to live through them are all about us. There are many Christians who find their churches to be places which discourage rather than encourage, which are willing to use them but which have little to give in return. And some give it up, quit going to worship because they get nothing out of the sermons, quit working because they get criticism instead of thanks, lose all desire to associate with church members whose lives are negative, rather than positive examples of the saving power of Christ. Why should they go on? But—thank God!—not all do that. Again and again we find Christians who stick it out and keep on giving of themselves, without reward or satisfaction, and through them Christ keeps the church alive. Whether or not they know much about Habakkuk, they demonstrate with their lives what he meant by "the righteous one will live by his faithfulness."

There are other ways. How many marriages have lost their romance and yet faithfulness endures? I do not mean the mutually destructive marriages in which each partner is bound to the other to his and the other's hurt. I mean the one-sided marriage in which one partner has much to give but whose own needs may be left largely unfulfilled. Once again, that may lead to unfaithfulness, desertion, or divorce, but sometimes it does not. Today's society may scorn that person who chooses to be self-giving instead of using any means to gain one of our age's highest goals —self-fulfillment. And yet the man or woman who for some reason chooses to be faithful and to do the best that is possible for an unrewarding marriage is showing something which the Old Testament calls steadfast love, covenant love, loyalty to a partner. And it says of such faithfulness, that is how God behaves toward us.

A final example is drawn from my pastoral experience. I have known chronically ill persons who have had little to look forward to in this life except pain and increasing disability, yet who have not become bitter, have not given up on life, who have relished whatever good they could still find and have given whatever they had left to give. Surely these people, whether they ever thought about Habakkuk 2:4 or not, were living it.

In review, our First Lesson gives us four cues on how to live in the midst of trouble: (1) acknowledge the reality of evil; (2) take your complaints to God; (3) listen, even when God's answers seem unsatisfying; and (4) hang on through faithfulness.

We have more reason than Habakkuk had to hang in faithfully. Our Lord Jesus was faithful in his work of redemption. His faithfulness inspires our own.

ALLAN H. SAGER
Trinity Lutheran Seminary
Columbus, Ohio

THE LESSON OF HISTORY

Twenty-first Sunday after Pentecost
Ruth 1:1-19a

When the eminent historians Will and Ariel Durant recently finished compiling their monumental ten-volume lifework, *The Story of Civilization,* they decided to write one more volume entitled *The Lessons of History* to summarize what can be learned: that, given human selfishness, democracy seems to have done less harm and more good than any other form of government; that nations not only don't get along well, but tend to cooperate only when they face a threat from a common enemy; and that whenever a few people grab up most of the wealth, the rest have a tendency to rise up and insist upon a redistribution.

Then the Durants kept working, condensing, until finally they were able to encapsulate the lessons of history into three words.

By this time the Durants had long since ended their association with church or synagogue, so their choice does not reflect a religious bias. It was with surprise, therefore, and with delight, that many of us listened to their final three-word summary of all the lessons of human history: the words "Love one another."

These are the same three words that John uses again and again in his first epistle. He writes:

> This is what love is: it is not that we have loved God, but that he loved us and sent his son. . . . Dear friends, if this is how God loved us, then we should love one another. (TEV)

Tradition has it that when John was very old and about to die, the students of this man who had been with Jesus gathered around him. "Tell us," they urged him, "what is most important."

And the great old apostle John, aged and weak, answered them slowly, "Love one another."

"We already know that!" one of his students said impatiently. "What else? Tell us more!"

"If you love one another," John said slowly, "that is enough."

Whatever Became of Commitment?

There is much talk today of self-fulfillment. Husbands abandon their wives and children to find their real selves; wives leave their husbands and small children to seek what they hope will be a more fulfilling life. Ruth in our lesson today stands in sharp contrast.

The story of Ruth is often used in wedding sermons because it epitomizes the love needed to establish a good home. "Where you go, I will go. Where you live, I will live. Your people will be my people, and your God, my God."

Her words are a bit different from those of some of today's conditional marriage contracts: "I will live with you as long as you do the vacuuming, keep the car washed, and take out the garbage." Or "I will live with you as long as things go just right for us." What has become of commitment? What has happened to "for better for worse, for richer for poorer, in sickness and in health"? How can there be a marriage without sharing and caring, without forgiveness?

The Most Difficult Relationships

But the Ruth story also speaks to all of our other close personal relationships. Naomi and Ruth were, after all, mother-in-law and daughter-in-law, one of the most difficult of all relationships. They must many times have had their differences. No two people can live in such close proximity without problems. But they must have learned to talk things over, listening to each other, trying to understand the other's feelings and needs. They must have many times decided to forgive and forget, to laugh, to hug each other, and to celebrate that they were God's people. The story of Ruth shows us that even in the most difficult of human relationships love is possible.

The Center of the Universe

Certainly love, the kind of love that God has for us, is the center of all that is. Paul writes,

> Now abide these three: faith, hope, and love.
> And the greatest of these is love.

In the story of Ruth and Naomi we see, acted out, this kind of love. Naomi, her husband, and two sons have gone from their home in Bethlehem, which is west of the Dead Sea, around to the east side to the land of Moab, because there is a famine in their own land. And while they are there, the husband dies and the two sons take Moabite wives. And then the two sons die, leaving their mother, Naomi, and their wives, Ruth and Orpah.

At this point Orpah returns to her own people. But Ruth chooses to remain with Naomi. Does she do this because she sees Naomi's need to be cared for as she grows old? Ruth can perhaps remarry and provide a home for her.

Or has Naomi become a very good friend as well as a mother-in-law? Have they developed a close relationship that Ruth would like to continue?

Or does Ruth see Naomi's relationship to the Lord of all creation, a faith that she would like to make her own?

In this story that has rarely been surpassed in all of world literature it is perhaps all of these.

Ruth's Love Is Like Our Lord's

Ruth's love for Naomi shows us, on a smaller scale, the kind of love our Lord has for us:

> *Ruth said,* "Entreat me not to leave you or to return from following you."
>
> *Our Lord has said,* "I will never leave you nor forsake you" (Heb. 13:5).
>
> *Ruth said,* "for where you go I will go, where you lodge I will lodge."
>
> *Our Lord has said,* "Lo, I am with you always, even to the end of the world" (Matt. 28:19-20).
>
> *Ruth said,* "Your people shall be my people, and your God my God."
>
> *Our Lord has said,* "I will take you for my people, and I will be your God" (Exod 6:7)

But all of this can leave us saying, "Wonderful. A great story. But I don't have it in me to love my husband (or wife) or my mother-in-law (or father-in-law) or any of my relatives or friends in this way. I have all I can do to make it through each day. I never get involved in anything as idyllic and beautiful as the story of Ruth and Naomi."

The story *does* seem beautiful as we look back on it. It has inspired numerous works of poetry, music, and art. But to the people who actually *lived* it—the famine, the deaths, the widowhood—it was anything but idyllic.

All Ruth and Naomi have left is the love of God for them. But that, of course, is enough. It is, in fact, everything. With it they are able to make their way back to Bethlehem, taking perhaps the same route the wise men from the East would take more than a thousand years later to pay homage to one who would be a direct descendant of Ruth and Naomi.

The important part of this story is *where* Ruth and Naomi find the strength to pick up the pieces of their lives. Naomi has been greatly embittered by all she has had to go through. When they reach Bethlehem she tells her friends to call her "Mara," which means "bitter." "The Almighty has dealt very bitterly with me," she says. "I went away full, and the Lord has brought me back empty. Why call me Naomi (which means "my delight") when the Lord has afflicted me and the Almighty has brought calamity upon me?"

But gradually Naomi's bitterness leaves, and the dark night of her soul gives way to dawn, so that when Ruth returns one day from the fields to tell her that she has been helped by a good man named Boaz, Naomi is able to say, "Blessed be he by the Lord, whose kindness has not forsaken the living or the dead!"

How We Are Able to Love

Love, after all, originates with God. "We love," John says, "because he first loved us." Even Ruth's love looks pale in comparison with the love that God has for us. Ruth could stay with her mother-in-law as long as she herself were living, but our Lord promises to stay with his people through all time and eternity.

Ruth could die where Naomi died and be buried there, but our Lord can also raise us again to new life.

Ruth's love for Naomi goes to the limit of our imagination, but our Lord's love for us goes far beyond.

The story of Ruth reminds us that God has broken into human history, with all its selfishness, bloodshed, and greed, sending his Son. And we are able to love because he first loved us.

Thanks be to God for this great gift. Amen.

BARBARA JURGENSEN
First Lutheran Church
Chicago, Illinois

THE BLESSING OF STRUGGLE

Twenty-second Sunday after Pentecost
Genesis 32:22-30

God's Children Struggle

Jacob, your life was a wrestling match. You had your brother by the heel when you were born. On the bank of the Jabbok, you grabbed hold of God's toe and wouldn't let go. You were a person who wrestled with himself. In our age many claim that the life of the faithful should be all bliss and sweet Jesus. But you, Jacob, showed us a different side of the faith. You showed us that the life of the faithful can often be described as a wrestling match. Indeed, you showed us that faithfulness includes struggle. It can even be said in stronger words. There are times when struggle itself is faith. There are times when we struggle with God, neighbor, and ourselves; all within the context of being faithful.

A faith that does not struggle is a dead faith. A faith that does not struggle indicates that a person or people are comfortable for the wrong reasons. Throughout the history God has sent his prophets and teachers to engage his people in a wrestling match of faith, and when there was no one to send, God himself entered the ring. Jacob found that out as he sat alone on the riverbank across from his family.

It is good to keep this in mind should we ever be tempted to follow the leadership of many of the alleged Christian programs now shown on television. Many of these programs have the image of being a kind of "Jesus Chamber of Commerce." A parade of smiling faces, endomorphic wastelines, and rags to riches stories seem to tell us that "you, too, could become a Christian with a Cheshire smile. All you have to do is dial the following toll-free number and we'll fill you with the Holy Ghost for a modest donation."

Jacob's night on the Jabbok was more realistic. In the intensity of a sleepless night he sweat and struggled. It is not clear what his feelings were. Perhaps there was a continuation of the fear and distress he had known. Perhaps there was guilt. Perhaps there was apprehension about the future. We can only make assumptions. One thing, however, is very clear. God was there. In the midst of it all he wrestled with the purpose to make everyone a winner. He wrestled with the purpose to make everyone a blessing.

One wonders how Israel might have understood this story when the monarchy seemed impervious to other powers or to destruction. Whenever Israel reached a position of power and security there was always the danger of giving up the wrestling match. There was always the danger of coasting along, having little regard for others, and assuming that God was "on your side." One can almost hear the Yahwist exegete this text to make clear something quite different. The text suggests that if we cease to wrestle with God and with life, then we have already given up and have been pinned to the earth by another power; be it prosperity, dependence on military power, or a desire to deny that there is a world out there beyond our electric can openers or twelve-year-old Scotch.

Jacob wrestled. Jacob struggled, as do all of God's chosen people.

Trickery or Treat

Jacob also wrestled with himself. His greatest strength was also his greatest weakness. He was very good at getting what he wanted. His entire history demonstrated an ability to master people and situations. He was a master of trickery. He outwitted his brother of his birthright and outwitted Laban when he fled without losing his possessions. Jacob's name meant supplanter, one who acquires through deception or force. Underneath his obvious success lay serious questions. Could he continue to depend on his trickery? What did it mean to be one of God's people? What did it mean to be blessed? How would he face his brother whose birthright he had stolen?

Jacob may have tried to forget that much of what he had had been stolen from his brother. He knew that things just didn't fall into his lap. He knew that he could not boast about ill-gotten power and ill-gotten possessions. Hidden away in a back closet were the bones of his treachery. He could not take pleasure in having stolen a birthright. And yet, God had not destroyed him. He survived and in good fashion. Still, there had to have been a nagging kind of uneasiness about how he had gotten his place at his brother's expense. The time called for him to be honest about his past. He had to be open to himself and to God.

There is an uneasiness in our own past. As individuals many of us have placed ourselves in front at the expense of others. Turkeys are currently growing plump for next month's Thanksgiving dinners. But what about the birthright of the people? What about the people who have been sacrificed and lost for our own gain? Does the stamping of "In God We Trust" on our homemade manna somehow legitimize our existence and convince God that our nation as a whole really does?

We must be honest. Haven't we also stolen the birthright from our own brothers? The copper in our wires was largely taken for pennies from our South American neighbors with little benefit to the common people. The diamonds which adorn our rings were dug by the sweat and struggle of our black brothers in Africa, who die an early death and earn incredibly low wages for their efforts. Many of our industrial giants had their beginnings through the exploitation of children, poor whites, poor blacks, and other immigrants. In the early 1800s children made up close to 45% of the work force in New England textile plants. Women and children would go to work at 4:30 in the morning and would generally work 12 to 13 hours a day. Many of our national leaders are wealthy because of the sacrifice of human life and dignity given by men, women, and children not too many years ago. The population of our native Americans has been decimated and the strengths of their culture have been largely crushed.

It is easy to say that God has blessed us. The words easily run off our tongues. Indeed, God has blessed us, but perhaps not in the way we often think. Perhaps the greatest blessing is that he has preserved us thus far in spite of our greed and folly.

Jacob had not been the only supplanter in history. We are not where we are by virtue of completely pure motives or ambitious drive. Even the history of many of our nation's communities shows that many people have created their own little kingdoms by supplanting their neighbors. Sometimes they have done so through betrayal. Sometimes it has been done through twisting words and bending promises. Sometimes it has been done through legal channels, which shows that what is legal is not always just.

Jacob's struggle has become ours. Can we live by our wits? Is trickery and double talk acceptable if it gives us what we want? Are we to deal with our neighbors, whether next door or nationally, on a position of fear? What does it mean to be a brother? What does it mean to share a globe with four billion other people? No doubt Jacob could have continued to live for a while longer by relying on his clever skills of manipulation and strategy. So can we, but is that really life? Is that the life God would have us or our nation lead? Is that what it means to be faithful? Is that how the blessed live?

Blessed to Be a Blessing

The answer is no. We do not live by trickery but, if you will, by treating. We do not live by betrayal but by blessing. We hear the echo of Genesis 12 where Yahweh told Abraham that he was blessed to be a blessing. Jacob's struggle with God confirms what it means to be one who is blessed. Power and wealth are insignificant. It can be a blessing but it can also be the product of stolen birthrights. Even Babylon and Syria had those things. To live by being a blessing to others is the point to which Jacob had been led. God blessed Jacob by struggling with him. It was that struggle with God which was more important than any of the possessions Jacob acquired. Jacob's struggle with God confirmed what it meant to be one of God's people.

The story of Jacob wrestling with God also confirmed what is hinted at in preceding and following verses. It confirmed what the blessed life is. It confirms what it means to be a blessing. In Genesis 32:18, Jacob offers gifts to the brother he had previously tricked and defeated. Of more significance, Jacob recognizes the face of God, not in some other mysterious wrestling match, but in the face of his weaker and less wise brother. In recognizing God in the face of his brother, he lives!

Jacob's struggle later became the monarchy's struggle as it had to determine what kind of people they would be to their neighbors, who had a history of being cruel to Israel before Israel conquered them. The answer goes against our grain, but not against the grain of God's graciousness. The answer is, once again, that one is to be a blessing.

Jacob's struggle is now our struggle as we enter the third century. As a whole our people have emphasized living by strength, cleverness, and even treachery. Our national benevolence to other nations is far less than one percent of our budget and ranks below a number of other countries. Could it be that God is calling us to be weak instead of strong? Could it be that he is telling us that there is more strength and life in being a blessing than in being belligerent? Could it be that he is calling us to be servants to the third and fourth world nations, instead of being lords? Could it be that he is calling us to look for his face in the face of the people we have rejected or given little consideration?

Perhaps the wrestling match is not yet over for us. Still, one thing remains clear, God will wrestle with us as long as he has to, and it is through wrestling with God that we are blessed, blessed to be a blessing.

JACK C. LEININGER
The Lutheran Churches of
Fort Peck, Frazer, and Nashua, Montana

THE CHOSEN

Twenty-third Sunday after Pentecost
Deuteronomy 10:12-22

When sides are being selected for a game, what child is there who does not long to be chosen quickly, surely, and with rejoicing? Certainly you remember those times of eager and anxious waiting, hoping against hope that you would not be left too long, hoping that your air of nonchalance was convincing, hoping to be chosen. And if such choosing came early, and eagerly, do you not recall that there was joy in your step and in your face?

Such memories are bittersweet for me. It is because the child is not ever quite gone from us and the longing to be chosen still lurks deep in our hearts. It is there when a student waits for a good word from a teacher. It is there when a merchant waits for someone to come into the store. It is there when a mother waits in the night for a child to return home. It is there when an old person waits for a visit from a son or daughter. Such memories are bittersweet, for the child is still within us; the child who wants to be selected, to be set apart, to be lifted up, to be chosen.

Sometimes we are chosen by a kind word, or by the sound of familiar steps in the night, or by a smile across a crowded room. This choosing is our daily joy and sorrow. But our text speaks of another choosing; a choosing which is not fleeting but lasting, both daily and once and for all. It is the choice which our Lord God has made of us, of you and of me. It is an amazing story; the story of how God himself, who has stretched out the heavens and formed the Pleidies and Orion, has set his heart on us. He has looked down on us from his celestial throne to see our wanderings and has chosen us to be his very own. That one who walks on the ethers of the far reaches and knows the deepest depths of the great seas has chosen us as his sons and daughters. It is quite a story, this choosing, and when we know that it is our own, it brings joy and peace to that deep place within us that longs to belong.

The Christian church is simply the company of the chosen. Once, when our fathers went down into Egypt, we were no people; but now we are God's people and he has made us as the stars in heaven in multitude. What is that ancient crossing of the sea but our history, our choosing? What is that promise to David but the calling of the church? And now, in these latter days, the God of the heavens has drawn near to us in his Son. In his suffering and death the church sees its choosing, the choosing of the Father in his love. How strange it is not to think of some other people as the chosen ones, but to know that we, the church, are his own.

It is strange because we already sense that to be chosen is to be called to live the life of sons and daughters, to stand as the church of Christ in the world. It is to trust in the one who has chosen us. It is to bear a calling that seeks our hearts and our deeds, a calling that longs to work its way into the world in love. To be his chosen ones means to fear God, to walk in his ways, and to serve him with heart and soul. Above all it means to be a sojourner in the earth, a wanderer who reaches out in service to other sojourners. It means to be at peace and yet not at peace, at rest and yet restless, at home and yet not at home. It means to be a sojourner who can reach out in love to other sojourners as they pass through these valleys and along the heights. It means to be a wandering minstrel in praise of that one who has chosen us through his mighty deeds.

I wonder if we really want to be the chosen ones of this God who wandered with Israel in the cloud and in the fire. I wonder if we really want to be the chosen ones of that dear son who turned steadfastly toward Jerusalem and death. I wonder if we want to be chosen if it means being an obedient and sojourning servant; I wonder if the church wants that. Is it not rather our youthful desire simply to be chosen to some fixed and sure position, as though we enjoy being recognized but cannot stand being loved? It is one thing to be chosen but quite another to be made an obedient sojourner by it.

Chosen sojourners of our Lord are to keep the Commandments; we are simply called and commanded to obey the laws of God. On this side of heaven our destiny as his chosen ones is not yet complete. This is why our sojourn has elements of both joy and sadness; joy because we are chosen and we know that one day all of our tears shall have been transformed into gladness, but sadness because we know that even as chosen ones we still live on the edge of chaos and death. Don't you sometimes sense around you the turbulent gathering of the water of chaos, the undertow of that river of lawlessness which seeks to bear us on its rushing course into the abyss? Our frightened glances communicate our fear: our fear of institutions that we don't trust, and our fear of a society without morality. It is almost as though we have forgotten the old words: "Thou shalt have no other gods before me," "Thou shalt not steal," "Thou shalt not bear false witness." We don't even teach these things to our children anymore. But the message is clear; we cannot be free sojourners in this world if we do not obey his commands. To be a disobedient wanderer is to be afraid of the chaos which always threatens to rush in.

Chosen sojourners of our God are to show love and mercy to other sojourners; we are to reach out to them with compassion. Isn't there a certain acceptable way for us to disobey this command, a virtuous way of remaining stubborn before God? It is the way of our pride; more particularly, the way of our religious pride. This is to remember only that we are chosen and not to remember that we are also sojourners. It is to try to build our permanent house out of our decent talk with religious people while at the same time we do not see the need and the pain in the eyes of our brothers and sisters. It is to be obedient but then to speak harshly of that one who has fallen into some agony and trouble. It is to keep clean hands to handle the articles of religious worship but to forget that our worship is of that one who died between two thieves. It is to succumb to the satisfaction of being with good and respectable people, but to forget the wanderers with hungry eyes who sit in shadows on sunny days. We want to be chosen but not to be sojourners; and so, we cannot look into the faces of the wanderers in our world for we know that if we do we shall see the face of Christ himself.

Dearly beloved, if we ask how we measure up to the demand of this text that we obey the commandments and show love and mercy to the needy, we may not like the answers that we find. And if we ask those same questions about the church in our time, the answers may not be much better.

Church history teaches us that the Christian church has always been marked by the sins of the world. Yet, it was said of those early Christians that they could be known by their obedience to God's commands. I wonder if that can be said now. Isn't it rather the case that we do not take the commandments very seriously, and that we cover our weak disobedience with the sounds of cheap benedictions?

And can it truly be said that the church is a wanderer showing love and mercy to other wanderers in the world? To much of the world it does not seem so. Rather the church seems indifferent, standing fast upon some height with doors closed. The church seems more and more turned in upon itself; like an old person whose task is done and who reminisces about former days.

I wonder if we really want to be the chosen ones of the God who wandered with Israel in the cloud and in the fire. I wonder if we really want to sojourn with that Nazarene who went down to his painful place between two thieves. I wonder if you want that, if I want that, if the church wants that. We want to be chosen but perhaps not to be obedient wanderers on the earth.

Certainly Israel questioned if she could be an obedient sojourner. Certainly now, after those years in the wilderness, Israel was ready to be at rest. Certainly now Israel did not want to hear the command to be obedient sojourners reaching out in love to widows and orphans. Yet, this word came to Israel from the very one who had given them life and traveled with them on the way. He was the one who had seen them from the great heights and set his heart upon them. He was the one who had raised up Moses to lead them out of bondage and now stood ready to give them a land. He was the one, the Lord God, who had given them little Isaac and had made them as numerous as the stars in heaven.

Certainly Israel did not want to hear this word now. That is, they did not want to hear this call until they recognized his voice; the voice of that one who had tended them in their youth, given them food in the passage through barren wastes, and now waited to give them those rolling hills beyond the river. When Israel heard the voice of the Lord God, then his call to obedience became a call to joy and his call to wandering service became a call to freedom. It was as when a dear, dear friend speaks and we are called into service by the speaking.

Dearly beloved, have you forgotten who has chosen you, whose voice it is that is your call? It is the very one whose path is the aurora borealis in the sky. It is the very one who bears the condor in its flight and sweeps away the darkness with the dawn; the very one who broods in the budding of each tree and rests beneath the sleeping face of a little child. It is this one, the almighty God, who has seen your wandering and made it his own; it is this one whose voice you hear. It is the voice of the wandering God in Israel who could not be contained in any place; the voice of the loving God of Israel who surprised old Sarah with new life and who stood by Moses in his task. It is the voice that came from Sinai's height, the voice of that one who tenderly bound up the wounds of Israel and cared for the orphan child. It is the voice of the one who in these latter days has come to us in his only son; his only son who was obedient even unto death, who loved us and loves us still. It is his voice that calls us in this text; that calls us into obedience with joy, into the life of a wandering servant in freedom.

Dear friends, do not be surprised, if you have heard that voice, that you should find new strength for obedience and new compassion for other sojourners. Do not be surprised if your heart goes out to those who look at you with a look that becomes the face of Christ himself. Do not be surprised if you find some way to dry their tears, to lighten their burdens, and give joy to their sadness. Do not be surprised; there is no telling what might happen when we are his chosen ones and he is with us in our wandering.

Dearly beloved, let it be our prayer that the Christian church might be enlivened by this calling. If the church is weak in its obedience, may it be given strength that it did not know and vigor that it did not possess. If the church is tempted to turn in upon itself, may it be reminded of that upper room where tongues of fire made messengers of ordinary folk. If the church does not dare to suffer with the suffering world, let it be given love and mercy by that one who healed the sick and calmed the troubled spirits. If the church does not want to be a loving wanderer, giving itself over to the world; let it know that it does not sojourn alone.

SHELDON TOSTENGARD
Luther-Northwestern Seminaries
St. Paul, Minnesota

STORIES OF GOD

Twenty-fourth Sunday after Pentecost
Exodus 34:5-9

We tell stories of God, and in the telling of them God speaks to us. The exodus is one such story, the most significant of the stories which make up our Old Testament. Of course, it is part of a larger story. We remember that before the exodus story we have the great prologue to the human story and the stories of the patriarchs. Following the exodus there are stories of wandering and conquest, of judges and kings, of exile and return, of rise and fall. Indeed, if we understand Paul correctly (Rom. 11:29), the story is still going on.

But somehow, the book called Exodus is at the heart of it. When the people formulated their creed, the exodus story was its content.

> We were Pharaoh's slaves in Egypt; and the Lord brought us out of Egypt with a mighty hand; and the Lord showed signs and wonders, great and grievous, against Egypt and against Pharaoh and all his house-

hold, before our eyes; and he brought us out from there, that he might bring us in and give us the land which he swore to give to our fathers. And the Lord commanded us to do all these statutes, to fear the Lord our God, for our good always, that he might preserve us alive, as at this day. And it will be righteousness for us, if we are careful to do all this commandment before the Lord our God, as he has commanded us (Deut. 6:21-25).

Or in another version of the creed,

A wandering Aramean was my father; and he went down into Egypt and sojourned there, few in number; and there he became a nation, great, mighty and populous. And the Egyptians treated us harshly, and afflicted us, and laid upon us hard bondage. Then we cried to the Lord the God of our fathers, and the Lord heard our voice, and saw our affliction, our toil, and our oppression; and the Lord brought us out of Egypt with a mighty hand and an outstretched arm, with great terror, with signs and wonders; and he brought us into this place and gave us this land, a land flowing with milk and honey. And behold, now I bring the first of the fruit of the ground, which thou, O Lord, hast given me (Deut. 26:5-10).

The story of the exodus is not one among Israel's stories. It is the formative, people-shaping story. It is the word through which the character of his people and the depth of God are revealed.

A National Saga

Think of how the story begins. We can hear it as if we were telling it. We were enslaved, the story goes, through no fault of our own. After all, "it was not unusual for families and clans of bedouins from Palestine and Sinai to enter Egypt in hard times and live along the border" (Wright and Fuller, *The Book of the Acts of God*, p. 76). How were we to know that there would arise "a new king over Egypt, who did not know Joseph" (Exod. 1:8), and that we would become slaves? It was hard, but we survived. And then, one day, we were rescued! True, we could hardly claim credit for that. We were not exactly ready to follow Moses (Exod. 2:14), nor was he all that eager to lead (Exod. 4:1ff.). But in one way or another, we were eventually delivered.

Justice at last. We were the "people whom the justice of the world had passed by, a people for whom there was no protecting law" (Wright, p. 73). That God delivered us shows that there is justice after all. The Egyptians got what was coming to them. And we got our rights. About time, too, after all those centuries of oppression.

That is a saga worthy of a nation. With variations it gets told again and again. Alexander Nevsky led the Russian people in battle against the conquering Knights of the Teutonic Order in A.D. 1242. The knights were eventually defeated on the ice of Lake Chud near Pskov, and many of the Germans were driven through the ice and drowned. This victory gave courage to the Russian people during the German invasion of World War II as they retold the story in the cantata by Sergei Prokofiev. The final chorus of the cantata is a mighty hymn of victory full of bells and shouts and national pride.

Even more like the beginnings of the exodus story is our own United States national saga. Emigrants, fleeing economic, military, and religious oppression, were given the untamed wilderness of North America. There they harnessed the land and its resources, built cities and linked them through commerce and communication, and created a "new order of the ages" (see the Great Seal's *novus ordo saeclorum* still printed on every dollar bill). Oppressed once again by the English king, they defeated the armies of the tyrant and won independence. It was a hard fight, but justice triumphed at last. We got our rights—and about time, too.

A Covenant God

Exodus doesn't end the story of Israel's beginnings on that note. As they traveled in their escape, every adversity they encountered evoked grumbling from the people and new wonders from God. At Sinai there was a great covenant. "I am the Lord your God, who brought you out of the land of Egypt, out of the house of bondage" (Exod. 20:2). They were to be his people and he their God. A great *Book of the Covenant* (Exod. 20:22-23:33) gave the people a form for their nationhood, a way to be identified as God's own people. They ratified the covenant with one voice: "All the words which the Lord has spoken we will do" (Exod. 24:3).

This is a great story of God, the kind of story we like to tell. Except that up to this point the story does not yet include those aspects of our experience which make our stories lies. So far the story reveals neither the dark side of our own character nor the depth of God's Word to us. The most important part of the exodus story still needs telling. The Old Testament Lesson for today is from that most important part—the narrative unit in Exodus 32–34. At the deepest level, we need a story big enough for our dark side. In the final analysis, the covenant is not that Israel received justice, but that she received mercy. "The depth of the riches and wisdom and knowledge of God," that which is unsearchable in his judgments and inscrutable in his ways (Rom. 11:33) is not his justice, but his grace!

Story of Sin

Exodus 34 is the astonishing revelation that concludes the story of Israel's beginnings. It is part of a tragic story. Moses' stay on the mountain evoked more grumbling. Coming on the heels of the offered and received covenant, the grumbling produced impatience, and the impatience produced catastrophe. Catastrophe? To us it might seem like harmless religious window shopping. Join the church of your choice, says our story. But if we are telling stories of *God*, then what followed was catastrophic. The people who had been delivered from bondage, fed in the wilderness, awed by the encounter at Sinai, consecrated by the covenant, the people who had responded "with one voice" now come to Aaron for new gods! Aaron makes them a bull, and now the people of *God* can worship just like their neighbors: with fertility games designed to evoke new beginnings from the gods!

That is the dark side—not our orgies, but our religions. We want gods that we can manipulate, religious stories that will justify our enterprises and privileges, rituals that will make us feel good, priests who will do our bidding. These self-made gods enable the affluent to know that their prosperity is only the divine reward for their industry and wisdom, that both affluence and poverty are simply economic justice. These self-made gods enable the pious emigrants to displace the heathen savages, enable whites to enslave blacks, enable the righteous to wage war on the godless. These self-made gods enable us to cover our greed and cruelty and pride with the comfortable rationalizations of piety. We are, after all, the chosen. We have covenanted with our gods.

Story and Judgment

The exodus story shatters that comfortable piety. It is a hard word: the story of God who wants to be left alone so "that my wrath may burn hot against them and I may consume them" (Exod. 32:10); the story of God who wants to start over with a new patriarch (Moses) and a new people; the story of a God who visits plague and death on a rebellious and idolatrous people.

But this is not yet the depth of the story of God. If it ended here, it would be predictable. Such judgments of God would be searchable, such ways scrutable. We understand that. We respond with hot anger and far less provocation. Washington columnist Colman McCarthy writes about a hot anger which justified increased military expenditures because we must be able to retaliate against our enemies and at the same time justifies decreased welfare expenditures because we must be able to retaliate against those who victimize the taxpayer. Yes, we can understand a God who has had it with a "stiff-necked people."

Story and Grace

What is incredible is that God would not give up on his people. When we tell the *whole* story of God, we encounter a God big enough for redemption! Come up, he says to Moses. Bring new tablets of stone. Hear the name of the Lord, that is, the depth of his being, that is, what dies at the heart of God. It is that to which we have no right. It is that upon which we have no claim. The consequence of our unfaithfulness is that there is no way in which we can tell the story of deliverance and covenant as if we were only getting justice. Now the deepest grounding of the covenant is evident:

> The LORD, the LORD, a God merciful and gracious, slow to anger, and abounding in steadfast love and faithfulness, keeping steadfast love for thousands, forgiving iniquity and transgression and sin . . .

Forgiveness

So we tell stories of God, and in the telling of them God speaks to us. He tells us in our stories that he forgives. When they are true stories, we know that forgiveness does not mean excusing us. There is no hiding behind excuses—leaders blaming the people ("you know the people, that they are set on evil," Exod. 32.22) or circumstances beyond their control ("I threw it into the fire, and there came out this calf," Exod. 32:24). When our stories are true, we know that forgiveness does not mean that God or we can act as if nothing went wrong.

> I will by no means clear the guilty, visiting the iniquity of the fathers upon the children and the children's children, to the third and fourth generation.

Forgiveness does not pretend there had been no breach of covenant. Forgiveness does not overlook the past. It *overcomes* the past. God commits himself to his people in the midst of, in spite of, our being a stiff-necked people. Forgiveness means that we are able to live with his judgment, to live with the consequences of sin, without despair.

The Ultimate Story

Moses offered to exchange his life for the forgiveness of the people (Exod. 32:32). This is the mark of a true story of God. The story knows that there is no forgiveness without cost. But Moses cannot bear the cost. The story is a true story because it knows that only the forgiver can bear the cost—by taking the hurt of sin into himself. Moses can plead for, but he cannot be the basis of, God's forgiveness.

When we tell the ultimate story of God, it includes that visit to Jericho and the dinner party at the house of Zacchaeus. No one in Jericho had less claim to the right of hosting the visiting rabbi. No incident could more vividly embody the God of the exodus covenant renewal:

> The LORD, the LORD, a God merciful and gracious, slow to anger, and abounding in steadfast love and faithfulness, keeping steadfast love for thousands, forgiving iniquity and transgression and sin. . . .

For the one who visits Zacchaeus is the one who renews the covenant. He has the authority to forgive because he takes the hurt of our sin into himself. In the ultimate story of God his name is Jesus, Deliverer!

WALTER R. BOUMAN
Trinity Lutheran Seminary
Columbus, Ohio

A DOXOLOGY

Twenty-fifth Sunday after Pentecost

Suggested hymn before the sermon:
"All Hail the Power of Jesus' Name" (328-329, LBW)

1 Chronicles 29:10-13

The most common doxology in our worship life is the one that comes at the end of The Lord's Prayer: "for thine is the kingdom, and the power, and the glory, forever." How interesting to see a larger version of it here in our text for the Twenty-fifth Sunday after Pentecost: "Thine, O LORD, is the greatness, and the power, and the glory, and the victory, and the majesty; for all that is in the heavens and in the earth is thine; thine is the kingdom, LORD, and thou art exalted as head above all. Both riches and honor come from thee, and thou rulest over all. In thy hand are power and might; and in thy hand it is to make great and to give strength to all."

If we were Jewish we would be even more drawn to the opening lines of the text—"Blessed art thou, O LORD, the God of Israel" for that is the formula with which most Jewish prayers begin. As they assemble at the table for food, pious Jews recite this blessing: "Blessed art thou, O Lord, ruler of the universe, for thou makest the earth to give bread." As they drink the sacred cup of wine they alter it only slightly to say, "Blessed art thou, O Lord, ruler of the universe, Creator of the fruit of the vine." Indeed, it may have been blessings like these with which our Lord blessed the bread and the wine on the night in which he was betrayed. Dear to the tradition of both Jews and Christians are the words of the text before us.

David...

And how fitting that they should come from the lips of great King David. We know King David, do we not? We know him as David the giant-killer, David the sweet singer of Israel, David the father of Judah's kings, the first one anointed by God to rule God's people.

Perhaps it would be well to review the story of David as we seek to understand our Old Testament text for the day.

... the Warrior

There is David the warrior, a story that appealed to many of us as we learned our Sunday school lessons in the years of childhood. David was sent to the battlefield, you may recall, to bring food to his brothers who were fighting against the Philistines in the army of King Saul. When young David arrived he found the armies at rest because the Philistines had a secret weapon that stopped the fighting for awhile—a giant of a man who stood nine feet tall and came out each day to challenge the army of Israel with these words, "Choose a man for yourselves and let him come down to me. If he is able to fight with me and kill me, then we will be your servants. But if I prevail against him and kill him, then you shall be our servants and serve us."

Day after day he made this challenge and none of the soldiers in the Israelite army of King Saul dared to accept the challenge. They all feared the giant Philistine.

But when David arrived, fresh from watching his father's sheep, and when he listened to the challenge of the boastful Philistine, he said, "Let no man's courage fail because of him. I will go and fight that Philistine."

The soldiers and David's own brothers were astounded. They took him to King Saul. "You can't fight this Philistine," said the king. "You are only a boy and he is a seasoned soldier."

"I have fought lions and bears to protect the sheep," replied David. "I can also fight this Philistine."

So it was that David was allowed to accept the challenge of the mighty Philistine, whose name, we may remember, was Goliath. The giant came out clad in heavy armor and carrying a spear as large as a small log. And David? He had only his shepherd's skirt, a weapon called a sling and five smooth, round stones he had picked out of the riverbed. The Philistine taunted him. "Come to me, sonny boy, and I will feed you to the birds and the beasts."

"You meet me with a sword and a spear and a javelin," said David. "I come to you in the name of the God of Israel." With that, David hurled one smooth stone with his sling and that stone struck Goliath between the eyes. David stepped forward and killed the giant with the giant's own sword.

That is David the soldier, the Robin Hood of the Judean desert.

. . . the Musician

David the sweet singer is one we also know from the earliest stories. When King Saul became ill-tempered, it was David with his harp and his songs who was alone able to calm the aging king's shattered nerves. And when Saul and his son Jonathan were killed in battle, David composed a beautiful psalm of sorrow in their honor. So famous was David as a singer of psalms that half of the psalms in the Book of Psalms are dedicated to him.

. . . the King

We may also remember from the history of Israel, that David became the first king of a dynasty of kings that ruled all of the tribes of Israel for three-quarters of a century and then ruled the little nation of Judah until it was conquered by Babylonians in 596 B.C. David is remembered—and especially in the books of Chronicles—as the greatest and best of all those kings. Our text for the day is part of what the chronicler knew was a last speech of David the king as he transferred his power and authority to his son Solomon. After that he died, "in a good old age, full of riches and honor," says the chronicler and ever since that all kings were judged by whether they were even nearly as good as King David.

David's Sons: The Messiahs

There was a special covenant between God and the house of David, according to Nathan the prophet and many other prophets and priests. According to that covenant God would rule his people forever through a descendant of David. So strong was the Jewish faith in that covenant that even when times were desperately bad, the people looked to the House of David for salvation. When Assyrian armies invaded their land in the eighth century B.C., Micah spoke of a ruler who would come out of Bethlehem to tend the flock of the Lord; and Isaiah, the prophet in Jerusalem spoke of a child who would be born, a son who would be given that the government might be put upon his shoulder and his name be called Wonderful Counselor, Mighty God, Everlasting Father, Prince of Peace.

As time went on and the fate of the Jewish nation was sealed by the war with Babylon, hope for a Son of David who would save his people became stronger rather than weaker. So it is that we read in the Book of Zechariah this marvelous hymn of hope.

> Rejoice greatly, O daughter of Zion!
> Shout aloud, O daughter of Jerusalem!
> Lo, your king comes to you;
> triumphant and victorious is he,
> humble and riding on an ass,
> on a colt the foal of an ass.
> I will cut off the chariot from Ephraim
> and the war horse from Jerusalem.
> The battle bow shall be broken
> and he shall command peace to the nations.
> His dominion shall be from sea to sea,
> from the River to the ends of the earth.

Jesus as Son of David

This is the vision that was acted out by Jesus on the day that we know as Palm Sunday, when his followers shouted, "Hosanna, Son of David!" And that, in turn, is why we, his disciples of today, all hail the power of Jesus' name and crown him Lord of all.

But what of Jesus himself? It was not his style to accept much glory very often. It was his style to serve and give all glory to his Father. This is that one who "emptied himself" of divine glory and took the form of a servant, according to the apostle Paul. This is that one who also taught us to say, "Give glory to God," so that even when we "confess that Jesus Christ is Lord, it is to the glory of God the Father" (Phil. 2:11).

This is that one who continues to come to us in the disguises of poverty so that we may give glory to God with deeds of mercy and not merely with words—by feeding the hungry, clothing the naked, visiting those who are sick or in prison and giving so much as a cup of cold water to the least of his brethren.

The very best way to speak the glorious words of our text, then, is by silent deeds of mercy. Here in public worship we can sing them to the swell of the organ or the blare of trumpets. In the days between we must declare God's glory through goodness in human living.

Is Jesus King?

In his own generation Jesus was known as "rabbi" or teacher to his disciples and as a prophet and worker of wonders to the people at large. Later generations, however, have consistently known him as *Christ*, which is the old Jewish title for a king. We even go so far to call him King of the World. But is he? Does he rule over presidents and prime ministers and generals and kings? Not in any way that is obvious at all.

Perhaps he rules through the needs of the world. Perhaps he rules us all through the hungry and the poor. Perhaps it is in honoring the poor and the needy that we best serve our king and live lives that do give all power and glory and victory to God.

What would happen to our world if we dared to believe such a thought?

Suggested hymn after the sermon:
"Where Restless Crowds Are Thronging" (430, LBW)

RICHARD SIMON HANSON
Luther College
Decorah, Iowa

WHAT KIND OF A KING?

Christ the King — Last Sunday after Pentecost
Jeremiah 23:2-6

One of the courses that I enjoyed in high school and college was the history course that dealt with the Middle Ages. One of the moments that thrilled me was in the year 1095, when Pope Urban II launched the First Crusade. It was a part of a reform movement that had its roots in Cluny of southern France. Its destination was Jerusalem, and its purpose was the liberation of Jerusalem from the Turks. Over the years, there were a number of crusades with this same objective.

The Church Year as Pilgrimage

This is the last Sunday of the church year. It is called Christ the King Sunday. I don't know whether you have ever thought of our liturgy as a crusade or pilgrimage, but a number of people have begun to consider it in these terms. A good example is Reginald Fuller's discussion on this Sunday in *Preaching the New Lectionary*. Fuller reminds us that the biblical God acted at certain times and in certain places. It would be safe to say that his acts in history centered around Jerusalem. This is why the liturgy seeks to take us on a pilgrimage, each Sunday, back to Jerusalem. Some of you will recall the anvil which blacksmiths used. Jerusalem is the historical anvil, as it were, on which God pounded out our salvation.

Our Gospel for this morning tells us about the climax of the historical drama which took place at Jerusalem. Our First Lesson from Jeremiah 23 tells us about a much earlier act in this drama.

The Turbulent Days of Jeremiah

The ministry of Jeremiah is interwoven with the final days of the southern monarchy. In some respects, his age is not much different from our age. It was fraught with all kinds of rebellion. Jeremiah contended that in response to this rebellion, God would act. For the purpose of judgment, God would use Nebuchadnezzar of Babylon as his servant. The king of Judah at this time was Zedekiah. He was to become the king of Judah. In our first lesson, we meet a wordplay on the part of the prophet. It centers around the name of Zedekiah. To this we shall return.

What is Jeremiah trying to say to the people of his day? He directs his message to the shepherds of Judah, who were the political and especially the religious leaders of these people. Jeremiah contends that they have been weak, with no clear grasp of the purpose of God. They did not have the courage to proclaim the word of God in its offensiveness. Because these shepherds were not faithful and because the people wandered after them, God acted in this Babylonian judgment to scatter them. Jeremiah witnessed the deportation of these people from Jerusalem to Babylon. However, this will not be the end of God's purpose, the prophet asserts. "The days are coming," says the Lord, "when I will raise up for David a righteous branch."

What Kind of a King for Latter Days?

What kind of a king will God raise up to rule over his people in the latter days? He will be like Zedekiah, and yet he will be different. The name Zedekiah means "The Lord is my righteousness." Zedekiah knew that the biblical God was righteous and that he expected the kings of Judah to rule with the norms and standards of righteousness and justice. In this respect, Zedekiah was not the ideal king. At the same time, he was not among the worst kings. Under pressure, he was weak; however, he did have some concern for righteousness.

Jeremiah and the other prophets were much concerned with how justice worked its way out in history. We shall not attempt to get into the details of their convictions on this point in this message. They believed in a person's right to own and develop property. At the same time, they realized that property was like Cracker Jacks. The more one eats, the more one wants. So they possessed equally strong convictions about equality.

The days are coming, Jeremiah says in the name of the Lord, that God will raise up an ideal Son of David, who will deliver these scattered people and restore them to Jerusalem. He will save them so that they can dwell securely once again on the land which was promised to their fathers. He will be a king who will combine in himself perfect power and perfect goodness. For this reason, he will be called *The Lord is our righteousness*. Notice the play on words: The name Zedekiah means *The Lord is my righteousness*. The ideal Son of David will be called *The Lord is our righteousness*. Jeremiah has in mind a righteousness that will happen in history. It will be something that God does for us.

How Did Luther Preach on This Text?

Some years ago I met with a group of people who were interested in biblical studies. They were discussing this passage from

Jeremiah. Some of them were asking questions like this: What did Jeremiah mean as he spoke to the people of his day? What kind of a king did Jeremiah have in mind? Would he be like Zedekiah? In what way would he be different? A few other members of this study group were interested in Luther's interpretation of Jeremiah. Luther took this text as a predictive prophecy about Christ. He contended that the name *The Lord is our righteousness* could point only to Christ. Then he ventured to point out the difference between the righteousness of life as over against the righteousness of faith. This distinction is rooted in the letters of Paul. The righteousness of life is something I create and is imperfect. The righteousness of faith is something that God does for us. It happened in history. Christ produced it and, as a believer, I am clothed with this righteousness.

As I listened to this discussion, I began to ask myself, "On what basis does Luther make his statements?" It soon became evident to me that on the one hand, the Old Testament does speak to its own day and age. On the other hand, there is a wholeness to the biblical message. It does point beyond itself. We can understand an Old Testament passage in the light of its end. This is what Luther sought to do.

What Kind of a King Seeks to Rule Now?

This morning we are taking a pilgrimage. It is a pilgrimage at the end of the church year. We are asking what kind of a king seeks to rule over us. Jeremiah asserts that he is a king who will combine in himself perfect power and perfect goodness. He will be the ideal Son of David. Now we must ask: Can such a king enter into this world of horizontal time? What if he were threatened by someone? Would he defend himself with his perfect power? There is only one way that he can enter into this world of history. Our Gospel for today gives us a glimpse. The enemies of Jesus made fun of him and sarcastically called him the "King of the Jews." They said, "He can save others; he cannot save himself." The Bible as a whole affirms that perfect power and perfect goodness can enter this world only as suffering love.

In our Gospel, we meet the two men who were crucified with our Lord. The one railed at Jesus and defied him. The other man began to view his situation in a new perspective. He rebuked his partner in crime. He even turned to Jesus and said, "Remember me when you come into your kingdom." Jesus spoke a promise to him. Within himself, this man experienced only pain. For his assurance he had to trust the promises of God.

We, too, have to trust these same promises that are written in the Scriptures. For this man, the name for the Son of David, *The Lord is our righteousness,* took on a new meaning. We have reason to believe that this man who was crucified with Jesus said to himself: There is a righteousness of life. It is something I produce, but what I have done gives me no hope. Thanks be to God, there is the righteousness of faith. It has happened in history. Jesus procured it when he died for us. God extends this righteousness to me as a pure gift. As a believer, I am clothed with it. This is the basis of my hope.

How Does This King Come Now?

Paul says in our lesson from Colossians that the experience of the man who died with Jesus transferred him from the dominion of darkness into the kingdom of God's beloved Son. If Christ is real, his rule and kingdom are real. What is your first contact with this kingdom? Has God acted to make you a part of this kingdom? This is what happened in your baptism. In the letter to the Colossians, Paul is concerned about your life within this kingdom. In other words, what will the rule of this king be like? In the thought of Paul, the rule of Christ is rooted in baptism. This act of God begins for us a life of endless striving. We are to become in life what we are already in Christ. For this striving, we need strength and power. Our King has chosen to come to us with food and drink. There is a mystery about communion. It is a moment of breakthrough for the kingdom. Our King comes with his body and blood in, with, and under bread and wine.

There is something unique about the exhortation of the New Testament. It does not just nudge us to become good persons. Rather, the exhortation is rooted in an act of God. This is what gives it bite and power. Our Lord says to you and to me: "I have acted in your baptism. I come to you with my promises which are written in the Scriptures. I come to you in a very personal way in communion. I, the Lord, extend to you my hand. You may accept it as you are. However, I shall not let you remain as you are. You must seek to love the Lord and your neighbor as I have loved you."

How then does our King rule? He rules with his righteousness. He extends the righteousness of faith to us as a pure gift. He affirms that we can receive this gift just as we are. At this point, we meet another mystery. This gift does become a task in life for you and me as believers. My great hope in life is that in the midst of striving, I can appropriate the promise of forgiveness. God bless you in your striving, and God bless you with his promise. Amen.

JOHN V. HALVORSON
St. Olaf Lutheran Church
Austin, Minnesota